Arts & Entertainment Fads

"A DELIGHTFUL ROMP THROUGH AMERICAN CULTURAL HIS-
TORY. The alphabetically organized resource guide focuses on
fleeting figures of fact (Horatio Alger) and fantasy (James Bond);
it explores trends both brief (surf music) and sustained (popularity of the song "White Christmas"); it notes the influences of
technology (video games), film innovations (stereoscopy: 3D), and
mechanics (optical toys); it recognizes cartoons (Mickey Mouse),
comic strips (Peanuts), commercial visuals (pop art and psychedelic posters), and paintings (American gothic); and it confronts
international ideological issues (anti-Iran Ayatollah songs) along
with uniquely American social topics ("Casey at the Bat," Beatlemania, and The Keystone Kops).*

"Editors Frank W. Hoffmann and William G. Bailey are thorough
in their descriptions, yet not verbose. Their prose is both clear
and readable. The illustrations they provide are succinct and invariably accurate in capsuling the event, personality, or trend
they are depicting. It is especially helpful to have a supplemen-
tary bibliography, often containing five or more citations, to
allow additional investigation of each fad topic. The best part
about discovering such a unique reference work on American
fads and entertainers is the announcement that . . . additional
volumes are forthcoming. Scholars, trivia buffs, sociologists,
librarians, and newspaper writers should treasure this initial
encyclopedia . . .

"Hats off to Hoffmann and Bailey! They have confronted the
shifty goddess of fads and fancies and conquered her. The tale
of their conquest is written in individual skirmishes with barbershop quartets, P. T. Barnum, Batman, Milton Berle, Betty Boop,
and Busby Berkeley."

B. Lee Cooper, PhD, Professor of History, Olivet College, Olivet, Michigan;
Author of Images of American Society in Popular Music and The Popular Music
Handbook

Arts & Entertainment Fads

Frank W. Hoffmann, PhD
William G. Bailey, MA

The Haworth Press
New York • London

Encyclopedia of Fads Volume 1: Arts & Entertainment Fads is Volume Number 1 in the Haworth Series on Fads.

The Haworth Press, Inc., 10 Alice Street, Binghamton, NY 13904-1580
EUROSPAN/Haworth, 3 Henrietta Street, London, WC2E 8LU England

All illustrations courtesy of the Library of Congress.

Library of Congress Cataloging-in-Publicatin Data

Hoffman, Frank W., 1949-
    Encyclopedia of fads / Frank W. Hoffman, William G. Bailey.
      p. cm.
    Includes bibliographical references.
    Contents: 1. Arts and entertainment fads.
    ISBN 0-86656-881-6 (v. 1)
    1. Fads—United States—Dictionaries. 2. United States—Social life and customs—Dictionaries. 3. United States—Popular culture—Dictionaries. I. Bailey, William G., 1947- . II. Title.
E161.H63   1990
306.4'03—dc20
                                              89-24570
                                              CIP

CONTENTS

ILLUSTRATIONS

About the Authors

Frank W. Hoffmann, PhD, MLS, is an associate professor at the School of Library Science, Sam Houston State University. His teaching responsibilities include library collection development, reference/information services, and a seminar of popular culture. His publications include *The Development of Collections of Sound Recordings in Libraries* (Marcel Dekker), *Popular Culture and Libraries* (Library Professional Publications), *The Literature of Rock* series (Scarecrow), and *The Cash Box* chart compilation series (Scarecrow). He received his doctorate from the University of Pittsburgh and his BA in History and MLS from Indiana University.

William G. Bailey, MA, MLS, has worked in the Information Services division of the Newton Gresham Library, Sam Houston State University, for the past 12 years. He is currently Head of the Reference Department. Due to his daily routine, he is constantly looking for new writing projects to fill information gaps. A fad encyclopedia appeals to his eclectic mind; he is already the editor/compiler of books on such diverse topics as police, longevity, and Americans in Paris. He holds an MA degree in English and American literature from the University of Houston, and an MLS from the University of Texas at Austin.

 ALL HAWORTH BOOKS & JOURNALS ARE PRINTED ON CERTIFIED ACID-FREE PAPER

Introduction

Arts and Entertainment Fads represents the first volume of the Haworth Series on Fads.

Other volumes to follow will concern sports and recreation, science and society, and fashions and merchandising. The rationale behind such a plan is to make evident the diversity of American fads — which would be difficult in a one-volume work — and to arrange them in discrete volumes. Past efforts at compiling anything resembling an encyclopedia of American fads have resulted in a mere taste of their infinite variety. We hope to change that by offering a balanced collection of entries that is well-documented, provocative, and simply fun to read. Even though we have the luxury of several volumes to fill, our choices must remain selective. The large number of past fads and the ever-growing number of present ones necessitates a judicious culling. We include fads from the colonization of America right up to the very latest craze. We stick with those fads that garnered national attention while attracting a lot of followers — not regional ones, certainly interesting in their own right, but little heard of outside of their breeding place. Once this encyclopedic survey is complete it will provide a unique history of American popular culture.

Now to turn to the most pressing question: What is a fad? Before starting work on this encyclopedia we asked colleagues to venture a definition. Most of them admitted they could not define fad any more precisely than Webster's, i.e., "A transitory fashion adopted with wide enthusiasm." In fact, the more we explored the parameters of a definition the more indistinct things got. All agreed hula hoops and bell-bottom pants were fads, but after that who can say? What was faddish to one colleague seemed less so or mislabeled to another, while a couple of skeptics suggested that most everything cultural and intellectual, at one time or another, has been a fad. Searching for further opinion, we moved on and asked non-academic friends for a definition. The typical response was, "Why, a fad is something here today and gone tomorrow. Like hula hoops and bell-bottom pants.'' Then we asked both groups a series of related questions, such as: How long can a fad run before it becomes a trend? Is a fad always frivolous? Is there such a thing as intellectual faddism? What do fads tell us about ourselves? Have there always been fads, or just recently? Does our appetite for constant novelty insure the continuance of fads? And so on, their answers exhibited such divergence that we knew an encyclopedia of American fads would prepare the groundwork for further discussion.

At this juncture we consulted any literature on the subject. According to the *Oxford English Dictionary* the etymology of fad is unknown. The word came into usage in 19th century England. Two early meanings were "a crotchety rule of action" or "a fussy, over-particular person." Closer to our modern definition, fad also denoted "a pet project, esp. of social or political reform, to which exaggerated importance is attributed; in wider sense, a crotchet, hobby, craze." For the 1931 edition of the *Encyclopedia of the Social Sciences*, Edward Sapir wrote that fads "are objectively similar to fashions but differ from them in being more personal in their application and in connoting a more or less definite social disapproval" (Volume VI, p. 139). His touchstone was dress neglecting the multitude of fads in other aspects of life. Rolf Meyersohn and Elihu Katz were the next notable writers to attempt a definition. In their "Notes on a Natural History of Fads" (*American Journal of Sociology* 62 (1957): 594-601), they postulated these laws:

Each new fad is a functional alternative for its predecessor.

Since most fads are of a minority or subculture, they may of course exhibit contradictory or countervailing trends all at once.

Fads are not born but rediscovered.

The birth of a fad is really accompanied by two labels; the phenomenon is given a name, and it is named as a fad. The fad is defined as real and in consequence becomes so.

The old drives in the new. The story of fads is, then, one of constant change.

As Sapir did with dress, Meyersohn and Katz focused on only one source of fads—the popular music industry—to the exclusion of other sources. When the revised and retitled International Encyclopedia of the Social Sciences appeared in 1968, Hubert G. Blumer broadened the definition:

> Fads, like fashion, may occur in widely different areas of group life, such as games, recreation, entertainment, dietary practice, health and medical practice, dress, ornamentation, language, and popular beliefs. . . . Fads have no line of historical continuity; each springs up independent of a predecessor and gives rise to no successor. . . . Fads do not require endorsement by a qualified prestige group in order to gain acceptance; they may spread from any section of hierarchized society. Fads are ephemeral . . . Fads follow the pattern of a craze or boom, thriving on spectacular and excitatory appearance . . . only to exhaust their attractiveness and undergo a rapid demise. (Volume V, p. 344)

A final definition comes from Ken Hakuta, a graduate of the Harvard Business School, who calls himself "Doctor Fad." He maintains a toll-free number so inventors can call him with ideas for marketable fads. His advice and support bolster their dreams of striking it rich. In addition, he sponsors a Fad Fair every year to showcase newly invented fads. Hakuta's definition is more laconic than Webster's: whatever sells. "The days of spending $20 million over three years to develop a new product are over," says Doctor Fad. "As consumers become more fickle, marketers have to learn to get products out there fast and change them quickly."

What a fad is has been bandied about from 19th century England to today with some consensus on its meaning. Our definition follows the high road. We do not believe that every fad must conform to the skyrocket theory—rapid ascent, rapid fall, then disappearance. Some fads have lingered on for years especially those prior to the frenetic 20th century before mass communications. We do believe that a fad dies out, but not always overnight, and it can reappear at any time in the same or altered manifestation—there is nothing new under the sun. Furthermore, for a fad to be called such it

must affect a sizeable number of people and be of enough importance to warrant documentation. We also believe that practically
every area of life has been touched by fad, and that within some of
those areas evolution has taken place. To cite an example of how a
fad can evolve, take opera. In Colonial America English ballad opera was all the rage; it gave way to pasticcio; which gave way to bel
canto; which gave way to the first native American musicals; which
gave way to opera bouffe; which gave way to operetta; which gave
way to grand opera. All were the rage at one time or another, and as
theatrical art forms have experienced reinvigoration over and again,
only to fall out of favor eventually. Of course, the musicologist sees
opera's evolution as one of form and not fad. However, for the
average American theater-goer this evolution, not perceived as
such, was decidedly one of fad turning into fashion. Delving
deeper, the public embraced certain faddish behavior in association
with opera. Wearing fancy evening clothes was once de rigueur —
even impoverished opera buffs accessorized with an old silk hat and
paste jewelry, as was Italian-style pandemonium after each aria.
Peering through a lorgnette to "leer" at the opera singers was once
chic, as was attending the opera in the first place — why endure an
endless performance sung in a foreign language? More contemporary, during Christmas 1988 music stores across America sold out
of Verdi and Puccini after the public heard operatic compositions in
movies (e.g., *Moonstruck*) and television commercials (e.g., Tott's
Champagne). All of a sudden Italian opera resounded in American
homes and swept away our hearts. But for how long? It is doubtful
the same faddish buying spree will occur during Christmas 1989. In
no sense of the word are Verdi and Puccini faddish, for they are
immortal, but the public's rush to "have" them is. The example of
opera points out the interrelatedness of fad and fashion. At present
distinguishing between the two is a simple matter. Today's fads fit
the common definition of being short-lived, whereas yesterday's
verged on or entered into fashion more readily due to a slower pace
of living. We, in the latter part of the 20th century, are riddled with
fads and heed the fadmongers more than is probably healthy. Our
ancestors were less capricious, therefore fads stood more of a
chance of becoming fashion; and they had less leisure and money
than we do which slowed the fad machine.

A besetting problem in studying any fad is how to establish its existence as a mass phenomenon. Psychologist Armando Simon accepted this challenge and reported his findings in an article, "A Quantitative Nonreactive Study of Mass Behavior with Emphasis on the Cinema as Behavioral Catalyst" (*Psychological Reports* 48 (1981): 775-785). For his study he selected these fads: the film *Jaws*, the fantasy of talking to your plants, and peak-year UFO sightings. During the course of his research Simon attempted to collect every scrap of quantitative data. For instance, after the film *Jaws* (1975)—about a killer shark that ravages a beach resort— achieved extreme popularity he discovered that sales of shark jaws and teeth rose to unprecedented levels. Marine Specialties in Wilmington, California witnessed an increase in individual orders for shark items from a normal 10-100 to 20,000-100,000. Other marine curio shops on both coasts likewise reaped the benefits of *Jaws*. Nationwide bookstores stocked more reading material on sharks which sold easily. A proliferation of newspaper articles, photographs, and cartoons about sharks fueled the mania. More and more people crowded around shark exhibits in city museums. Public library statistics showed that shark books, which had gathered dust for years, were in great demand. And the number of entries for sharks in the *Reader's Guide to Periodical Literature* nearly doubled from the previous year before *Jaws*. Once Simon had gathered his statistics he could state with more certainty that the film *Jaws* had indeed produced a faddish interest in sharks. As authors of this encyclopedia we wish we could emulate Armando Simon's research in every detail. To be able to substantiate the existence of a fad with quantitative data would strengthen our work immeasurably. But this is best done when the fad is current and if it is merchandised to the hilt (stuffed shark toys and shark water playthings sold well which would have rendered more hard data).

Some of our most sobering moments come when an outsider analyzes us. An anonymous British journalist did just that for *The Economist* in a perceptive article, "America's Unfading Passion for What's New" (December 20, 1986: 35-36, 43). The writer declared that health, technology, and sex fads obsess us and guarantee big profits for merchandisers. It seems we can't go jogging unless we wear the latest light-weight, ventilated, rapid-dry, sporty-striped, night-glo, Velcro fastening outfit. To count miles jogged, calories burned, and heart rate, we must strap on a watch that gives us such essential information. Jogging shoes have to be ergonomically correct and as light as a feather. Among our other obsessions were (and still are): wearing skin-tight leotards as regular dress, breast augmentation, giving "intimate photographs" as presents, adults smiling through dental braces, every kind of exercise machine, surgical correction of shortsightedness for cosmetic reasons, Fuzzbusters, video telephones, massage chairs, bottled water in flavors, pasta dishes sprinkled with basil, and decorative condoms. For many Americans who read the article, it must have been somewhat embarrassing.

Adult Westerns

Despite its inauspicious start during the 1955-1956 season, "Gunsmoke" proved to be a highly influential program, paving the way for a new wave of TV Westerns, including "Broken Arrow," "Dick Powell's Zane Grey Theater" and "Tales of Wells Fargo." From nine Westerns scheduled by the three major networks they would peak at thirty-one during the 1958-1959 season, in addition to holding down seven out of the top ten series positions.

"Gunsmoke" — which ascended to the number one ranking in the late 1950s — differed from earlier kids' Westerns like "The Lone Ranger" and "Hopalong Cassidy" in that it was geared to adults much in the style of contemporary movie fare (e.g., *High Noon*, *Shane*, *The Searchers*). As opposed to the mythological status given heroes in the first wave Westerns, the second wave addressed adult issues and relationships; e.g., "Gunsmoke's" Marshall Dillon did not relish violent shoot-outs and, while accepting their necessity, chose to focus upon the interpersonal aspects of his job. This adult orientation attracted the involvement of Hollywood film studios, which endowed the new Westerns with a cinematic depth and subtlety missing from earlier TV entries. The genre also profited from the troubles of its chief competitor, the quiz shows, which were all pulled off the air as a result of the 1958-1959 scandals.

The TV Western proved to be remarkably versatile, branching off into a third wave — i.e., the anti-hero who, while devoting his energies to the assistance of those in need, was ultimately guided by self-interest, rather than by a mythical "Code of the West" — as early as the 1957-1958 season. Notable proponents of this approach included "Maverick," "Sugarfoot" and "Have Gun Will Travel." In the meantime, the second wave continued to thrive, generating such long-running programs as "Wagon Train," "Bonanza" and "The Virginian."

1

The genre entered a decline in the early 1960s due to the following factors:

1. The overabundance of oaters; many were competing against each other, and new entries found it hard to attract attention.
2. The growing concern of the American public over TV violence, which centered on crime programs (e.g., "The Untouchables," "The Roaring Twenties," "Bus Stop"), but embraced Westerns as well. By 1961, the U.S. Congress was investigating the issue, and the networks began feeling the pressure to moderate things.
3. Perhaps most important of all, research into TV viewer demographics indicated that Adult Westerns were favored largely by older people, while children and young adults preferred sitcoms. Given that the latter two groups comprised a majority of the American population (and were more active consumers), advertisers shifted their support away from the Western. "Gunsmoke" proved to be the casualty of this policy, being pulled off the air by CBS in the mid-1970s despite reasonably strong ratings (its audience consisted largely of senior citizens who had remained loyal to the program throughout its long run).

BIBLIOGRAPHY

Barrett, M., and S. Bourgin. "Just Wild About Westerns," *Newsweek*. 50 (July 22, 1957) 51-54.

Brooks, Tim, and Earle Marsh. "Introduction," In: *The Complete Directory to Prime Time Network TV Shows, 1946-Present*. New York: Ballantine, 1985, pp. x-xxi.

Castleman, Harry, and Walter J. Podrazik. *Watching TV*. New York: McGraw-Hill, 1982.

Ellis, G. "TV Western Craze; How Long Will It Last?," *Look*. 22 (June 24, 1958) 66ff.

"Freewheeling Slick; Maverick," *Time*. 70 (December 30, 1967) 37.

"Happy Larceny; Maverick," *Newsweek*. 53 (January 19, 1959) 82.

Hargrove, M. "This is a Television Cowboy?," *Life*. (January 19, 1959) 75-76ff.

"Have Guns, Will Teach," *Newsweek*. 51 (January 27, 1958) 64-65.

Scott, J. "Adult Gunslingers," *Cosmopolitan*. 143 (December 1957) 44-51.

Shayon, R.L. "Togetherness on the Range," Saturday Review. 41 (October 4, 1958) 28.

"TV Goes Wild Over Westerns," *Life*. 43 (October 28, 1957) 99-102ff.

Horatio Alger, Jr.

Horatio Alger, Jr. (1834-1899) wrote nearly 130 books for boys, all based on the principle that hard work and resistance to temptation would ultimately lead to wealth and fame. His literary output was generally organized in series of eight or ten volumes each; e.g., *Ragged Dick, Luck and Pluck, Tattered Tom*. In addition, he wrote biographies of self-made statesmen (e.g., *From Canal Boy to President*, 1881; *Abraham Lincoln: The Backwoods Boy*, 1883) and a book of verses, *Grandfather Baldwin's Thanksgiving* (1875).

Alger was considered by critics to be a poor writer. His books were endlessly repetitious; often characters intruded themselves into the wrong volume. However, his stories were exactly in accord with the temper of the 1870s and 1880s. In sheer bulk of readers, Alger may well have been the most popular author who has ever lived. It is estimated that more than twenty million copies of his novels were published. He was thought of as an authority on youth; his fan mail was enormous, his visitors multitudinous.

Changing tastes and the emergence of new writers for juveniles (e.g., Edward Stratemeyer, L. Frank Baum) have consigned his works to oblivion. However, his name remains a part of the vernacular, referring to the high-minded, rags-to-riches quest typified by his fictional heroes.

BIBLIOGRAPHY

"Alger, Horatio, Jr.," In: *American Authors, 1600-1900*, edited by Stanley J. Kunitz and Howard Haycraft. New York: Wilson, 1938, pp. 24-25.

Allen, F.L. "Horatio Alger, Jr.," *Saturday Review of Literature*. 18 (September 17, 1938) 3-4ff. Abridged version reprinted in November 1938 issue of *Readers' Digest* (Volume 33; pages 54-57).

Benet, W.K. "Monument to Free Enterprise," *Saturday Review Of Literature*. 28 (September 1, 1945) 15-16.

Cowley, M. "Alger Story," *New Republic*. 113 (September 10, 1945) 319-320.

Gustaitis, Joseph. "Horatio Alger; Creator of the American Success Story," *American History Illustrated*. 22 (October 1987) 36-37.

Holbrook, S.H. "Horatio Alger Was No Hero," *American Mercury*. 51 (October 1940) 203-209.

Levy, N. "They Make Me What I Am Today," *Atlantic*. 172 (November 1943) 115ff.

Meelan, T. "Forgettable Centenary; Horatio Alger's," *New York Time Magazine*. (June 28, 1964) 22-23ff.

Tebbel, J. "Horatio Alger Revisited; excerpts from From Rags to Riches, Horatio Alger, Jr., and the American Dream," *Publishers Weekly*. 183 (February 18, 1963) 121-125.

One of the many novels that made Alger (1834-1899) a fortune. His heroes were all honest lads who through perseverance and good humor succeeded in life against every obstacle. Reading Alger novels for motivation was a popular pastime underscoring the notion that any boy in America become President if he wanted to.

American Gothic

American Gothic, an oil on composition board painting by Grant Wood measuring 29 7/8 by 24 7/8 inches, was completed in late 1930. Depicting a lean, dour-faced farming couple (father and daughter) — the man holding a pitchfork, thereby evoking a nineteenth century setting — standing in front of a Mission-style bungalow located in Eldon, Iowa, the work was awarded the Norman Wait Harris Bronze Medal and a $300 prize at the Forty-Third Annual Exhibition of Painting and Sculpture at the Art Institute of Chicago. It was then purchased by the Friends of American Art at the Art Institute for $300; not only was it an overnight success with the public, the painting attracted critical acclaim throughout the nation. The work, with its protean image, capable of addressing an infinite number of issues, was eventually adopted by mass America as a national portrait.

The capacity of American Gothic for multiple interpretations inspired a second life as a popular icon. This phase began at some point in the late 1950s. Meredith Willson's musical, *The Music Man* (1957), had the actors briefly replicating the couple's pose behind an empty frame so as to set the scene in River City, Iowa. In 1961 the celebrated Charles Addams published a cartoon in the *New Yorker*, which depicted the couple startling a guard as they walked out of an exhibition in a modern art museum. By the late 1960s, a virtual torrent of takeoffs of the work began surfacing. Amateurs and professionals, cartoonists and illustrators, advertisers and advocates of various causes began using American Gothic as a sort of "blackboard" on which to write their messages, voice their concerns or hawk their wares.

The grafting of heads onto the painting was a particularly prevalent motif. The results of this practice have tended to be outrageously funny, including

—*Mad*'s mating of Spiro Agnew (wearing the apron) and Richard Nixon in its June 1971 issue.

—Richard Locker's depiction of Jimmy and Rosalyn Carter in "Just Plains Folks" (*Chicago Tribune*, 1981).

—Alfred Gescheidt's pairing of two dissimilar candidates for the Democratic presidential nomination, Shirley Chisholm and George Wallace.

The farm couple—in the role of Mr. and Ms. Average American—have sold a wide-ranging array of products and ideas. Because of their old-fashioned appearance, ads in which they have endorsed products far beyond their realm of experience—e.g., skis, Ford Mustangs, pocket calculators, radios, computers—were particularly successful.

Wanda Corn notes that the couple's universality has rendered them an effective mouthpiece for a host of social and political issues during the past generation.

> In statements on contemporary relations between the sexes, the American Gothic woman has traded in her apron for a business suit or a judge's robe, spoken out on women's rights, and picketed for the Equal Rights Amendment. Embodying our belief in clean living, the couple have protested pornography and fought for clean air and less congestion and noise in our cities. As average Americans, they have felt the gas shortages, suffered soaring prices in the recession, and seen foreclosure notices posted on their front door.

In short, they have acted as a barometer of our times, reflecting changes in national priorities, values, worries and aspirations. As a result, it can be said that no painting, with the possible exception of da Vinci's *Mona Lisa*, has been so widely and intensely consumed by the American public.

BIBLIOGRAPHY

Corn, Wanda M. "American Gothic: The Making of a National Icon," in: *Grant Wood: The Regionalist Vision*. New Haven, CT: Yale University Press, 1983, pp. 128-142.

Corn, Wanda M. "The Birth of a National Icon: Grant Wood's American

Gothic," in: *Art: The Ape of Nature*, edited by Moshe Barasch and Lucy Freeman Sandler. New York: Abrams, 1981, pp. 749-769.

Corn, Wanda M. "The Painting That Became a Symbol of a Nation's Spirit," *Smithsonian*. 11:8 (November 1980) 84-97.

Dennis, James M. *Grant Wood: A Study in American Art and Culture*. New York: Viking, 1975.

Guedon, Mary Schulz. *Regionalist Art, Thomas Hart Benton, John Steuart Curry, and Grant Wood: A Guide to the Literature*. Metuchen, NJ: Scarecrow, 1982.

Answer Songs

An "answer song" is broadly defined as a commercial recording that is directly related to a previously released record either by title, by lyrical content, or by melody. Although generally issued only weeks after the original tune has achieved popularity, response recordings occasionally appear months — or even years — later. Usually regarded as a novelty item by most artists, record company executives and pop music enthusiasts, the answer song has served to launch careers, revive others and provide a continuing vehicle for a select few to exercise their talents as satirists. Despite the rich diversity of material falling within this genre, it is possible to discern at least five major subcategories: (1) answers to direct questions; (2) responses to statements or commands; (3) challenges to stated positions or ideologies; (4) continuations of distinct storylines or themes; and (5) follow-up statements to general ideas or themes (see Figure I).

Although they have appeared throughout the rock era (earliest examples were based upon rhythm and blues hits from the early 1950s such as The Dominoes' "Sixty Minute Man," Muddy Waters' "Manish Boy" and Bo Diddley's "I'm A Man"), answer songs were released in particularly large numbers during 1960-1962. The impetus for this deluge of recordings appears to have been the notable success of Jeanne Black's "He'll Have to Stay" (Capitol). Based upon Jim Reeves' "He'll Have to Go," Black's record entered Billboard's "Hot 100" on May 2, 1960, peaking at number four. Skeeter Davis followed with an answer to Hank Locklin's "Please Help Me, I'm Falling, entitled "(I Can't Help You) I'm Falling Too," which dented the Top Forty in late summer.

Both Black and Davis continued to successfully mine the genre in 1960 with "Oh, How I Miss You Tonight" and "My Last Date

(With You)," respectively. The former was part of its own mini-phenomenon; Elvis Presley's number one smash, "Are You Lonesome Tonight," spawned numerous answer songs, including "Yes, I'm Lonesome Tonight" (which hit the charts with versions by both Thelma Carpenter and Dodie Stevens). Damita Jo also experienced great success recording answer songs on the Mercury label. "I'll Save the Last Dance For You" (modelled after The Drifters' number one hit, "Save the Last Dance For Me") and "I'll Be There" (Ben E. King's "Stand By Me") both just missed the Top Ten.

The genre appears to have been popular for the following reasons:

1. Given the long odds against achieving hit status with any particular entry, answer songs had the built-in advantage of appropriating the residual popularity and name recognition of the original.
2. The existence of the original rendered the follow-up relatively easy to compose.
3. The answer song peaked at a time when pop music was uniformly mediocre; the major record companies had recently succeeded in harnessing the vigor and spontaneity of classic rock 'n' roll and were milking the formula for all it was worth.

FIGURE I
Examples of Answer Songs by Category

Original Song Title/Artist . . . Response Song Title/Artist

1. Answer to a Direct Question

"Why Do Fools Fall in Love" — Frankie Lymon & The Teenagers (1956) . . . "I Found Out Why" — Lewis Lymon & The Teenchords; "Who Can Explain?" — Frankie Lymon & The Teenagers

"Book of Love" — The Monotones (1958) . . . "Reading the Book of Love" — The Monotones

"Will You Love Me Tomorrow" — The Shirelles (1960) . . . "Not Just Tomorrow, But Always" — Bertell Dache; "Yes, I Will Love You Tomorrow" — Jon E. Holiday; "You Know I'll Love You Tomorrow" — Colly Williams

"Who Put the Bomp (in the Bomp, Bomp, Bomp)" — Barry Mann (1961) . . . "We're the Guys" — Bob & Jerry; "I Put the Bomp" — Frankie Lymon

"Who Stole the Keeshka?" — The Matys Brothers (1963) . . . "Jashu Found the Keeshka" — The Matys Brothers

"Who Shot J.R.?" — Gary Burbank with Band McNally (1980) . . . "I Don't Give a Diddly Damn Who Shot J.R." — Hook McCoy

2. Response to a Statement or Command

"Get a Job" — The Silhouettes (1958) . . . "Got a Job" — The Miracles; "I Found a Job" — The Heartbeats

"Shop Around" — The Miracles (1960) . . . "Don'cha Shop Around" — Laurie Davis; "Don't Let Him Shop Around" — Debbie Dean; "Don't Have to Shop Around" — The Mad Lads

"Wooden Heart" — Joe Dowell (1961) . . . "I Know Your Heart's Not Made of Wood" — Marie Ann; "You Don't Have a Wooden Heart" — Bobby Martin; "Your Heart's Not Made of Wood" — Terri Dean; "Your Heart's Not Made of Wood" — Joyce Heath

"Bring It On Home to Me" — Sam Cooke (1962) . . . "I'll Bring It Home to You" — Carla Thomas

"Dang Me" — Roger Miller (1964) . . . "Darn Ya" — Teresa Brewer; "Dern Ya" — Ruby Wright

"In the Midnight Hour" — Wilson Pickett (1965) . . . "You Can't Love Me in the Midnight Hour" — Ann Mason

3. Challenge to a Stated Position or Ideology

"You Talk Too Much" — Joe Jones (1960) . . . "I Don't Talk Too Much" — Martha Nelson; "I Talked Too Much" — Valerie Carr

"This Diamond Ring" — Gary Lewis & The Playboys (1965) . . . "Gary, Don't Sell My Diamond Ring" — Wendy Hill

"Eve of Destruction" — Barry McGuire (1965) . . . "Dawn of Correction" — The Spokesmen

"An Open Letter to My Teenage Son" — Victor Lunberg (1967) . . . "Hi Dad (An Open Letter)" — Dick Clair; "Letter From a Teenage Son" — Brand Wade; "Letter to Dad" — Every Father's Teenage Son; "An Open Letter to My Father" — Bob Randon; "A Teenage Son's Open Letter" — Robert Tamkin; A Teenager's Answer" — Keith Gordon

"Okie From Muskogee" — Merle Haggard & The Strangers (1969) . . . "The Only Hippie in Muskogee" — C. Dean Draper

"The Logical Song" — Supertramp (1979) . . . "The Topical Song" — The Barron Knights

4. Continuation of a Distinct Storyline or Theme

"Stagger Lee" — Lloyd Price (1958-1959) . . . "The Ballad of Stagger Lee" — The Senders; "The Return of Stagger Lee" — Don ReVels; "Return of Stagolee" — Titus Turner; "Trail of Stagger Lee" — Stella Johnson

"Say Man" — Bo Diddley (1959) . . . "Say Man, Back Again" — Bo Diddley

"Mr. Custer" — Larry Verne (1960) . . . "Custer's Last Man" — Pop Corn & The Mohawks; "Ho Ho Mr. Custer" — Moe Nudenick; "Return of Mr.Custer" — Larry Verne; "We're Depending on You, Mr. Custer" — The Characters

"Mother-in-Law" — Ernie K-Doe (1961) . . . "My Mother-in-Law is in My Hair Again" — Ernie K-Doe; "Son-in-Law" — The Blossoms; "Son-in-Law" — Louise Brown

"Hit the Road Jack" — Ray Charles (1961) . . . I'm Changed My Mind, Jack" — Jo Anne Campbell; "Well I Told You" — The Chantels

"Duke of Earl" — Gene Chandler (1962) . . . "Duchess of Earl" — The Pearlettes; "Duchess of Earl" — Bobbie Smith; "Walk on With the Duke" — Gene Chandler

"Party Lights" — Claudine Clark (1962) . . . "I'm Sorry I Went" — The Cannon Sisters

"Wolverton Mountain" — Claude King (1962) . . . "I'm Going Down Wolverton Mountain" — Betty Luther; "I'm the Girl From Wolverton Mountain" — Jo Anne Campbell; "Keep Off My Mountain" — Cliff Adams

"My Girl Sloopy" — The Vibrations (1964) . . . "(My Girl) Sloopy" — Little Caesar & The Consuls

"Hang On Sloopy" — The McCoys (1965) . . . "Sloopy's Gonna Hang On" — The Debs

"Mrs. Brown You've Got a Lovely Daughter" — Herman's Hermits (1965) . . . "A Frightful Situation," — Mrs. Brown's Lovely Daughter Carol; "Mother Dear You've Got a Silly Daughter" — Sharon Black; "Mrs. Green's Ugly Daughter — Kenneth Young & The English Muffins; Mrs. James, I'm Mrs. Brown's Lovely Daughter" — Connie Holiday; "Mrs. Schwarts You've Got an Ugly Daughter" — Marty

"These Boots Are Made for Walkin'" — Nancy Sinatra (1966) . . . "Put Your Boots Back on the Shelf" — Boots Walker; "These Spurs are Made for Ridin'" — Gene Goza

"They're Coming to Take Me Away, Ha-Haaa!" — Napoleon XIV (1966) . . . "Don't Let Them Take Me Back, Oh No" — Henry IX; "Down on the Funny Farm" — Josephine XIII; "I'm Normal" — The Emperor; "They Took You Away (I'm Glad, I'm Glad)" — Josephine

"Snoopy vs. The Red Baron" — The Royal Guardsmen (1966) . . . "Red Baron's Revenge" — The Delicatessen; "The Return of the Red Baron" — The Royal Guardsmen

"Ode to Billie Joe" — Bobby Gentry (1967) . . . "Mystery of the Tallahatchie Bridge" — Roger White; "The Return of Billie Joe" — Tommy Lee

"Skinny Legs and All" — Joe Tex (1967) . . . "I'll Take Those Skinny Legs" — Syl Johnson; "I'm Leroy — I'll Take Her" — Bobby Patterson & The Mustangs

"By the Time I Get to Phoenix" — Glen Campbell (1967) . . . "By the Time You Get to Phoenix" — Wanda Jackson; "By the Time You Get to Phoenix" — Joanna Moore

"A Boy Named Sue" — Johnny Cash (1969) . . . "A Girl Named Harry" — Joni Credit; "A Girl Named Johnny Cash" — Jane Morgan; "A Girl Named Sam" — Lois Williams; "My Name is Sue (But I'm a Girl)" — Johnny & Phil

"Ruby, Don't Take Your Love to Town" — Kenny Rogers & The First Edition (1969) . . . "Billy, I've Got to Go to Town" — Geraldine Stevens; "Ruby's Answer" — Dori Helms

"Taxi" — Harry Chapin (1972) . . . "Sequel" — Harry Chapin

"Short People" — Randy Newman (1977) . . . "Mr. Small" — The Mr. Men; "Tall People" — The Short People; "Tall People" — Wee Willie Small

5. Follow-Up Ideas and Themes

"Oh, What a Night" — The Dells (1956) . . . "Oh, What a Day" — The Dells

"At the Hop" — Danny & The Juniors (1958) . . . "Back to the Hop" — Danny & The Juniors

"Itsy Bitsy Teenie Weenie Yellow Polka Dot Bikini" — Brian Hyland (1960) . . . "Four Shy Girls" — The Girlfriends; "1967 Itsy Bitsy Teenie Weenie Yellow Polka Dot Bikini" — Tommy Dae & High Tensions; "Poor Begonia Caught Pneumonia" — Jeri Lynne Fraser

"The Twist" — Chubby Checker (1960) . . . "Do You Know How to Twist" — Hank Ballard & The Midnighters; "La Paloma Twist" — Chubby Checker; "Let's Twist Again" — Chubby Checker; "Slow Twistin' '" — Chubby Checker with Dee Dee Sharp; "Twist It Up — Chubby Checker; "Twistin' U.S.A." — Chubby Checker

"The Lion Sleeps Tonight" — The Tokens (1961) . . . "The Lion is Awake" — Sammy & The 5 Notes; "The Tiger's Wide Awake" — The Romeos

"Little Sister" — Elvis Presley (1961) . . . "Hey, Memphis" — LaVern Baker (1961)

"The Dog" — Rufus Thomas (1963) . . . "Can Your Monkey Do the Dog" — Rufus Thomas; "Somebody Stole My Dog" — Rufus Thomas; "Walkin' the Dog" — Rufus Thomas

"Hi-Heel Sneakers" — Tommy Tucker (1964) . . . "Slip-in Mules" — Sugar Pie DeSanto

"King of the Road" — Roger Miller (1965) . . . "Queen of the House" — Jody Miller

"Papa's Got A Brand New Bag" — James Brown (1965) . . . "Mama's Got a Bag of Her Own" — Anna King; "Mama's Got a Brand New Box" — Vicky Lewis

Answer songs have given rise to at least two spinoff genres, the parody song and song cycles centered around a particular theme. Parodies differ from the hardcore answer song in that they usually don't take up where the original left off; rather, they recycle the thematic material of the original in a humorous — sometimes satirical — manner. Classic examples include The Detergents' Top Twenty hit, "Leader of the Laundromat" (Roulette, 1964), which reworked the Shangri-Las' "Leader of the Pack," and Phil McLean's "Small Sad Sam" (modelled after Jimmy Dean's 1961 chart topper, "Big Bad John"). Sheb Wooley, under the alias of Ben Colder, had the longest string of hits in this genre, including "Don't Go Near the Eskimos" (after Rex Allen's "Don't Go Near the Indians," 1962), "Still No. 2" (1963), "Detroit City No. 2" (1963), "Almost Persuaded No. 2" (1966), and "Harper Valley P.T.A. — Later That Same Day" (1968).

The Midnighters (featuring Hank Ballard) and The Heartbeats were both notable for recording a successive string of singles which continued to build upon one central storyline. The Midnighters' "Annie songs" (e.g., "Work With Me Annie," "Sexy Ways," "Annie Had A Baby," "Annie's Aunt Fanny") had the heroine dancing, engaging in various sexual activities, becoming a mother and settling down into a more conventional adult-oriented lifestyle. The Heartbeats' saga featured less specific allusions to any given plot. However, the doo-wop group's material always concerned itself with the ups and downs of a young couple's relationship. Best known examples of the cycle are "A Thousand Miles Away" (Hull, 1956) and its answer song, "Daddy's Home," released in 1961 under the nom de plume Shep & the Limelites for legal reasons.

BIBLIOGRAPHY

Adams, Roy. "I Put the Bomp," *Record Exchanger*. n13 (1973) 24, 26.

Cooper, B. Lee. "Bear Cats, Chipmunks and Slip-in Mules: The Answer Song in Contemporary American Recordings, 1950-1985," *Popular Music and Society*. XII:3 (1988) in press.

Cooper, B. Lee. "Response Recordings as Creative Repetition Answer Songs and Pop Parodies in Contemporary American Music," *OneTwoThreeFour: A Rock 'N' Quarterly*. 4 (Winter 1987) 79-87.

Cooper, B. Lee. "Sequel Songs and Response Recordings: The Answer Song in Modern American Music, 1950-1985," *International Journal of Instructional Media*. XIII (1986) 227-239.

Grevatt, Ren. "Answer Songs Aren't New!," *Melody Maker*. 35 (November 5, 1960) 6-7.

Moonogian, George. "The Answer Record in R & B," *Record Exchanger*. n22 (1976) 24-25, 28.

Moonogian, George. "Oh, That Annie!," *Record Exchanger*. n23 (1977) 20-21.

"Same to You, Mac," *Time*. 77 (January 6, 1961) 52.

AromaRama
and Smell-O-Vision

The movie, *Behind the Great Wall* (1959), introduced the public to AromaRama with this come-on: "You must breathe it to believe it." Italian Count Leonardo Bonzi had filmed the travelogue of Red China as an art for art's sake piece with no pretense to judge the sleepy communist giant. His film would be pure entertainment and nothing else. Bonzi got with Charles Weiss, a public relations man and developer of AromaRama, and decided that the new process was ready to unveil. Weiss incorporated a scent track directly on the film which transmitted cues to an electronic device. Once triggered the device fired a special scent into the theater through the air-conditioning system. The scent rode in on a quickly evaporating base of Freon. Then after another cue the air-conditioning system sucked out the scented air through a filter to remove the smell. *Behind the Great Wall* dispersed thirty-one smells which didn't work as well as planned. The movie reviewer for *Time* saw on screen a beautiful old pine grove in Peking but smelled "a subway rest room on disinfectant day." For a scene of the Gobi Desert the smell of spring grass still lingered in the air. Another problem was the intensity of the smells. To fill a large theater a large dose of smell had to be discharged evenly. Those in the audience sitting closest to the air conditioning vents got the strongest blasts. A final difficulty arose with the supplier of scents. Rhodia, Inc., a manufacturer of industrial perfumes — among them leather smell for plastic briefcases, new-car odor for used cars, and strawberry scent for embalming fluids — produced some inaccurate AromaRama smells.

The second and last film to employ "realistic smells" for the pleasure of its audience was *Scent of Mystery* (1960), the first picture made by Mike Todd, Jr., son of the famous producer. It acquainted the public with Smell-O-Vision, a sensation far superior to AromaRama. Each Smell-O-Vision customer sat in a movie seat equipped with a system to pipe in smells directly to the nose. Advance publicity ballyhooed the precise science behind it. "Osmologist" Hans Laube, using a "library of essences," had carefully perfected each "olfaction" to insure authenticity—all of which made the $3.50 ticket a bargain. Theater-owners knew AromaRama and Smell-O-Vision wouldn't be around long. Curious customers came and went without getting too excited. The processes cost extra money to build-in and were problematic. But not to waste a good idea, some of the more enterprising theater-owners thought the piped-in smell of steam heat might make people feel warmer, or the olfaction of buttered popcorn might send them scurrying back to the refreshment counter.

BIBLIOGRAPHY

Alpert, Hollis. "Aromatics," in *The Dream and the Dreamers*. New York: Macmillan, 1962.
Lightman, Herb A. "The Movie Has Scents!" *American Cinematographer* (February 1960): 92-93, 120.
"Nose Opera." *Time* (February 29, 1960): 98.
"A Sock in the Nose." *Time* (December 21, 1959): 57.

Ayatollah Songs

The imprisonment of American hostages by Iran in 1978-1979 spawned a number of recordings which spoofed the feelings held by U.S. citizens for the Ayatollah. Two, in particular, received a considerable amount of radio play. "Bomb Iran," as performed by Vince Vance and the Valiants, appropriated the melody and arrangement of "Barbara Ann," a hit for both The Regents (1961) and The Beach Boys (1966). Recorded in Nashville and released on the Paid label, the song's lyrics included the following lines:

> Went to a mosque, gonna throw some rock,
> Tell the Ayatollah gonna put him in a box . . .
> Old Uncle Sam's getting pretty hot,
> Time to turn Iran into a parking lot.

A similarly slanted exercise in invective, albeit more witty, was cut by Steve Dahl and Teenage Radiation on the Renta-Hits label. "Ayatollah" was modelled after The Knack's "My Sharona," a monster hit in the summer of 1979 (it was number one on the pop singles charts for six weeks). Released with the catalog number "KOMEN I," sample lyrics read as follows:

> You've got a real nice beard, a real nice beard,
> You know it really caught my eye, Ayatollah,
> But your mind is weird, your mind is weird,
> You really are a nutty kind of guy, Ayatollah.
>
> When you get the Shah back, the Shah back home,
> We know you're going to eat him on rye, Ayatollah.
> But we kind of need your oil to make our gas,
> You know you're such a pain in the eye, Ayatollah.
> Don't get us too upset, or we'll do something
> nuclear . . . Bye, Ayatollah . . .

Americans are mostly cool, mostly cool,
But now we're really starting to fry, Ayatollah,
And you know, if you were here, if you were here,
We'd hit you in the face with a pie, Ayatollah . . .

BIBLIOGRAPHY

Raker, Muck. "Singularly Painful—Singles and EPs," in: *Rock Bottom; the Book of Pop Atrocities*. New York: Proteus, 1981, p. 41.

Barbershop Quartet

The Society for the Preservation and Encouragement of Barber Shop Quartet Singing in America (SPEBSQSA) would heartily disagree that their type of vocalizing was ever faddish. Founded in 1938 with a current membership of 38,000 and a yearly budget of $2,500,000 the Society maintains a library of 650,000 old songs, sponsors singing contests, and convenes annually. Furthermore the Society traces its roots at least to Shakespeare's England where friendly barbers provided entertainment. Musicologist P.A. Scholes tells us:

> One of the regular haunts of music in the 16th, 17th, and early 18th centuries was the barber's shop. Here, customers awaiting their turn found simple instruments on which they could strum. The barbers themselves in their waiting time between customers took up the instruments and thus acquired some skill as performers. (*Oxford Companion to Music*)

Here barbershop singing flourished in the American West of gold-rush days reaching its apex in the 1890s. The prototypic appearance of quartet members — pomaded hair parted in the middle, handlebar mustache, mutton-sleeves bound on each arm with a red garter — came about then. Technically, using close harmony a male quartet sings by ear with the first tenor always singing above the melody carried by the lead singer. Some favorite barbershop ballads are "Sweet Adeline," "Say Au Revoir But Not Good-Bye," "Workin' On the Railroad," "My Old Kentucky Home," and "Red River Valley."

At the turn of the century Tin Pan Alley songs replaced barbershop vocalizing in popularity. But with the advent of Prohibition, speakeasies, and bathtub gin, Americans began to harmonize in groups again. Though with a difference, now they slurred the words of drinking songs like, "And When I Die" or "How Dry I Am."

After a few illegal drinks the inebriates sang loud and long displaying an astonishing range of voices. Hardly a rebirth of true barbershop vocalizing, the rage to join in and defy the law was irresistible. By 1938 when Tulsa attorney, Owen C. Cash formed the SPEBSQSA his favorite type of singing was near extinction. Since then revivalist groups around the country have performed on a regular basis for public gatherings. But barbershop singing hasn't regained the popularity it once knew in the 1890s.

BIBLIOGRAPHY

Martin, Deac C.T. *Deac Martin's Book of Musical America*. Englewood, NJ: Prentice-Hall, 1970.
Spaeth, Sigmund. *Barber Shop Ballads and How to Sing them*. NewYork: Prentice-Hall, 1940.

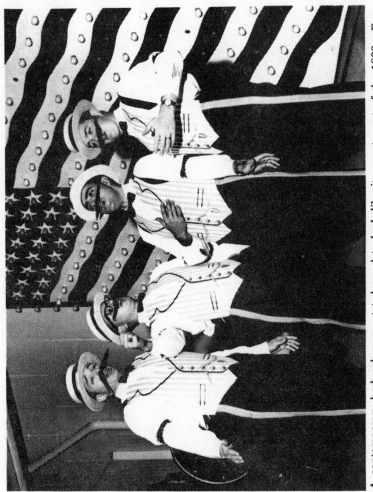

A contemporary barbershop quartet dressed to look like its counterpart of the 1890s. Even though barbershop singing still prevails today primarily through the Society for the Preservation and Encouragement of Barber Shop Quartet Singing in America (SPEBSQSA), its heyday was a century ago.

Barnum

Phineas Taylor Barnum (1810-1891) revitalized the circus making it "The Greatest Show On Earth." He succeeded through imagination, diligence, and effective publicity, but also in part through pure humbuggery. One can claim with justification that he is the father of fad entertainment in America. At age 25 Barnum began his meteoric rise in New York City. A salesman, Coley Bartram, called at his grocery store and while engaged in conversation revealed that he had recently owned an interest in a Negro woman, Joice Heth. She was reputed to be 161 years old and had been George Washington's nurse. Her current owner, R.W. Lindsey, was then exhibiting the venerable woman in Philadelphia. Barnum states in his autobiography that he checked into Heth's longevity:

> This whole account appeared to me satisfactory, and I inquired the price of the negress. Three thousand dollars was the sum named, but before leaving Philadelphia I received from Mr. Lindsay a writing, stipulating that I should have the right at any time within ten days to become her owner upon paying to him the sum of one thousand dollars.

Joice Heth made good money for Barnum until she was exposed as a fraud. Because of her he saw how the public reacted to the unusual—his first lesson in showmanship. His next "rare" find was the Feejee Mermaid, a dead though well-preserved female monkey sprouting a fish tail. The bogus tail was so expertly joined to the dried body that even on close inspection, people, including skeptical newspapermen, believed it natural. Barnum used this curiosity to headline his exhibit, "The Mermaid, and Other Wonderful Specimens of the Animal Creation." Before its opening he released the news to three New York City papers and mounted a saturation ad campaign.

> The mermaid fever was now getting pretty well up. . . . My
> 10,000 mermaid pamphlets were then put into the hands of
> boys, and sold at a penny each (half the cost) in all the princi-
> pal hotels, stores, etc. etc.

Barnum didn't miss an angle — charging for the ad pamphlets!

Not all of his curiosities were fakes. For example, he employed
midgets, a tattooed man, a bearded lady, and the Siamese twins,
Chang and Eng. These and other attractions filled a dilapidated museum at Broadway and Ann Street, later famous as Barnum's American Museum (1841). In 1842 he discovered Charles Stratton, a resi-
dent of Bridgeport, Connecticut. Immediately recognizing Stratton's
potential, Barnum taught him how to dance, sing, tell jokes, and
imitate Napoleon. Now he had a bona fide star attraction; Stratton,
a five-year-old midget outfitted in military regalia, strutted the
boards as General Tom Thumb. With profits from Tom Thumb's
successful tours of the United States and Europe, Barnum built an
Oriental palace, Iranistan, in Bridgeport. Not long after that he negotiated with Jenny Lind, the "Swedish Nightingale," to tour the
United States. He secured her by mortgaging Iranistan, his museum, and other property. Due to his reputation as an opportunist
she had demanded that he place $187,500 on deposit for her in a
London bank. Ninety-five concerts later Barnum tallied gross re-
ceipts of $712,161.34.

Never dull Barnum's saga winds through bankruptcy, recovery,
and more new ventures. At age sixty he and William C. Coup, a
seasoned circus manager, began organizing a colossal traveling
show. It would have everything: a museum, menagerie, caravan,
hippodrome, acrobats, tight-rope walkers, and clowns. But the big
dream had to wait for a few more years until Barnum formed another partnership with James Anthony Bailey. From their union
"The Barnum and Bailey Greatest Show On Earth" brought kids
running from all corners in every town they stopped at. How
Barnum obtained and promoted his amusements is instructive reading. Expert at topping himself he, in his own words, only gave the
people what they wanted. Interest in an ancient woman flagged
quickly, so bring on the Feejee Mermaid. Mark Twain saw enough
of Barnum, the humbug:

There is little or nothing in the place worth seeing, and yet how it draws! It was crammed with both sexes and all ages. . . . Barnum's Museum is one vast peanut stand now, with a few cases of dried frogs and other wonders scattered here and there, to give variety to the things.

What there is in the human psyche that craves the exotic, even if false, was clay in Barnum's hands.

BIBLIOGRAPHY

Barnum, P.T. *Barnum's Own Story*. New York: Dover Publications, 1961.
Harris, Neil. *Humbug: The Art of P.T. Barnum*. Boston-Toronto: Little, Brown and Co., 1973.
Saxon, A.H., ed. *Selected Letters of P.T. Barnum*. New York: Columbia University Press, 1983.
Wallace, Irving. *The Fabulous Showman*. New York: Knopf, 1959.

Commander Nutt, Miss Lavinia Warren, P.T. Barnum, and General Tom Thumb
(out of uniform). Barnum's midgets attracted immense crowds wherever they
appeared, feeding the public appetite for unusual specimens of humanity. This
photograph was taken in 1862 just before Miss Warren married Tom Thumb.

Batman

Batman was already a vintage fictional character when he took television by storm in early 1966. A creation of cartoonist Bob Kane, he first appeared in a comic book, *Detective Comics #27*, in 1939. Always a strong contender in the superhero sweepstakes, the character was featured in radio's "Superman" series and in two movie serials in the 1940s.

First telecast on January 12, 1966 as part of ABC's "second season," "Batman" represented the quintessential flowering of the pop 1960s, in which many diverse elements of the decade's popular culture—i.e., comic books, camp, Pop Art, superheroes and television—were blended in a package that captured the American public's imagination right from the beginning. The show's popularity—both weekly installments (the two-part stories ran on Wednesday and Thursday) ranked among the ten most popular programs of the 1965-1966 season—was attributed to the following features:

1. the vast array of marvelous gadgets (e.g., the Batmobile, the Batcopter, the Batboat, the Batlab);
2. the delightful absurdity of special effects such as the bat-noises—animated words (e.g., "crunch!," "klonk!," "pow!," "splatt!," "kapow!," "whap!," "zlonkk!") that flashed on the screen when a blow was struck during fight scenes;
3. a long list of flamboyant bat-villains, including Art Carney (The Archer), Tallulah Bankhead (Black Widow), Joan Collins (The Siren), Burgess Meredith (The Penguin), Vincent Price (Egghead), Cesar Romero (The Joker), Rudy Vallee (Lord Phogg), and Otto Preminger/George Sanders/Eli Wallach (Mr. Freeze).
4. Adam West's studiously wooden behavior as Batman amidst

contrived plot twists and the overdone acting of the rest of the cast;

5. Robin's terrible puns (e.g., attempting to scale a building with Batman during the first episode, he exclaimed, "Holy fire escape, Batman!").

By the fall of 1967, the program's novelty had subsided, and preteens became the primary audience, rendering it too risky a proposition for sponsors at its time slot. Therefore, "Batman" was cut back to one night per week in September 1967, and was terminated in March 1968. However, the character has returned to television in a number of series: "The Batman-Superman Hour" (CBS, Saturday morning, 1968-1970); "Super Friends" (1973-); and "The New Adventures of Batman" (CBS, 1977-1978). In addition, a number of episodes from the original show have been re-edited and released as *Batman – The Movie* both theatrically and as a videotape (Playhouse, 1985).

Batman has also experienced a resurgence of interest in the comic book medium since the mid-1980s as a result of National Periodical Publications' celebration of the fiftieth anniversary of the *Detective Comics* title and the character himself. A talented stable of scripters and artists have contributed to the creation of several mini-series and graphic novels which have explored new dimensions of the character's basic premise.

BIBLIOGRAPHY

Brooks, Tim, and Earle Marsh. "Batman," in: *The Complete Directory to Prime Time Network TV Shows, 1946-Present*. Third Edition. New York: Ballantine, 1985, pp. 71-72.

Edelstein, Andrew J. "Batman," in: *The Pop Sixties*. New York: World Almanac Publications, 1985, pp. 64-59.

Gilmore, Mikal. "Comic Genius," *Rolling Stone*. n470 (March 27, 1986) 56ff. Focuses upon Frank Miller's work with the Batman character.

"Here Come Capes and Capers and Genuine Barman Blood; Commerce Exploits Cult," *Life*. 60 (March 11, 1966) 26-26A.

"Holy Flypaper! Batman," *Time*. 87 (January 28, 1966) 61.

LeShan, E.J. "At War With Batman," *New York Times Magazine*. (May 15, 1966) 112ff.

Levy, R. "Friend of Batman," *Duns Review & Modern Industry*. 87 (March 1966) 51-52.

Shayon, R.L. "All the Way to the Bank: Batman," *Saturday Review*. 49 (February 12, 1966) 46.

Skow, J. "Has TV Gasp! Gone Batty? Batman TV Program," *Saturday Evening*. 239 (May 7, 1966) 93-97.

"Superfans and Batmaniacs," *Newsweek*. 65 (February 15, 1965) 89-90.

Beatlemania

Beatlemania refers to the hero worship of four young male musicians, collectively known as the Beatles, from Liverpool, England—rhythm guitarist John Lennon, bassist Paul McCartney, lead guitarist George Harrison, and drummer Ringo Starr (aka Richard Starkey)—experienced in North America as well as much of Europe, Japan, and the British Commonwealth. It is more than coincidence that *Meet the Beatles*, the band's first major American release, was issued in England on November 22, 1963, the same day President Kennedy was assassinated. In retrospect, the Beatles have come to represent a dose of lighthearted escapism, a vital prescription for curing a nationwide case of the blues. For most Americans, the initial introduction to the band took place in the early weeks of 1964 via radio plays of "I Want to Hold Your Hand" and the visual impact of their two appearances on the "Ed Sullivan Show." However, in almost no time the group's persona was seemingly everywhere. It has been alleged that some Beatles song could be heard at any time of the day somewhere on the AM radio band during the peak period of Beatlemania in the spring of 1964.

The following chronology encapsulizes the highlights of Beatlemania from 1964:

> *January*. Backed by a $50,000 advertising campaign, Capitol Records releases "I Want to Hold Your Hand" on the 13th; the January 18 issue of *Billboard* magazine shows it debuting on the pop music charts at number eighty-three. On the 20th, *Meet the Beatles* is released by Capitol; it becomes the largest-selling album up to that time.
>
> *February*. "I Want to Hold Your Hand" reaches number one on the Billboard "Hot 100." On the 7th, 100 policemen, 200 reporters, and more than 10,000 youth greet the Beatles at

New York's Kennedy Airport. The group appears on the "Ed Sullivan Show" on February 9 and 16, enabling the program (viewed by 73,000,000 Americans) to achieve the highest rating in TV history to that time. It is alleged that the band accounted for sixty percent of all singles sold in America during the month.

March. After seven weeks at the top, "I Want to Hold Your Hand" is finally overtaken by "She Loves You." Capitol reveals that "Can't Buy Me Love" had first-day sales of 940,225. On the March 31 *Billboard* chart "Can't Buy Me Love" is number one, followed by "Twist and Shout," "She Loves You," "I Want to Hold Your Hand," and "Please Please Me" at positions two through five, respectively, with five other Beatles songs in the "Hot 100." Beatles singles sales in the U.S. had grossed $17.5 million up to this point.

May. "Love Me Do" reaches number one. The group has fourteen songs in the "Hot 100" for one particular week.

June. In only six months, the group has placed twenty songs on the U.S. charts.

July. The film, *A Hard Day's Night*, is released; it is both a commercial and artistic success. Three songs from the movie are released as singles.

August. The Beatles tour America; they receive $1,933 for each minute onstage at the Hollywood Bowl.

September. The merchandising boom continues to be strong, encompassing such products as dolls, games, buttons, books, magazines, wigs, T-shirts, jewelry, hair spray, trading cards, wallpaper, ice cream, and instruments.

November. Capitol releases "I Feel Fine," backed by "She's A Woman"; both reach the top five.

December. *Beatles '65* is released; it becomes the eleventh Beatles album to chart in 1964. Others are: *"Meet the Beatles"; "Introducing the Beatles"; "The Beatles vs. the Four Seasons"; "Jolly What!" "The Beatles and Frank Ifield"; "The Beatles with Tony Sheridan and Their Guests"; "The Beatles' Second Album"; "Something New"; "A Hard Day's*

Night"; "The American Tour with Ed Rudy"; Songs, Pictures and Stories of the Fabulous Beatles.

While the intensity of the initial wave of Beatlemania had worn off by 1965, the band continued to set a torrid commercial pace throughout the sixties. Challenges to their hegemony by a succession of pretenders (e.g., the Monkees, Herb Alpert & the Tijuana Brass) merely encouraged the mass media to further hype the Beatles. More movies appeared. With the appearance of *Rubber Soul* in late 1965, each album release took on the trappings of a full-scale media event. Controversy entered into the equation with John Lennon's misquote that the Beatles were more popular than Jesus (1966), their admission to using LSD (1967), the flirtation with transcendental meditation (1968), and the naked John Lennon/Yoko Ono cover of the *Two Virgins* LP (1968). During the six-year period culminating in their decision to disband in early 1970, the group placed more than sixty songs on the U.S. singles charts, over half of which reached the top ten. At that time, they had sold more than eighty-five million albums and 120 million singles, enough to encircle the globe four times.

The influence of the Beatles is incalculable. They stimulated many to grow long hair, wear wire-rimmed glasses, take drugs, and wear Carnaby Street fashions. With respect to music, they brought the singer-songwriter and self-contained groups to the forefront. Artistic growth and social respectability became the modus operandi in rock; the LP was adopted as the primary vehicle of expression, often with conceptual overtones. In short, the Beatles acted as cultural gurus for the post-World War II baby boomer generation; they were a source of inspiration, style, and moral leadership. And now, ironically, they represent a marketing bonanza for nostalgia peddlers attempting to serve up a refried version of Sixties artifacts. The release of all of the group's British albums on compact disc in the U.S. in 1987 was arguably the biggest musical event of that year. Michael Jackson, current owner of the Beatles' song catalog, has begun leasing rights to the Big Business sector (e.g., "Revolution" to Nike). It appears probable that the vestiges of Beatlemania will be around for many years to come.

BIBLIOGRAPHY

Brown, Peter, and Steven Gaines. *The Love You Make; An Insider's Story of the Beatles*. New York: McGraw-Hill, 1983.

Catone, Marc A., ed. *As I Write This Letter: An American Generation Remembers The Beatles*. Ann Arbor, MI: Pierian, 1982.

Edelstein, Andrew J. *The Pop Sixties: A Personal and Irreverent Guide*. New York: World Almanac Publications, 1985.

Gilbert, Bob, and Gary Theroux. *The Top Ten; 1956-Present*. New York: Fireside, 1982.

Schaffner, Nicholas. *The Beatles Forever*. New York: McGraw-Hill, 1978.

Schaumburg, Ron. *Growing Up With the Beatles*. New York: Harcourt Brace Jovanovich, 1976.

Stokes, Geoffrey. *The Beatles*. New York: Rolling Stone/Times Books, 1980.

Milton Berle
and Texaco Star Theater

In retrospect, it would be easy to underestimate the impact of Milton Berle on the television medium. While his time at the top was comparatively short in duration—his program, "Texaco Star Theater," ranked number one for three seasons (1948-1951), at a time when few Americans even owned TV sets—Berle became television's first superstar. "Uncle Miltie," as he came to be affectionately known, was largely responsible for the upsurge in TV ownership, from less than two percent of U.S. homes to over seventy percent during the period (1948-1956) he was on the air.

Berle's program, shown on Tuesday evenings, was the model for the earliest wave of prime time programming. It was rapidly paced and corny, with a premium placed upon the visuals. The prevailing wisdom at the time was that if the average American was going to spend $400 for a small-screen "radio with picture," large amounts of movement and action would have to be provided. Berle excelled in this respect, offering fall-down slapstick accented with an abundance of crazy costumes and sight gags.

A host of imitators followed: Ed Sullivan serving up a potpourri of comedians, musicians, scenes from plays and circus acts as well as "The Ed Wynn Show," "The All Star Revue" with Jimmy Durante, "Your Show of Shows" featuring Sid Caesar, "Fireball Fun-For-All" with Olsen and Johnsen and "The Colgate Comedy Hour" which utilized some of the biggest names in show business (e.g., Eddie Cantor, Martin and Lewis, Abbott and Costello, Bob Hope). The variety format employed by these and other programs struck some as so old fashioned that the term "vaudeo"—signifying a wedding of vaudeville and the newly established video medium—was coined to describe it.

BIBLIOGRAPHY

Ace, G. "Berle's Still Berling," *Look*. 17 (April 7, 1953) 52-54.

"Berle and His Ace," *Newsweek*. 40 (September 29, 1952) 60.

Brooks, Tim, and Earle Marsh. "Introduction," in: *The Complete Directory to Prime Time Network TV Shows, 1946-Present*. Third Edition. New York: Ballantine, 1985, pp. x-xxi.

Edwards, J. "Behind the Scenes with Milton Berle," *Coronet*. 29 (April 1951) 83-87.

"Mama Remembers Milton Berle's Forty Years in Show Business," *Look*. 17 (November 3, 1953) 115-121.

Millstein, G. "Bringing Things to a Berle," *New York Times Magazine*. (April 8, 1951) 17ff.

Shayon, R.L. "Old Star With New Tricks," *Saturday Review*. 35 (October 4, 1952) 41.

Betty Boop

Betty Boop was created as a canine character by Grim Natwick, first appearing as the girl friend of another dog, Bimbo, in the Talkartoons series produced by Max and Dave Fleischer for Paramount in the twenties. After a few cartoon shorts her long ears developed into earrings, with the result that she looked like a cute little girl. Betty's figure parodied Mae West's, while her singing style was based on that of Helen Kane (the "Boop Boop a-Doop Girl"), who sued Max Fleischer but lost. The voice for Betty Boop was supplied by Mae Questal, who also the voice of Olive Oyl in the Popeye series.

Her cartoons were a phenomenal success; more than one hundred were produced in the 1930s. The comic inventiveness of the series has rarely been equalled; the basic premise called for Betty to sing and dance her way through a variety of far-fetched plots, in a surreal world populated by anthropomorphized clocks, flowerpots, toys and furniture. But the prime reason for the appeal of these cartoons was the Betty Boop persona; she played a vamp with a heart of gold, who threw kisses with wild abandon and batted her long eyelashes in suggestive provocation. At the peak of her popularity, Betty Boop was made into numerous toys and dolls; in 1934, King Features Syndicate introduced a newspaper strip version of the character.

Max Fleischer's decision to terminate production of the cartoons resulted from

1. a wave of puritanical attacks, mostly emanating from women's clubs, against the character (the 1933 short, "Boilesk," was actually banned in Philadelphia);
2. a costly strike in 1937; and
3. their gradual decline in popularity.

After years of being relegated to PBS television channels and art film theaters, Betty Boop has undergone a revival since the sixties.

Many products again bear her likeness and many cartoon festivals have centered on the classic Fleischer cartoons, most of which are also available in the video format (via both the colorization process and in the original black-and-white).

BIBLIOGRAPHY

"Betty Boop," in: *The World Encyclopedia of Cartoons*, Volume 1, edited by Maurice Horn. New York: Gale/Chelsea House, 1980, pp.115-116.

Big Little Books

Big Little Books were extremely popular with juvenile readers in the 1930s and early 1940s. They were small, but extremely thick in size; the covers were made of stiff cardboard and featured colored illustrations. Inside, the usual format consisted of a full-page illustration opposite a page of printed text. An offshoot of comic strips (sans the "balloon" text), many titles featured the notable characters from that medium. Adventure stories and fables were also popular. The following list represents a sampling of titles from the heyday of Big Little Books:

Ace Drummond
Alley Oop and Dinny
Andy Panda and Presto the Pup
Bambi
Barney Google
Big Little Mother Goose
Blondie and Baby Dumpling (1937; 1939)
Brer Rabbit (1945; 1948)
Buck Jones and the Night Raiders
Dick Tracy, Adventures of
Donald Duck and the Ducklings
Flash Gordon and the Monsters of Mango
G-Man on Lightning Island
Gene Autry in Gunsmoke
Huckleberry Finn
John Carter of Mars
Little Orphan Annie
Lone Ranger and His Horse Silver
Mickey Mouse
Popeye in Choose Your Weppins
Red Ryder, Acting Sheriff

Smilin' Jack and the Border Bandits
Tarzan of the Apes
Tom Mix and the Hoard of Montezuma

BIBLIOGRAPHY

"Books—Big Little Books," in: *The Official Price Guide to Paper Collectibles*, edited by Thomas E. Hudgeons III. Third Edition. Orlando, FL: House of Collectibles, 1983, pp. 125-129.

Lowery, Lawrence F. *The Collector's Guide to Big Little Books and Similar Books*. Danville, CA: Educational Research and Applications Corp., 1981.

James Bond, Agent 007

Although James Bond first appeared in the 1950s in Ian Fleming's spy novels, the character didn't became a national obsession until the 1960s. The impetus for this development was the cinematic interpretation of Bond by Scottish actor Sean Connery. Connery's portrayal of Bond would come to epitomize the ideal of the 1960s male hero — cool under pressure, assured and adventuresome with women, equally familiar with weaponry and wine, emotionless, noncommittal, cynical tonque planted firmly in cheek.

Connery made five Bond films during that decade (as well as *Diamonds Are Forever* in 1971 and 1983's *Never Say Never Again*). While the first two — *Dr. No* (1962) and *From Russia With Love* (1963) — were only modest successes, they established the formula which later captivated the nation: larger-than-life villains, gorgeous women, spectacular action sequences and a host of memorable gadgets, most notably Bond's Aston-Martin DB-V, which shot oil slicks at pursuers, dispatched unwanted occupants via an ejector seat and further confused enemies with its chariot scythe, smoke screen and rotating license plate. *Goldfinger* (1964) and *Thunderball* (1965) pushed the series to the top of the box office sweepstakes, spinning off hit songs (e.g., Shirley Bassey's "Goldfinger"), countless TV imitations (e.g., "The Man From U.N.C.L.E.," "Mission: Impossible," "I Spy"), substantial sales for Fleming's novels in paperback and a wide array of 007 merchandise (e.g., aftershave, clothing, attaché cases, games, toys). Fleming — who died in August 1964, before the craze hit full stride — attributed the success of the Bond books and films to the fact that they were in sync with the times: "We live in a violent era . . . In our last war, thirty million people were killed. As for sex, seduction has to a marked extent replaced courtship."

After *You Only Live Twice* (1967) — a film markedly inferior to its predecessors — Connery took a long sabbatical from the 007 role.

Films featuring other actors as Bond (e.g., George Lazenby, Roger Moore) have been commercially profitable, but these titles have lacked the edge inherent in the multi-dimensional performances provided by Connery in his prime.

BIBLIOGRAPHY

Amis, Kingsley. "Does James Bond Really Hate Women? Excerpt from the James Bond Dossier," *Ladies Home Journal*. 82 (July 1965) 47ff.

"Bond Phenomenon," *Newsweek*. 65 (April 19, 1965) 95-96.

"Bondanza; 007 Products Boom," *Newsweek*. 65 (May 10, 1965) 92ff.

Boyd, A.S. "James Bond: Modern-Day Dragonslayer," *Christian Century*. 82 (May 19, 1965) 644-747.

Cockburn, Alexander. "James Bond at 25," *American Film*. 12 (July/August 1987) 26-32.

Cohn, Lawrence. "Broccoli Bonds Spawned Imitators," *Variety*. 327 (May 13, 1987) 62ff. Focuses upon the work of Cubby Broccoli.

Corliss, Richard. "Bond Keeps Up His Silver Streak: After 25 Years, the 007 Formula Remains Stirring But Not Shaken," *Time*. 130 (August 10, 1987) 51-52.

Edelstein, Andrew J. "James Bond Galore," *The Pop Sixties*. New York: World Almanac Publications, 1985, pp. 138-141.

Gelman, Morris. "From MGM-UA Communications With Love, 14 James Bond Pics to be Sped to World TV Marts," *Variety*. 324 (October 15, 1986) 17ff.

Greenberg, James. "'Daylights' Beats All Bond Openers to Lead Natl. B.O.," *Variety*. 328 (August 5, 1987) 3ff.

Greene, Bob. "So . . . We Meet at Last, Mr. Bond; an Encounter With Sean Connery, Whose 007 Set the Standard for Cool," *Esquire*. 107 (April 1987) 15-16.

Hirshey, Gerri. "Meet the New Bond: In 'The Living Daylights,' Timothy Dalton Does it Better," *Rolling Stone*. (July 16, 1987) 37ff.

Olesky, J.F. "Incredible James Bond; Merchandizing Program," *Dun's Review and Modern Industry*. 86 (October 1965) 75-76.

Sragow, Michael. "Heroes We Don't Deserve," *Atlantic*. 256 (October 1985) 89-91.

Boogie Woogie

I want you to pull up on your blouse,
   Let down on your skirt,
Get down so low you think you're in the dirt . . .
Now when I say 'Boogie!' I want you to boogie;
When I say 'Stop!' I want you to stop right still . . .

These lyrics are from "Pinetop's Boogie Woogie" (1928) by Clarence "Pinetop" Smith and they started a new musical rage. That is, among those who regularly attended Chittlin Struts, Gumbo Suppers, Fish Fries, Egg Nog and rent parties. It took a while for the rest of America to get infected. Of these diversions the rent party is the most interesting. Among blacks who lived on Chicago's South Side (and elsewhere) some couldn't pay their rent so they threw parties called "pitchin' boogie." Anyone in the neighborhood could stop by and for fifty cents, a bag of sandwiches or a bottle of gin, join in on the fun. Musicians who were no more flush than the renters went from party to party playing a rapid, incessant rhythm on piano. For their contribution of boogie woogie they got free food and plenty of adulation. The revelers stuffed sandwiches in their mouths to keep them scorching the keys all night long. Both hands of the boogie woogie artist dazzled the crowd, the left on bass patterns and the right improvising. Before long the landlord pocketed the rent.

Ragtime, its progenitor, sounded sedate next to boogie woogie. Even the artists' names were more flamboyant; compare rag pianist Scott Joplin with Cripple Clarence Lofton, Cow Cow Davenport, Romeo Nelson, Montana Taylor, and Speckled Red. The exciting new sound wasn't meant to stay bottled up in tenement buildings. Once white-owned record companies heard boogie woogie they had to have it; first with Pinetop (his recording named the style of music), then with Tommy Dorsey's "Boogie Woogie" (1938), Char-

lie Barnet's "Scrub Me, Mama, with a Boogie Beat" (1940), and
the Andrews Sisters' "Boogie Woogie Bugle Boy" (1941). Ten
years had elapsed between Pinetop and Dorsey attesting to white
conservative record production. Of course, in the meantime, a lot of
rent parties went on where boogie woogie was king and had nothing
to do with mainstream popular music. Real boogie woogie bespoke
joy in the face of hardship, a devil-may-care attitude. Homogeniz-
ing black culture to make it palatable and then linking it to a dance,
insured that boogie woogie would only be a fad—and it was for the
general public. But black blues pianists continued to incorporate the
style of playing in their renditions and new music well into the
1950s.

Then in the late 1970s half of the name reappeared. "To boogie"
and "to boogie down" meant to dance hard and fast mainly to disco
music. The original black dance, though, combining high kicks,
knee and lower body twists, and swaying was completely lost on
the young inebriates. White kids just didn't know what it was like to
really boogie woogie. Nor would they have understood, if told, that
the music had once been a safeguard against despair. Black writer
LeRoi Jones recalls the Depression-era rent parties one more time:

> The parties could last all weekend, and for some intrepid
> souls, well into the week. The Third Ward of Newark once
> boasted for several months, until the law moved in, a rent
> party promoted by two blues singers which was called 'The
> Function' and which advertised that one could "Grind Till
> You Lose Your Mind." It was at these kind of parties that
> boogie woogie developed.

BIBLIOGRAPHY

Hitchcock, H. Wiley, and Stanley Sadie. *The New Grove Dictionary of American Music*. Vol. I, A-D. New York: Macmillan, 1986, pp. 257-258.

Jones, LeRoi. *Blues People: Negro Music in White America*. New York: William Morrow, 1963.

Ramsey, Frederic, Jr., and Charles E. Smith. *Jazzmen*. New York: Harcourt, Brace and Co., 1939.

British Invasion

The British Invasion refers to the onslaught of U.K. musicians on American television, radio and record charts during the mid-1960s. Following close on the heels of the enthusiastic reception given the Liverpool Merseybeat band, the Beatles, by Americans, beginning in January 1964, U.S. record companies began signing — and promoting — British acts at a feverish pace. Some of the more notable hitmakers included:

The Animals — "House of the Rising Sun," "We Gotta Get Out of This Place"

Chad & Jeremy — "Yesterday's Gone," "A Summer Song"

The Dave Clark Five — "Glad All Over," "Bits & Pieces," "Do You Love Me," "Can't You See That She's Mine"

Petula Clark — "Downtown," "I Know A Place"

Donovan — "Catch the Wind," "Universal Soldier"

Wayne Fontana & The Mindbenders — "Game of Love"

The Fortunes — "You've Got Your Troubles"

Freddie & The Dreamers — "I'm Telling You Now," "Do the Freddie"

Gerry & The Pacemakers — "Don't Let the Sun Catch You Crying," "How Do You Do It?"

Herman's Hermits — "Can't You Hear My Heartbeat," "Mrs. Brown, You've Got A Lovely Daughter"

The Hollies — "Look Through Any Window," "Bus Stop"

The Honeycombs — "Have I the Right," "I Can't Stop"

Tom Jones — "It's Not Unusual," "What's New Pussycat"

The Kinks — "You Really Got Me," "All Day and All of the Night," "Tired of Waiting for You"

Billy J. Kramer & The Dakotas — "Little Children," "Bad to Me"

Manfred Mann — "Do Wah Diddy Diddy," "Sha La La"

The Moody Blues—"Go Now"

Peter & Gordon—"A World Without Love," "Nobody I Know"

The Rolling Stones—"Time Is On My Side," "The Last Time," "Satisfaction"

The Searchers—"Needles & Pins," "Love Potion No. 9"

Silkie—"You've Got to Hide Your Love Away"

Dusty Springfield—"I Only Want to Be With You," "Wishin' & Hopin'"

The Swingin' Bluejeans—"The Hippy Hippy Shake"

Unit 4 + 2—"Concrete & Clay"

The Who—"I Can't Explain," "My Generation"

The Zombies—"She's Not There," "Tell Her No"

The extent of the mania for all things British—many of these acts were virtually unknown in their own country—forced many long established American performers out of the public eye, including Neil Sedaka, the Everly Brothers, Fats Domino and, to some degree, even Elvis Presley. The success of this music wave has been attributed to the national state of depression brought on by the Kennedy assassination, which rendered the United States open to something completely fresh and new. Ironically, the music that Americans found so unique and invigorating had been a part of American culture, albeit underground, for almost a generation; i.e., the British had simply taken rhythm and blues and adapted it to three- and four-part harmonies, complete with English accents.

In the face of successive challenges by indigenous American styles (e.g., soul music, folk rock, various California sounds such as surf music, car songs, etc.), the British presence waned somewhat by 1966. However, the pipeline between the U.S. and U.K. music scenes—only strictly a one-way proposition—has remained open to the importation of British talent. The cross-fertilization of styles and cultures has rendered it virtually impossible for the casual listener to distinguish between rock artists hailing from either side of the Atlantic.

BIBLIOGRAPHY

"Beatles' Success in U.S. A Trend for the British?," *Variety*. 233 (February 5, 1964) 46.

Cohn, Nik. "London 1964-65," in: *Rock; From the Beginning*. New York: Stein & Day, 1969, pp. 203-227.

Cross, C., and others. *Encyclopedia of British Beat Groups and Solo Artists of the Sixties*. New York: Omnibus, 1981.

Ewen, David. "Rock Around the Clock, 1-3," in: *All the Years of American Popular Music; A Comprehensive History*. Englewood Cliffs, NJ: Prentice-Hall, 1977, pp. 611-626.

Lucie-Smith, Edward. *The Liverpool Scene*. Garden City, NY: Doubleday, 1968.

Schoenfeld, Harold. "Britannia Rules Airwaves; Beatles Stir Home Carbons," *Variety*. 233 (February 12, 1964) 63.

Shaw, Arnold. "The British Invasion," in *The Rock Revolution*. London: Crowell-Collier, 1969, pp. 95-112.

"U.K. Rock 'n' Rollers Are Called Copycats," *Billboard*. 77 (June 19, 1965) 12.

Busby Berkeley

During World War I Berkeley fought with the U.S. Army in France, but more importantly for the history of cinema, after the war he choreographed parade drill teams. He taught soldiers how to march in precise, intricate patterns. All it took was discipline to please the crowd as the moving mosaic of stalwart men crisscrossed in ranks. A little over a decade later he would direct, not soldiers, but chorines through even more complex patterns for the pleasure of a worldwide audience.

Discharged from the army Berkeley spent most of the 1920s on Broadway where he quickly achieved success staging dance numbers. So much so that Hollywood beckoned. Samuel Goldwyn hired him as a dance director to work on a couple of Eddie Cantor films. They were lackluster though it didn't matter much since the film industry conceded that movie musicals were on the decline anyway. Berkeley must have wondered why he had been brought out to California to minister to a dying market. Then in 1932 Darryl F. Zanuck at Warners decided to beat the odds. He gave Berkeley complete control over the dance production numbers in a film vehicle called, *42nd Street*. The plot mirrored real life – a Broadway director on his last leg must produce a hit show or else. The drama unfolds, tensions mount, leading up to the big production numbers that have to surpass the usual hackneyed fare. Berkeley met the challenge by using overhead camera shots and shifting perspectives, sharply contrasting black and white sets, and playful song interpretations. For "Shuffle Off to Buffalo" the chorines' train car opens to reveal the girls getting ready for bed. As each girl sings, the lyrics disclose something about her personality. That way the voyeur audience gets to know them better, not to mention gets to see more of them. For "Young and Healthy" the girls flaunt ribbon-entwined flesh and tilt their heads back to smile up at the camera. The finale has the star, Ruby Keeler, singing and dancing center stage, then her tapping feet magically land on top of a taxicab without missing a step. She rides along in the heart of 42nd Street still dancing as Manhattan skyscrapers sway to the beat. Keeler and the whole cast of Broadway dancers take over the street and finish the number.

42nd Street was one of the top moneymaking films for 1933. Berkeley had found his formula: pretty girls seen from all angles (he even ran a camera through a tunnel of chorine legs), songs he could interpret with wit to tantalize the audience, and extravagant fantasy. His innovations of the overhead kaleidoscopic shot and collective dancing to fill the screen renewed interest in the movie musical. Berkeley production numbers became a fad and usually overshadowed the storyline. Audiences could hardly wait to see what his clever mind would invent next. In *Gold Diggers of 1933* he treated them to "Pettin' in the Park." Couples snuggle outdoors until a rain shower sends them scurrying indoors; the drenched girls take off their wet clothes behind translucent curtains. Not much dancing but the choreographed silhouettes elicited audience approval. Another number, "The Shadow Waltz," had sixty chorines playing violins while shifting in and out of lacy patterns. For a climax they melded into one huge neon-lit violin and bow seen from overhead. In *Dames* the title said it all—girls and more girls twisting in and out of geometric patterns as if drawn through their motions by a compass and protractor. Berkeley gave each girl an illustrated board which was a piece of a jigsaw puzzle, so when put together and filmed from above the pieces formed a giant-size picture of the star, again Ruby Keeler.

As visually stimulating as these production numbers were they were short-lived. The public applauded their novelty, but once seen they lost their element of surprise. What Berkeley did achieve was to refurbish the musical, gather a new audience, and open the door for the great Hollywood musicals to come. After a few years the classic Berkeley signature went into dormancy until Jackie Gleason revived it. Then television audiences looked down on the June Taylor Dancers forming mosaics every week at the beginning of the "Jackie Gleason Show" (1952-1970). Recent summer Olympics Games have incorporated spectacular human picture-making in their ceremonies, as do many football half-time activities, both relayed by blimps. But Berkeley was the first to popularize dancers moving fluidly from one set position to another to create stunning kaleidoscopic images. His work remains the best.

BIBLIOGRAPHY

Altman, Rick. *The American Film Musical*. Bloomington & Indianapolis: Indiana University Press, 1987.

Hirschhorn, Clive. *The Hollywood Musical*. New York: Crown Publishers, Inc., 1981.

Wolfe, Charles. "Busby Berkeley," in *American Directors*, Volume I, edited by Jean-Pierre Coursodon. New York: McGraw-Hill, 1983.

The Cakewalk

An Afro-American dance associated with a syncopated music related to ragtime, it appears to have originated with slaves parodying the genteel manners and formal dances of their white owners. The term evidently refers to the prize (i.e., a cake) given to the best dancers among a group of slaves; by the 1890s, "cakewalk contests" were organized as public entertainment in cities above the Mason-Dixon line. The cakewalk was popularized amd further refined via blackface minstrel shows, the all-black musicals of the late 1890s (e.g., Will Marion Cook's *Clorindy*, or *The Origin of the Cakewalk*, 1898), and later, vaudeville and burlesque. In particular, the vaudeville team of Bert Williams and George Walker were instrumental in spreading its fame in the early 1900s through their performances in *In Dahomey* (1902) and *In Abyssinia* (1905).

While no specific steps were associated with the cakewalk, it was performed — albeit following years of continued refinements — as a grand march in a parade-like fashion by couples prancing and strutting arm in arm, bowing and kicking backwards and forwards (sometimes with arched backs and pointed toe), and saluting to the spectators. Its popularity resulted in the assimilation of some features of the cakewalk into white dances in America.

BIBLIOGRAPHY

Butler, Albert and Josephine. "Cakewalk," in: *Encyclopedia of Social Dance*. New York: 1967.

Cooper, H.E. "A Cycle of Dance Crazes; the Jouchi-Couchi, Cakewalk and Charleston are Birds of a Feather That Now Find a Warm Nest in the Revue," *Dance Magazine*. (February 1927) 28-29, 50.

Emery, L.F. *Black Dance in the United States from 1619 to 1970*. Palo Alto, CA: 1972.

Hitchcock, H. Wiley, and Pauline Norton. "Cakewalk," in *The New Grove Encyclopedia of American Music*, edited by H. Wiley Hitchcock and Stanley Sadie. Volume One, A-D. London: Macmillan, 1986, p. 343.

Stearns, M., and J. Stearns. *Jazz Dance: the Story of American Vernacular Dance*. New York: 1968.

Calypso

The roots of the brief calypso vogue can be found in the first wave of rock 'n' roll. As the music industry establishment attempted to put the latter development into perspective, attitudes such as the following were widespread:

1. Elvis Presley, Little Richard and others of that ilk were a threat to the American (read: Judeo-Christian) way of life and/or my financial security; therefore, an acceptable substitute must be found.
2. Rock 'n' roll was a passing fad and, given the propensity of youth for things new and different, let's go find the next "big thing."

Calypso was hardly a new development, having been a part of the musical landscape in Trinidad since the late nineteenth century. Half-hearted efforts had even been made to sell the genre in the States in the 1930s as well as the early 1950s. It certainly had some highly saleable features; e.g., a catchy rhythm and English lyrics which were in some cases highly literate. When Harry Belafonte — an unknown folk interpreter of West Indian extraction who had languished at RCA for several years — was given calypso material to record, he quickly achieved superstar status. His "Jamaica Farewell" hit the Top Twenty pop charts in late 1956 and "Banana Boat (Day-O)" peaked at number five early in the following year.

By now, the market was flooded with releases attempting to capitalize on the calypso trend. The folk camp was represented by the Tarriers' "Banana Boat Song" (number four, 1957) and Terry Gilkyson's "Marianne" (number four, 1957) while Tin Pan Alley artists came up with their inevitable cover versions. The Fontaine Sisters, Steve Lawrence and Sarah Vaughan all reached the Top Twenty in 1957 with "Banana Boat Song," The Hilltoppers scored with "Marianne," and Stan Freberg had a hit with his spoof of "Day-O."

Calypsomania ran out of steam by mid-1957 in part due to the oversaturation of the U.S. airwaves with a style which had not secured any base of support other than novelty appeal. In addition, there was a dearth of native Caribbean talent performing calypso. Reporters and tourists found that Fats Domino and other New Orleans artists were the rage in Jamaica as a result of powerful clear-channel radio stations beaming from the southern states. While other artists identified with calypso sank from public view without a trace, Belafonte continued to be successful as an album artist (e.g., *Calypso, Belafonte, An Evening with Harry Belafonte, Harry Belafonte at Carnegie Hall, Jump Up Calypso, The Midnight Special*), playing a major role in the commercial folk boom of the early 1960s.

BIBLIOGRAPHY

"The Calypso Craze," *Newsweek*. 49 (February 25, 1957) 72.
"Calypso is Stone Cold Dead," *Variety*. 206 (May 22, 1957) 41ff.
"Calypsomania," *Time*. 69 (May 25, 1957) 55-56.
Castagne, Patrick. "This Is Calypso," *Music Journal*. 15 (January 1958) 32-33ff.
Crowley, Daniel J. "Toward a Definition of Calypso," *Ethnomusicology*. 3 (May 1959) 57-66; 3 (September 1959) 17-24.
Holder, G. "That Fad from Trinidad," *New York Times Magazine*. (April 21, 1957) 14ff.
"Natural Death or Murder?," *Variety*. 207 (June 12, 1957) 61.
Nilson, J.S. "Belafonte and Others in Calypso Variety," *New York Times*. 106 (May 5, 1957) Section 2, p. 15.
Schoenfeld, Harold. "Calypsongs Father Bother," *Variety*. 207 (March 20, 1957) 55.

Belafonte, Harry

Shaw, Arnold. *Belafonte*. New York: Pyramid, 1960.
"Today's Top Record Talent," *Billboard*. 74 (April 7, 1962) 48.

The Tarriers

"New Acts," *Variety*. 206 (May 15, 1957) 69.

Car Songs

An offshoot of "surfing music," car songs sold millions of records during 1963-1964. Built around the West Coast Sound – airy harmonies, jangling guitars and pulsating rhythms – merged with hot-rod terminology and atmospheric background effects such as revving engines and squealing brakes, the genre was dominated by a surprisingly small, close-knit family of Southern California musicians. At the center of the phenomenon were the Beach Boys, whose "409" (1962) – the popular B-side of the hit single, "Surfin' Safari" – was the first song of this type. "409" had all of the major ingredients of a car song: lyrics praising a particular vehicle's positive qualities (usually speed) geared to the intellect and sensibilities of a twelve- to-sixteen-year-old male. Brian Wilson, chief composer of the Beach Boys, also wrote material for "competing" acts such as Jan and Dean. When Wilson ceased touring in 1965, the Beach Boys replaced him with Bruce Johnston, formerly of the car song duo Bruce and Terry.

Notable car songs included the following:

"Shut Down" – The Beach Boys (Capitol, 1963)
"Fun, Fun, Fun" – The Beach Boys (Capitol, 1964)
"Custom Machine" – Bruce and Terry (Columbia, 1964)
"Little Honda" – The Hondells (Mercury, 1964)
"Drag City" – Jan and Dean (Liberty, 1963-1964)
"Dead Man's Curve" – Jan and Dean (Liberty, 1964)
"The Little Old Lady (From Pasadena)" – Jan and Dean (Liberty, 1964)
"G.T.O." – Ronny and The Daytonas (Mala, 1964)
"Bucket 'T'" – Ronny and The Daytonas (Mala, 1964-1965)
"Hey Little Cobra" – The Rip Chords (Columbia, 1963-1964)
"Three Window Coupe" – The Rip Chords (Columbia, 1964)

The listing omits pretenders such as The Routers, whose instrumental, "Sting Ray" (1963), featured fruity horn effects which sounded like something on a child's tricycle.

Car songs eventually fell victim to the "relevancy quotient" which infiltrated pop music with the rise of folk rock and protest songs in 1965. The genre's inherent dumbness, even in the hands of an accomplished lyricist like Wilson, turned off youth who by then were preoccupied with weighty matters such as Vietnam and the Civil Rights movement.

BIBLIOGRAPHY

Alexander, Shana. "Love Songs to the Carburetor," *Life*. 57 (November 6, 1964) 33.

Cooper, B. Lee. "'Cruisin' and Playin' the Radio': Exploring Images of the American Automobile Through Popular Music," *International Journal of Instructional Media*. 7 (1979-1980) 327-334.

Lewis, David L. "Sex and the Automobile: From Rumble Seats to Rockin' Vans," *Michigan Quarterly Review*. (Fall 1980/Winter 1981) 518-528.

Wright, John L. "Croonin' About Cruisin'," in: *The Popular Culture Reader*, compiled by Jack Nachbar, Deborah Weiser and John L. Wright. Bowling Green, OH: Bowling Green University Popular Press, 1978, pp. 109-117.

Casey at the Bat

Despite the efforts of its author to disassociate himself from it, *Casey at the Bat* has come to be regarded as the most famous American sport poem ever written. Although written by a Harvard philosophy scholar, Ernest Lawrence Thayer, the work—which first appeared on Sunday, June 3, 1988, in the fourth column of the fourth page of the *San Francisco Examiner*—merely bore the signature "Phim," Thayer's college nickname.

Casey's immortality was the result of the decision of a young vaudevillian, William de Wolf Hopper (husband of Hollywood columnist Hedda Hopper), to incorporate it into his stage routine. Beginning with a rousing recitation in New York's Wallock Theatre in 1888 to an audience including the personnel of two major league baseball teams—the New York Giants and the Chicago White Stockings—Hopper went on to re-enact the drama over 10,000 times during his career. His success touring the country with *Casey* led many publications to reprint the poem; by the turn of the century it appeared that every baseball fan in America was familiar with the pathetic hero of Mudville.

The poem's ability to capture the imagination of the American public is reflected in the large body of works which parody, imitate, build upon, etc., the Casey theme. One of the more notable examples was *Casey's Revenge*, a 1906 revision of the legend, written by famed sports writer Grantland Rice for the Nashville *Tennessean*, which has Casey hitting the ball. In addition, the poem has inspired films (e.g., a Disney animation short appearing in the 1944 feature, *Make Mine Music*), recordings (e.g., narrations by Lionel Barrymore and New York Yankees announcer Mel Allen), TV productions and an opera by William Schuman. The theme has even been employed in Penn and Teller's magic act; the skit has Penn speed-reading the poem as Teller, bound in a straitjacket and suspended by his ankles above a bed of spikes, attempts to free himself before the completion of the poem. More recently, Casey's one-hundredth birthday inspired a renewed outburst of articles (e.g., Frank Deford's mythological exploration of the days in Casey's life leading up to the fateful moment when he struck out which appeared in the July 18, 1988 issue of *Sports Illustrated*) and sports commentaries during the summer of 1988.

While Thayer eventually admitted that he was the legitimate author of *Casey*, he continued to consider it a maudlin and overdramatic piece of doggerel. However, Americans have found these very flaws compelling; it continues to connect with an audience that identifies with the poem's premise, its tragedy and the pathos of misplaced bravado.

BIBLIOGRAPHY

Deford, Frank. "Casey at the Bat," *Sports Illustrated*. 69 (July 18, 1988) 52-62ff. A continuation of the story beyond Thayer's poem.

Hall, D. "In Mudville, Hope Springs Eternal: Mighty Casey's 100th Season," *The New York Times Book Review*. 93 (June 5, 1988) 16ff.

Isaacs, Benno. "Casey Hits 100," *The Saturday Evening Post*. (May/June 1988) 20, 112.

Turkin, Hy, and S.C. Thompson. "Baseball Ballads," in: *The Official Encyclopedia of Baseball*. 7th ed., revised by Pete Palmer. New York: Barnes, 1974, c1951, pp. 679-683.

David Cassidy

David Cassidy has proven to be the most notable teen idol of the rock era. Following sporadic acting assignments on Broadway and television as a teenager, he achieved overnight fame in fall 1970 as Keith Partridge on the TV series, "The Partridge Family" (modelled after the 1960s pop-rock group, The Cowsills). The Partridge Family's debut single, "I Think I Love You," sold almost six million copies. With Cassidy as its centerpiece, the group was featured on a wide array of products, including coloring books, lunch boxes, dolls, comic books, postcards, clothing, books and a succession of hit recordings.

In order to capitalize on his teen idol potential, Cassidy embarked upon a solo recording career in 1971 with a remake of the Association's "Cherish," which achieved million seller status in short order. His tours inspired mass hysteria throughout the early 1970s.

In 1974 Cassidy left the TV series and signed a long-term recording contract with RCA in February of the following year with the aim of attracting a more mature audience. Various projects — including collaborations with Mick Ronson and Brian Wilson, respectively — have met with hostility from rock critics and indifference from record buyers.

BIBLIOGRAPHY

Deck, Carol. *The David Cassidy Story*. New York: Curtis, 1972.

Fayard, J. "David," *Life*. 71 (October 29, 1971) 70-73.

Green, R. "Naked Lunch Box: The David Cassidy Story," *Rolling Stone*. n108 (May 11, 1972) 36-42.

Gregory, James, ed. *David, David, David*. New York: Curtis, 1972.

Hudson, James A. *Meet David Cassidy*. New York: Scholastic Book Services, 1972.

"1 Dies as Hysteria Grips Kids at Cassidy U.K. Gig," *Variety*. 275 (June 5, 1974) 57.

Stambler, Irwin. "David Cassidy," in: *Encyclopedia of Pop, Rock and Soul*. New York: St. Martin, 1974, pp. 99-100.

Vernon and Irene Castle

Vernon and Irene Castle parlayed extraordinary grace and good looks to reign over the dancing craze gripping America during the second decade of the twentieth century.

The Castles came upon their seemingly effortless style almost by accident. As unemployed actors taking a break from Broadway slapstick for a honeymoon trip to Paris in 1912, the couple got a job as a dance team at the sumptuous Café de Paris. The night before beginning work, they went to the cafe to see what the place was like. Because Irene was using her wedding dress as an evening gown, they found it necessary to tone down the high-stepping gymnastics then in vogue. Their grace and ingenuity entranced the management, which insisted that they repeat the performance the following night. Soon the Castles were the rage of Paris.

Returning in triumph to New York later in the year, the Castles proceeded to make a profound impact via Broadway musicals (e.g., *Watch Your Step*, 1914), cabaret engagements and ballroom exhibitions. The couple originated and introduced the fox trot, the Castle walk and the Castle polka. In addition, they popularized such dances as the maxixe, the tango, the hesitation waltz, the bunny hug and the turkey trot. The couple starred in a film, *The Whirl of Life*, and Irene's bobbed hair and slim, uncorseted figure were envied — or imitated — by the majority of American women.

The Castles' career was prematurely cut short when Vernon — a flying instructor during World War I — was killed in a training mission on February 15, 1918. However, their legacy lived on through a book of instruction, *Modern Dancing* (1914).

BIBLIOGRAPHY

"Artists of the Tango," *Cosmopolitan*. 55 (August 1913) 408-410.

Castle, Irene. *My Husband*. New York: Scribner's, 1919.

Castle, Irene, as told to Bob and Wanda Duncan. *Castles in the Air*. Garden City, NY: Doubleday, 1958. Reprinted by Da Capo in 1980.

Cohen-Stratyner, Barbara Naomi. "Castle, Irene"; "Castle, Vernon," in: *Biographical Dictionary of Dance*. New York: Schirmer, 1982, pp. 157; 158-159.
"Darlings of the Dance Craze," in: *This Fabulous Century; Volume II, 1910-1920*, edited by Ezra Bowen. New York: Time-Life, 1969, pp. 276-279.
Duncan, Donald. "Irene Castle in 1956; an Exclusive Interview with the Fabulous First Lady of Ballroom Dance," *Dance Magazine*. (October 1956) 87-89.
Erenberg, Lewis A. "Everybody's Doin' It: The Pre-World War I Dance Craze, the Castles and the Modern American Girl," *Feminist Studies*. 3 (Fall 1975) 155-170.
"Vernon Castle, Redeemed from Frivolity by War," *Literary Digest*. 56 (March 2, 1918) 66-68.

Vernon and Irene Castle got American dancing prior to the First World War. They were poetry in motion and the personification of litheness. Imitators of their style came later, most notably Fred Astaire and his many supple female partners.

Charlie Chaplin

It is hard to cover Charlie Chaplin's career without resorting to superlatives. Gerald Mast succinctly set forth the Chaplin legacy as follows:

> Charles Chaplin was the first and the greatest international star of the American silent comic cinema. He was also the twentieth century's first media "superstar," the first artistic creator and popularized creature of our global culture, whose face, onscreen antics, and offscreen scandals were disseminated around the globe by new media which knew no geographical or linguistic boundaries. But more than this, Chaplin was the first acknowledged artistic genius of the cinema, recognized as such by a young generation of writers and artists whose number included George Bernard Shaw, H.G. Wells, Bertolt Brecht, Pablo Picasso, James Joyce, Samuel Beckett, and the surrealist painters and poets of both Paris and Berlin. Chaplin may be the one cinema artist who might truly be called a seminal figure of the century — if only because of his influence on virtually every other recognized seminal figure of the century.

Chaplin virtually exploded upon the American film scene. Commencing work with Keystone in January 1914, Chaplin — frequently combining the functions of director, script writer and actor — produced thirty-five one- and two-reel shorts as well as a feature, *Tillie's Punctured Romance*, for that company. Although Marie Dressler had been recruited from the stage to star in the latter film, it proved to be the launching pad to stardom for Chaplin. With each succeeding release, letters poured into the studio asking for information about and pictures of the "Little Tramp." Given the moviegoing audience's insatiable appetite for his work, countless actors appeared who were both directly (e.g., Billy West) and indirectly (e.g., Harry Langdon, Harold Lloyd, Buster Keaton) derivative of Chaplin's style.

In the meantime, Chaplin proceeded to change studios with regularity in order to garner the financial renumeration and artistic control he considered his due. Chaplin left Keystone to do fourteen films with Essanay (1915-1916), eleven for Mutual (1916-1917) and nine for First National (1918-1923). Although he became more methodical and painstakingly meticulous in his work as time passed, Chaplin reaped progressively larger aesthetic and commercial dividends. By 1921, he would receive $600,000 plus seventy-five percent of $2,500,000 grossed by the mini-feature, *The Kid*. As he evolved into the multi-faceted creator of feature films (he even produced the music for his films following the advent of sound; his composition, "This Is My Song," was a bestseller well into the rock era) in the early 1920s, Chaplin stood as the acknowledged master of cinematic comedy, a man whose name was a household word. Co-owner of his own film company (United Artists), and fabulously wealthy, he mingled with the world's social elite. Kalton Lahue *World of Laughter*, University of Oklahoma, 1966) has attributed Chaplin's popularity to

> . . . his universal appeal and the greatness of his vigorous talent. He could be looked up to, laughed at, and pitied, almost at once. It was part of Chaplin's genius that he could make audiences become aware of and sympathetic to the human condition . . .

Changing fashions, Chaplin's relative inactivity as an artist beginning in the mid-1920s and the lurid divorce proceedings of 1927 contributed to the erosion of Chaplin's popularity with the American public. While his films continued to make money, they became more and more elitist in their approach and intent. Chaplin's ultimate fall from grace took place within a relatively short period of time. His outspoken defense of liberal political causes led to his being vilified by the press and right-wing activist groups as a communist sympathizer in the late 1940s. His *Monsieur Verdeux* (1947) was widely criticized for its handling of taboo subject matter; i.e., an updating of the Bluebeard theme in which Chaplin murders successive wives in order to support his invalid first wife. While abroad in 1952, the State Department summarily revoked his automatic re-entry permit. Chaplin retaliated by not returning to America for twenty years, by refusing to let any of his films circulate in America during that period and by releasing *A King in New York* (1957), which satirized American democracy.

BIBLIOGRAPHY

"Chaplin, Charlie," in: *The International Dictionary of Films and Filmmakers: Volume II; Directors/Filmmakers*, edited by Christopher Lyon. Chicago: St. James, 1984, pp. 89-92.

Lyons, T.J., comp. *Charles Chaplin – a Guide to References and Resources*. Boston: 1977.

Manvell, Roger. *Chaplin*. Boston: 1974.

McCabe, J. *Charlie Chaplin*. Garden City, NY: Doubleday, 1978.

McDonald, Gerald, and others. *The Films of Charlie Chaplin*. Secaucus, NJ: 1965.

Moss, Robert. *Charlie Chaplin*. New York: 1975.

Payne, Robert. *The Great God Pan: A Biography of the Tramp Played by Charlie Chaplin*. New York: 1952.

Sobel, Raoul, and David Francis. *Chaplin, Genesis of a Clown*. London: 1977.

Charlie Chaplin's signature incorporating the accouterments of his world famous Little Tramp character. For avid fans dressing up in bowler, mustache, and floppy shoes á la the Little Tramp has been all the rage time and again.

The Charleston

According to Pauline Norton (*The New Grove Dictionary of American Music*), the charleston symbolized the "Roaring Twenties," the jazz age, the Black Renaissance, flappers, the prohibition, organized crime, "big spending" and the frenzied social gaiety of that era. Believed to have originated in Charleston, South Carolina, as part of the Afro-American culture, it surfaced in the black musical comedy, *Liza* (1922). The following year it achieved enormous popularity as a dance song, "The Charleston," by James P. Johnson and Cecil Mark, in the black musical *Runnin' Wild* and was featured as a dance in *How Come?* and the *Ziegfeld Follies*.

Derived from other Afro-American exhibition dances built around a syncopated rhythm, the movements of the charleston included shimmying (i.e., rapid shaking of the upper torso, hips, thighs and buttocks), kicking of the legs and swinging of the arms with wild abandon, and slapping of the body with the hands, all of which were performed in the seemingly awkward posture of a half-squat, with hunched shoulders, knees together and toes pointing inward. It was gradually modified during the 1920s by the English gliding style of dance, and the abrupt motions were replaced by subtler ones with hands on the knees or swaying of the torso while rotating the hands with the palms out.

The charleston died out in the late 1920s due to the decline of New Orleans jazz as well as the sudden shift in the socio-economic mood of the country following the Wall Street crash of 1929. It was revived as a stage dance in the 1950s and 1960s, particularly for nostalgic musicals.

BIBLIOGRAPHY

Emery, L.F. *Black Dance in the United States from 1619 to 1970*. Palo Alto, CA: 1972.

"On With the Charleston!," *Literary Digest*. 86 (September 19, 1925) 40-42.

Seldes, Gilbert. "Shake Your Feet; the Charleston," *New Republic*. 44 (November 4, 1925) 283-284.

Silvester, Victor. "Why Bring Back the Charleston?," *The Dancing Times*. (1950) 751.

Stearns, M., and J. Stearns. *Jazz Dance: the Story of American Vernacular Dance*. New York: 1968.

Walker, Bemis. *How to Charleston Correctly*. Minneapolis: Great Northern Publishing Company, 1926.

Winslow, Thyra Samter. "The Charleston Thirty Years After," *Dance Magazine*. (January 1955) 26-33, 69.

Chautauqua

If a banner announced a traveling Chautauqua was coming to town, people rejoiced. It meant that for a couple of days to a week they would get to see a variety show, hear stirring lectures, and stop all work for the duration. Gaining its greatest popularity during World War I, the traveling Chatauqua grew out of a 19th century educational movement. John Heyl Vincent, a clergyman, and Lewis Miller, an Akron manufacturer, established a school for Sunday school teachers on Chautauqua Lake in New York State (1874). The new summer academy provided lectures, study courses, and for entertainment after the day's lessons—music recitals. From this simple beginning sprang other outdoor, pedagogical endeavors that broadened to include instruction on all manner of subjects. Concurrent with the Chautauqua movement the Lyceum lecture circuit brought such noted speakers as Ralph Waldo Emerson and Mark Twain to America's cities and towns. People everywhere appreciated both educational experiences since few of them had the chance to attend a college or university. Hearing a Plato in one's own backyard was a wonderful innovation for the culturally-minded.

In 1904 Keith Vawter, an officer of the Redpath Lyceum Bureau, had a bright idea. He would combine the lakeside Chautauqua and the urban Lyceum and take them on the road to enlighten even more people. Soon Vawter's tents were seen in just about every small town. He and other entrepreneurs democratized the high-brow Chautauqua and Lyceum garnering enthusiastic public support. Crowds overflowed the tents to hear William Jennings Bryan, politicians, divines, Rear Admiral Peary, Ida Tarbell, and others expound on what was dear to their hearts. The speakers were no longer mere educators but demagogues. They played the crowds well wanting as much control of mass thought as possible for whatever they had to sell. Politicians made sure to include "heaven, home, and mother" in their lectures, and they succeeded more often than not in directing public opinion on important matters of state (for example, from an isolationist stand during World War I to one of intervention to save Europe). Brass bands galvanized the people, as did other pure entertainment offerings. Humorists, magicians, singers, and some Shakespeare made the thick speechmaking more palatable. Still in all, the traveling Chautauqua evolved rapidly into a political forum for the expression of patriotic ideals, and into a social forum for correcting what was thought evil in human nature.

The war years witnessed the biggest expansion of Vawter's dream. According to estimates, at least 5,000 towns and cities hosted a summer Chautauqua with a total attendance of over 20,000,000 people. The horror of the first global war drew Americans together so that the need for community and wisdom became paramount. Conviviality lightened a dark time. After the war the traveling Chautauqua slowed to almost a crawl. The main reason was it exchanged education for entertainment which could be gotten elsewhere. Music hall frolic replaced pedagogy and local bands substituted for intelligent speakers. Instead of appealing to the mind by instructing it wisely, amusement and evangelism dictated. William Jennings Bryan, who died in 1925, epitomized the type of speaker who made the traveling Chautauqua an overnight success. He spoke brilliantly about the popular election of senators, the advisability of an income tax, and women's suffrage, all much debated topics. For his efforts — two lectures a day, six days a week — he earned $3,000. But he also represented the type of speaker who killed the movement. There were few men his equal, though many who thought they were and demanded his same compensation. The traveling Chautauqua paid its way through subscription and advance ticket sales. As the up-front money dwindled so too did the ability to hire top lecturers. Concerned citizens had nourished the original Chautauqua by contributing time and money to bring lasting educational value to their communities. When the traveling version lost sight of its impetus and degenerated into a flashy show it died out quickly.

BIBLIOGRAPHY

Dalgety, George S. "Chautauqua's Contribution to American Life." *Current History* (April, 1931): 39-44.
Gould, Joseph E. *The Chautauqua Movement*. Albany: State University of New York Press, 1961.

Panorama of a Chautauqua Assembly in Clarinda, Iowa (1908). While the main speakers harangued the crowd in the permanent building, other meetings, lectures, and demonstrations took place in the tents. Predominantly a liberal arts experience for country folk, in this way rural America became cultured.

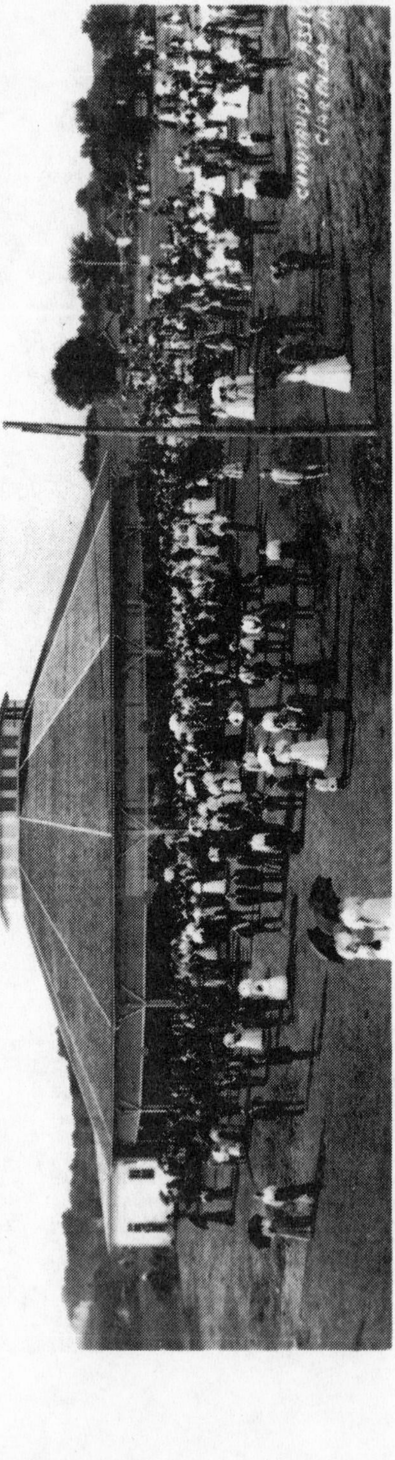

The Chipmunks

The Chipmunks were a music studio creation of Ross Bagdasarian, then a recording artist for Liberty Records. The speeded-up vocal effects, the prime identifying feature of these three imaginary characters, had actually been used earlier in his song, "Witch Doctor," a number one hit on the pop music charts in April/May 1958. Bagdasarian allegedly came up with the idea of the name when driving through Yosemite, California. When a chipmunk refused to leave the road clear for his car, inspiration struck.

The three Chipmunks were named after executives at Liberty Records: Alvin for Al Bennett, president of the label; Simon for Bennett's partner, Si Waronker; and Theodore for recording engineer, Ted Keep. The role model for the mischievious Alvin was Bagdasarian's youngest son, Adam, who had a penchant for asking in September if it was Christmas yet. Bagdasarian's deduction that other children were probably doing the same thing led him to compose the group's first—and biggest—hit, "The Chipmunk Song." In addition to selling more than 4,000,000 copies within seven weeks of release and remaining atop of the charts for four weeks during December 1958/January 1959, the song swept three categories at the first annual Grammy Awards: Best Recording for Children, Best Comedy Performance and Best Engineered Record.

The Chipmunks' mass popularity continued well beyond the novelty song that spawned them. A follow-up single, "Alvin's Harmonica," reached number three on the chart in March 1959. Many singles and albums followed during the next few years. A prime-time animated TV series, "The Alvin Show," premiered on CBS on October 4, 1961 and ran for one season. The series continued on Saturday morning for three more years, beginning in June 1962.

In 1967 Bagdasarian retired the Chipmunks in order to pursue serious songwriting and leave behind the novelty artist appellation. The revival of the act began in 1980 with a radio station playing

Blondie's "Call Me" at a faster speed and announcing, tongue in cheek, that it was the Chipmunks. In the wake of many requests for the "new" Chipmunks song, Ross Bagdasarian, Jr. (his father had died of a heart attack in 1972) and his wife, Janice Karman, recorded an album entitled, *Chipmunk Punk*. A sequel LP, *Urban Chipmunk*, followed along with a "live" touring Chipmunk show. A new TV series, "Alvin and the Chipmunks," premiered on the NBC Saturday morning schedule in September 1983 and has continued its successful run to the present day.

BIBLIOGRAPHY

Alexander, Shana. "Alvin!," *Life*. 46 (March 23, 1959) 43-44.
Bronson, Fred. "The Chipmunk Song (by) The Chipmunks With David Seville," in *The Billboard Book of Number One Hits*. New York: Billboard Publications, 1985, p. 47.
"Chipmunks Return as Punk Rockers," *Billboard*. 92 (July 5, 1080) 74.
Henderson, C. "How Alvin Chipmunk Hopes to Earn Some $7 Million in 1959," *Wall Street Journal*. 153 (March 9, 1959) 1.
Sherwood, Lydia. "The Chipmunks Chatter—A Talk with Ross Bagdasarian, Jr.," *Goldmine*. n79 (December 1982) 16-18, 23.
Stambler, Irwin. "Chipmunks' Christmas Song," in: *Encyclopedia of Popular Music*. New York: St. Martin, 1965, pp. 49-50.
"Whiz Kid with a Jingle," *Newsweek*. 52 (December 22, 1958) 49.

Buffalo Bill Cody's
Wild West

Beginning with a performance at Omaha, Nebraska in 1883, Buffalo Bill Cody's Wild West reigned as America's favorite show for two decades. Hailed by reporters as "the best open-air show ever seen," and its organizer as the showman who "out-Barnumed Barnum," the spectacle set attendance records across the nation as well as throughout Europe. During one five-month season more than a million people paid to see the show. A single performance in Chicago in 1884 attracted 41,448 customers.

In addition to rave reviews, the popularity of The Wild West was largely a result of the fame of Buffalo Bill. Given a national fascination with the Old West, most Americans were well aware of his background — e.g., hunting buffalo for railroad-building crews (which earned him his nickname), Pony Express rider, Indian fighter, eleven years as a professional actor — and gladly paid the price of admission merely to catch a glimpse of the star.

The show lived up to its hype, employing a cast of trail-hardened cowboys to put on an exciting display of stunt riding, rope tricks and marksmanship. Cody, as producer, steadily upgraded the quality of his personnel. In 1885, for example, he added Sitting Bull, the Sioux chieftain responsible for the defeat of General George Armstrong Custer at Little Big Horn in 1876, and sharp-shooter Phoebe Ann Butler (billed as "Annie Oakley, Little Sure Shot").

BIBLIOGRAPHY

Arpad, Joseph J., and Kenneth R. Lincoln. *Buffalo Bill's Wild West*. Palmer Lake, CO: Filter, 1971.

Cody, William. *The Life of Buffalo Bill*. New York: Dorchester, 1976.

Fiedler, Leslie A., et al. *Buffalo Bill and the Wild West*. Pittsburgh: University of Pittsburgh Press, 1982.

"The Greatest Showman on Earth," in: *This Fabulous Century, 1870-1900*, edited by Ezra Bowen. New York: Time-Life, 1969, pp. 266-269.

Russell, Donald B. *Lives and Legends of Buffalo Bill*. Norman: University of Oklahoma Press, 1973. Reprint of 1960 edition.

Yost, Nellie S. *Buffalo Bill: His Family, Friends, Fame, Failures, and Fortunes*. Athens: Ohio University Press, 1979.

Pawnee Bill and Buffalo Bill (1846-1917) kept the Wild West alive for a long as people wanted to see their show. Rampaging Indians, fire-snorting steeds, trick shooting, hairy buffaloes, it was all there and much more for incredulous audiences.

Columbia Comedy Shorts

From 1933 to 1958 Columbia Pictures produced a motley assortment of funny two-reelers for showing before the feature film presentation. Sixteen to twenty minutes long the shorts relaxed the audience and were sometimes more entertaining than the main entree. The guiding genius behind them was Jules White, former child actor and an experienced director. Given the job of making the best comedy shorts he could, White rounded up a stock company of proven ability — writers, comedians, stunt men, and other requisite talent. These people were easy to hire since the major movie studios were casting them off thinking that shorts were passé. But White laughed last every time one of his comedy gems had the public rolling in the aisles.

The comedy shorts relied on tried-and-true formulas perfected by Mack Sennett, the master of non-stop gags. Slapstick was the thing and the more horseplay the better. White launched series built around a zany character or characters, hoping to make them screen fixtures. Some of his zanies survived, other didn't. Vaudevillians Sidney and Murray played two hapless old gents who never quite succeeded at anything in shorts like *Stable Mates* (1934) and *Back to the Soil* (1934). Walter Catlett impersonated an indecisive worrier who was putty in other people's hands; two of his shorts were *Get Along Little Hubby* (1934) and *Fibbing Fibbers* (1936). More successful, Andy Clyde portrayed a humble to the bone, old man type whom audience adored. He had developed the character earlier when he worked for Mack Sennett and it continued to provide him with steady work for thirty-five years. Small-town comedies were his forte: *Love Comes to Mooneyville* (1936), *Stuck in the Sticks* (1937), and *Wolf in Thief's Clothing* (1943). Harry Langdon, Collins and Kennedy, El Brendel, Charley Chase, Hugh Herbert, and Vera Vague also starred at Columbia with varying degrees of success.

One major disappointment, Buster Keaton, already known for his great comedy talent, didn't fare well at Columbia. He made only a handful of so-so shorts there. It was not Keaton's fault; he had to work from lackluster scripts, crowded with old gags, all poorly timed. But not to worry, those fabulous knight-errants of the shorts, the Three Stooges, picked up the slack. First, Larry, Moe, and Curly; then Larry, Moe, and Shemp Howard; then Larry, Moe, and Joe Besser played the rubber-faced imps. Whatever the combination they squealed, whimpered, and complained like children; they fought constantly, poking each other in the eyes and stomping each other's feet; and they were the most naive human beings ever seen on the face of the earth. Watching grown men act like idiots (far beneath the antics of the Marx Brothers) may seem faddish today, but the very popular Three Stooges series ran from 1934 until 1959. Movie historians continue to marvel at their success and wonder why Americans found, and still find, them entertaining. Jules White directed almost all of their shorts and because of their popularity Columbia prospered.

A nagging question is: How to assess the comedy shorts? Audiences must have laughed at them; they endured for twenty-five years demonstrating that slapstick and outrageous characters still worked; and they provided the transition from Mack Sennett to television. Moreover, they were never meant to stand alone in lieu of the main feature. As part of fad history it would be interesting to know whether movie-goers hurried to the theater not wanting to miss the comedy shorts. Or did they take their time realizing they had approximately twenty minutes to kill before the real movie started?

BIBLIOGRAPHY

Howard, Moe. *Moe Howard & the Three Stooges*. Secaucus, NJ: Citadel Press, 1977.
Matlin, Leonard. *The Great Movie Shorts*. New York: Crown, 1972.
Okuda, Ted, and Edward Watz. *The Columbia Comedy Shorts*. Jefferson, NC and London: McFarland, 1986.

Commercial Folk Music

Commercial folk music first burst onto the music scene in 1950, when the Weavers' rendition of Leadbelly's "Goodnight Irene" was a number one hit on the *Billboard* pop singles chart for thirteen weeks. The group's overtly leftist political stance encouraged suppression during the McCarthy era; after their record label (Decca) dropped them from its roster, the folk movement went underground until the emergence of the Kingston Trio in 1958 with a chart-topping single, "Tom Dooley."

The continued success of the trio, particularly through the medium of the record album, proved that folk songs as a genre had commercial potential, and the record industry reacted in its customary fashion by signing countless imitators. These acts—and others—produced a lengthy list of folk hits, including

Joan Baez—*Joan Baez* (1960)

Joan Baez—*Joan Baez 2* (1961)

Joan Baez—*Joan Baez in Concert* (1962)

The Brothers Four—"Greenfield" (1960)

The Glencoves—"Hootenanny" (1963)

The Highwaymen—"Michael" (1961)

The Chad Mitchell Trio—"Lizzie Borden" (1962)

The Chad Mitchell Trio—"The Marvelous Toy" (1964)

The New Christy Minstrels—*Ramblin'* (1963), including "Green Green"

Peter, Paul and Mary—*Peter, Paul and Mary* (1962), including "Lemon Tree" and "If I Had A Hammer"

Peter, Paul and Mary—*Movin'* (1963), including "Puff"

Peter, Paul and Mary—*In the Wind* (1963), including "Blowin' in the Wind" and "Don't Think Twice, It's All Right"

The Rooftop Singers—"Walk Right In" (1963)

The Serendipity Singers — "Don't Let the Rain Come Down" (1964)

The Singing Nun — "Dominique" (1963)

The Springfields — "Silver Threads and Golden Needles" (1962)

The Tokens — "The Lion Sleeps Tonight" (1961-1962)

In addition to recordings, folk-oriented musicians found a large and receptive audience at concerts and festivals. The success of the genre has been widely attributed to the desire of the audience — particularly youth — for music which challenged the intellect and had something important to communicate. Peter, Paul and Mary — the most successful folk act in terms of record sales — played a major role in expanding the socio-political consciousness of the movement beyond the Greenwich Village-collegiate axis, which embraced Joan Baez, Bob Dylan, Phil Ochs, Tom Paxton, Pete Seeger, Dave Van Ronk and other "purist" interpreters. In contrast to the goodtime, fraternity house ambiance projected by the Kingston Trio and others of that ilk, Peter, Paul and Mary gave voice to the younger generation's concerns regarding issues such as civil rights, war and free speech. The movement's crowning extramusical moment was probably the civil rights march on Washington, D.C. in 1963 led by Martin Luther King, Jr., which featured his famed "I have a dream" speech.

By early 1964 folk music had slipped out of the commercial mainstream, a casualty of the British beat invasion and its own ambivalence with respect to the starmaking process. ABC's TV hit, "Hootenanny," instituted in 1963 to capitalize on the folk music boom, alienated a large segment of the folk community — artists and audience alike — through its refusal to let Pete Seeger appear because he wouldn't sign a "loyalty oath" to the American government. Other manifestations of the "hootenanny" vogue proved even more embarrassing to folk purists; more than a hundred albums (largely slapdash compilations) trumpeting the term were released in less than one year while mindless films such as *Hootenanny Hoot* exhibited little in common with the sense of community it implied. In 1965 Bob Dylan and the Byrds forged the music industry's "next big thing," folk rock. Many folk artists experimented with this form; however, the rapidly changing face of pop music soon left them with a forced choice — they either joined the rock establishment and went electric or retreated back to the coffee-house circuit.

BIBLIOGRAPHY

Baez, Joan. *And A Voice to Sing With; A Memoir*. New York: Summit, 1987.

Belz, Carl. "Popular Folk Music," in: *The Story of Rock*. 2nd ed. New York: Oxford University Press, 1972, pp. 74-87.

Dachs, David. "Folk Music Boom," in: *Anything Goes: The World of Popular Music*. Indianapolis: Bobbs-Merrill, 1964, pp. 238-258.

Edelstein, Andrew J. "Folk Music," in: *The Pop Sixties*. New York: World Almanac Publications, 1985, pp. 17-23.

Ewen, David. "Rebels with a Cause," in: *All the Years of American Popular Music; A Comprehensive History*. Englewood Cliffs, NJ: Prentice-Hall, 1977, pp. 640-657.

Hopkins, Jerry. "Meet Me at Izzy's Place," in: *The Rock Story*. New York: Signet, 1970, pp. 53-67.

Jasper, Tony. "Songs of Protest and Social Commentary," in: *Understanding Pop*. London: SCM Press, 1972, pp. 92-110.

Lees, Gene. "The Folk-Music Bomb," *Stereo Review*. 13:5 (November 1964) 57ff.

Leisy, James. F. *Hootenanny Tonight*. Greenwich, CT: Fawcett, 1964.

Schmid, W. "Reflections on the Folk Movement," *Music Educators Journal*. 66 (February 1980) 42-46ff.

Shaw, Arnold. "Guitars, Folk Songs, and Halls of Ivy," *Harper's Magazine*. 229 (November 1964) 33-43.

Shelton, Robert. *No Direction Home; The Life and Music of Bob Dylan*. New York: Beach Tree Books/William Morrow, 1986.

Ward, Ed, Geoffrey Stokes and Ken Tucker. "Roll Over, Frankie Avalon," in: *Rock of Ages*. New York: Rolling Stone Press/Summit Books, 1986, pp. 249-279.

Davy Crockett

In December 1954, *Disneyland* (Walt Disney's one hour prime-time TV series on ABC, which premiered in late October 1954) sparked a nationwide craze with the broadcast of the first of five programs, starring Fess Parker, which fantasized the life of frontier hero Davy Crockett. The mini-series was shown three times during the 1954-1955 season (in keeping with *Disneyland's* 20-20-12 schedule); surprisingly the ratings for the Crockett episode actually increased for the reruns, while the drop-off in viewers for the third runs was nowhere near what was expected.

The popularity of the Disney program stimulated a merchandizing bonanza. Sales of Davy Crockett coonskin caps, T-shirts, blue jeans, rifles, powder horns, cap pistols, peace pipes, lunch boxes, guitars, records and many other items surpassed $100 million in the early months of 1955. Stores in Los Angeles and Dallas set up Crockett clubs and marked off special sections containing products bearing the frontiersman's name. Denver's May Co. advertised a bath towel with this pitch to mothers: "Your bath-time struggles are over . . . They'll run to use Davy Crockett towels." Bill Hayes had a number one hit with his recording. "The Ballad of Davy Crockett," one of seventeen versions competing for the attention of fans. The sheet music for the song, endorsed by Parker, sold over half a million copies. Advance orders alone for *The Picture Story of Davy Crockett*, a twenty-five cent Wonder Playbook, exceeded one million. At least three new editions of Crockett's autobiography (*Davy Crockett's Own Story*, Citadel; *The Adventures of Davy Crockett*, Scribner's; *The Life of Davy Crockett*, N.A.L.) had appeared by July 1955. Even institutions of high culture jumped into the fray; the Boston Museum of Fine Arts exhibited a rare contemporary portrait of Crockett (John Neagle's 1828 work) while a freshman Congressman wearing a flowing tie.

Walt Disney, known for wringing every possible cent from his enterprises, found himself embroiled in heated competition for use of the Crockett name. One oldtime Baltimore garment maker named Morey Schwartz proved particularly troublesome; first registering the Davy Crockett Enterprises trademark in Texas, and then in 1947 at the U.S. Patent Office, he began putting out clothing under the Davy Crockett label. With the advent of the Disney-inspired boom, Schwartz began licensing clothing manufacturers to use the Davy Crockett label.

By the summer of 1955, the entertainment phenomenon of the decade had attracted a substantial debunking element. Brendan Sexton, educator of the United Auto Workers, denounced Crockett in a Detroit radio address as "not at all an admirable character." The New York *Post* launched a four-ply idol-smashing series by Murray Kempton in 1955 entitled "The Real Davy" while John Fisher's editorial in *Harper's Magazine* noted

> . . . infant brainwashers have been bedazzled into worshipping a Crockett who never was — a myth as phony as the Russian legend about Kind Papa Stalin . . . He proved himself — according to accepted historical authority — "a poor farmer, indolent and shiftless." He also was an unenthusiastic soldier; during the Creek War he weaseled his way out of the army by hiring a substitute to fill out his term of service.
>
> Since work was distasteful to Davy, he became, in turn, a backwoods justice of the peace who boasted about his ignorance of law; an unsuccessful politician; a hack writer, heavily dependent on some unidentified ghost . . . He never was king of anything, except maybe The Tennessee Tall Tales and Bourbon Samplers' Association. When he claimed that he had shot 105 bear in nine months, his fellow tipplers refused to believe a word of it, on the sensible grounds that Davy couldn't count that high.

Supporters of the Crockett legend fought back with a vengeance. One band of youngsters, supported by a Coney Island concessionaire, picketed the New York *Post's* office with placards reading, "Davy killed a b'ar at 3 — What did Murray Kempton ever shoot —

except the bull???" and "Who you gonna expose next—Santa Claus?"

By early 1956 the Crockett craze had wound down to a noticeable degree, a casualty of oversaturation and the rise of new heroes, most notably Elvis Presley and the new constellation of rock 'n' roll stars.

BIBLIOGRAPHY

"Crockett and Circulation," *Newsweek.* 46 (July 18, 1955) 60-62.

Davis, K.S. "Coonskin Superman," *New York Times Magazine.* (April 24, 1955) 20.

"Davy: Row and a Riddle," *Newsweek.* 46 (July 4, 1955) 56.

Fisher, John. "Personal and Otherwise: The Embarrassing Truth About Davy Crockett, the Alamo, Yoknapatawpha County, and Other Dear Myths," *Harper's Magazine.* 211 (July 1955) 16-18.

Lofaro, Michael A. *Davy Crockett; the Man, the Legend, the Legacy*, 1786-1986.

"Portrait: Davy in Bean Town," *Time.* 66 (August 8, 1955) 59.

"The Wild Frontier," *Time.* 65 (May 23, 1955) 90-92.

Currier & Ives

Nathaniel Currier and James M. Ives were proprietors of the largest lithographic company in the United States during the latter half of the nineteenth century. The firm produced roughly ten million prints on nearly 10,000 subjects; for many years it accounted for three-quarters of the American print market.

Currier & Ives outdistanced their competitors not only because they were superb craftsmen but also because they were diligent merchandisers. The film handled mail orders as well as utilizing street vendors and retail shops. In addition, pedlars and agents distributed their wares throughout the nation and abroad; in Latin America, many prints were made available with Spanish titles. Currier & Ives displayed an uncanny knack for selecting subjects with mass-sales appeal — e.g., fires, shipwrecks, battles — as well as providing the prints with winning titles. They appealed to patriotism, love of family, courage and a reverence for middle-class virtues in general. In short, the company filled a need for inexpensive art works whose subjects had universal appeal.

Currier founded the firm in New York City in 1835 at the age of twenty-one following a five-year apprenticeship in Boston. In 1852 he took on his brother-in-law, James Ives, as bookkeeper. Ives' talent as both an artist and businessman led to his being made a partner in 1857; the imprint of the company's works was changed from "N. Currier" to "Currier & Ives." During its heyday the firm's regular staff included one man who prepared the lithographic stones, up to seven lithographers, and perhaps a dozen women who tinted the prints with watercolors. Experiments in printing skies and backgrounds in color were employed with some prints; however, the majority continued to be produced in black and white and then hand-colored, or occasionally sold "plain." The designs for the prints came from a variety of sources: (1) staff artists; (2) lesser painters, who received no credit for their contributions; and (3) adaptations of well-known American paintings, both old and contemporary. The least expensive small works sold for as low as twenty cents, whereas prices went as high as six dollars for large folios.

By 1907 the firm had run out of steam under the management of the founders' sons. As early as the 1880s its hand processes had become outdated due to the introduction of new, cheaper printing techniques such as chromolithography and photoengraving.

Despite going out of business, the firm has remained extremely popular by means of the activities of collectors and the preponderance of reproductions adorning every conceivable form of merchandise (e.g., tins, household nick-nacks, greeting cards). This continued appeal owes much to the fact that the work of Currier & Ives offers contemporary Americans a nostalgia glimpse of culture and events in the previous century.

BIBLIOGRAPHY

Crouse, Russel. *Mr. Currier and Mr. Ives, a Note on Their Lives and Times*. Garden City, NY: Garden City Publishing Company, 1930.

Cunningham, Frederic A. *Currier & Ives Prints, An Illustrated Checklist*, rev. ed., updated by Colin Simkin. New York: Crown, 1970.

"Currier, Nathaniel," in: *Dictionary of American Biography*, edited by Allen Johnson and Dumas Malone. Volume II. New York: Scribner's, 1958, c1929, p. 604.

"Currier & Ives," in: *Encyclopedia of American Art*, edited by Milton Rugoff. New York: Dutton, 1981, p. 131.

"Currier & Ives; A Heritage in Print," in: *The Encyclopedia of Collectibles*, edited by Andrea DiNoto. Alexandria, VA: Time-Life, 1978, pp. 82-99.

"Ives, James Merritt," in: *Dictionary of American Biography*, edited by Dumas Malone. Volume V. New York: Scribner's, 1933, c1932.

Rawls, Walton. *The Great Book of Currier & Ives' America*. New York: Abbeville, 1979.

Weaver, Warren A. *Lithographs of N. Currier and Currier & Ives*. New York: Holport, 1925.

Currier & Ives prints (c. 1840-1890). Combining precise draftsmanship and domestic appeal, these two and many others were framed by the millions. They were the Rembrandts for middle-class Americans.

BE NOT WISE IN THINE OWN EYES

"Dallas"

Soap operas have long been a staple of daytime television; however, ABC's "Peyton Place" (1964-1969) was the only prime-time representative of the genre to attract a large audience share prior to the 1980s. But "Dallas" changed all that. The program was only moderately successful during its early run, changing time slots on a frequent basis (Sunday, 10-11 EST, April 1978; Saturday, 10-11, September-October 1978; Sunday, 10-11, October 1978-January 1979; Friday, 10-11, January 1979-November 1981). The following for "Dallas" continued to build, however, and the show went on to become a national sensation, becoming the most popular series on television during the 1980-1981 season.

"Dallas" is best known for the "Who shot J.R.?" controversy. In the last episode (prior to the re-runs) of the 1979-1980 season, the program's chief character, the unscrupulous Texas oilman J.R. Ewing, was shot by an unknown assailant and brought to the hospital in critical condition. The person responsible for the deed as well as likely plot developments for the upcoming fall season were debated by viewers around the world. Gambling operations were extraordinarily busy that summer handling wagers. Extreme security precautions were taken at the studio where the upcoming episodes for "Dallas" were being filmed; the actors themselves were not given advance notice of the resolution of the controversy (several alternative plots were shot). The November 21, 1980 episode which opened the new season became the highest-rated individual show in history, attaining a 53.3 rating and 76 audience share. (Kristin Shepard, the sister of J.R.'s wife, was revealed as the assailant—the motive: she was pregnant with his child and about to be framed by him for prostitution because she refused his order to leave Dallas; J.R., of course, lived to commit many more nasty deeds.)

The program's success led to a spinoff ("Knots Landing") and countless imitators during the early part of the decade, including

"Dynasty," "Falcon Crest," "Flamingo Road," "King's Cross-
ing" and "Secrets of Midland Heights." Beginning with the 1981-
1982 season, "Dallas" lost momentum, largely the result of relatively staid, uninspired scripting. "Dynasty," featuring yet another
larger-than-life villain played by the ageless Joan Collins, eclipsed
it as the highest rated prime-time soap. However, "Dallas" continued to retain a solid following throughout the 1980s by incorporating a steady stream of fresh, new faces (e.g., Morgan Brittany,
Priscilla Presley) and plot twists (e.g., "Who killed Bobby?").

BIBLIOGRAPHY

Battele, P. "Larry Hagman Talks About Himself and Dallas' J.R.," *Good
Housekeeping*. 192 (January 1981) 105ff.
Brooks, Tim, and Earle Marsh. "Dallas," in: *The Complete Directory to Prime
Time Network TV Shows, 1946-Present*. Third Edition. New York: Ballantine,
1985. pp. 194-196.
Castleman, Harry, and Walter J. Podrazik. *Watching TV*. New York: McGraw-
Hill, 1982.
Emerson, G. "Dallas Fever—America's Got It Good," *Vogue*. 170 (June 1980)
194-195ff.
Fiore, M. "Larry Hagman," *Good Housekeeping*. 192 (January 1981) 106-109.
"Hats Off to 10 Years of Dallas! The Man Known as J.R. Reflects on a Decade
Backstage at TV's Southfork," *People Weekly*. 29 (April 4, 1988) 98-103.
Haven, S.P. "TD's Families of Fortune," *Redbook*. 161 (October 1983) 88-89.
Kitmas, M. "Searing for the Secret of 'Dallas'," *New Leader*. 64 (February 9,
1981) 21-22.
Lardine, B. "Tube," *People*. 13 (April 14, 1980) 88-90ff.
"Larry Hagman: vita celebration est," *Time*. 116 (August 11, 1980) 62.
Nuwer, H. "Larry Hagman: the Man You Love to Hate," *Saturday Evening Post*.
252 (October 1980) 50-53.
Pederson, R. "Larry Hagman: Why Women Love His Evil Ways," *Mademoi-
selle*. 86 (September 1980) 56ff.
Reilly, S. "What are Larry (J.R.) Hagman and the *Dallas* producers Feeling
From the Shots Cheered Round the World? Absolutely No Pain," *People
Weekly*. 14 (July 14, 1980) 87-90.
Rosenfield, Paul. "The Low-down on Low-down J.R.," *Saturday Evening Post*.
257 (November 1985) 58-61.

Death Songs

Death Songs flourished in the early 1960s — a period of general malaise in the pop music industry between the birth of rock 'n' roll and the English rhythm and blues revival spearheaded by the Beatles. The thematic core of this material was teen fatalities, usually of a grisly and/or melodramatic nature. Proposed explanations for the popularity of death songs have ranged from teenagers' love of both a good scare and whatever strikes adults as bad taste to the fact that they were a manifestation of the A-bomb generation's anxieties.

The first big hit belonging to this genre was Mark Dinning's "Teen Angel" (MGM). Released in late 1959 and reaching number one on the pop singles charts the following year, it tells of a girl who was crushed by the train after returning to the car stalled on the tracks in search of her steady beau's high school ring. Other classic entries included Ray Peterson's "Tell Laura I Love Her" (RCA, 1960), in which the hero was killed in an auto race accident, and J. Frank Wilson and The Cavaliers' number one hit, "Last Kiss" (Josie, 1964).

Some artists contributed multiple entries to the field. Dickey Lee utilized the recurrent theme of the angst of a modern day Romeo and Juliet in "Patches" (Smash, 1962). The rich boy-poor girl from "old shanty town" premise led to a rejected Patches floating face down in the river which divided the two socio-economic classes in the town. Lee's "Laurie (Strange Things Happen in This World)," released in 1965, represented a cross between Edgar Allan Poe and a gothic paperback. The plot had boy meeting girl, lending her his sweater and kissing her goodnight at her door; backtracking to her house to retrieve his sweater, the man at the door tells him, "You're wrong son, you weren't with my daughter . . . she died a year ago today." The boy goes to the graveyard, and finds his sweater lying upon her grave.

The Shangri-Las were undoubtedly the champions of the genre, contributing at least four death tracks. The best known of these, "Leader of the Pack" (Red Bird, 1964)—which reached number one—had the hero broadsided by a truck in full view of his teary-eyed girlfriend accompanied by a graphic soundtrack of squealing tires and shattering glass. "I Can Never Go Home Anymore" tells of a girl who breaks her mother's heart by leaving home in a dispute over a boyfriend and then makes an untimely exit from Planet Earth prior to patching things up. "Give Us Your Blessings" has Mary and Jimmy deciding to elope in the face of parental disapproval; we are left to believe that tears in their eyes results in a failure to see a sign on the road warning of a detour with the end result being that they plunge to their deaths.

It is perhaps just as well that most pop music fans have not heard the more tasteless variants of this genre. A prime case in point would be "Little Dead Surfer Girl" by the Incredible Broadside Brass Bed Band, which appears on an album entitled *The Great Grizzly Bear Hunt* (Poison Ring). Played in a typical surf music style, it tells of how the singer and his girlfriend Rhonda go to the beach and attempt to surf, going out some distance, before it transpires that Rhonda is unable to swim. As she sinks the singer laments,

> I'll never forget her last words to me —
> gurgle, gurgle, gurgle . . .
> Every night I go down to the beach,
> because I know that when the tide comes in,
> so does Rhonda.

To be fair, many of the above noted death themes have been exploited by other mass media as well, particularly television and films. However, the relative preponderance of this material in the early 1960s rendered the genre more visible within the pop music industry.

BIBLIOGRAPHY

Betrock, Alan. "Out in the Streets," in: *Girl Groups; The Story of a Sound.* New York: Delilah, 1982, pp. 98-111. Covers the career of The Shangri-Las.

"Death Rock," in: *The Rolling Stone Encyclopedia of Rock & Roll,* edited by Jon Pareles and Patricia Romanowski. New York: Rolling Stone Press/Summet Books, 1983.

"Dinning Sisters' Brother Hits Charts," *Billboard.* 72 (January 4, 1960) 24.

Raker, Muck. "Singularly Painful—Singles and EPs: Death Records," in: *Rock Bottom; the Book of Pop Atrocities.* New York: Proteus, 1981, pp. 31-32.

"Ray Peterson's 'Tell Laura' Leaping Charts," *Billboard.* 72 (July 4, 1960) 20.

Dime Novels

Dime novels—the popular name for cheap thrilling tales of history (usually set in America during the Revolution, Civil War or frontier period), romance, warfare, crime or any violent action—were the equivalents, in both appearance and content, of today's paperbacks. They served as literature for the masses, who either could not afford $1 or $2, or wanted faster-paced action than was being provided by regular novelists. Their compactness—they were similar in appearance to modern pamphlets and fit easily in the pocket, thereby rendering them easy to conceal from authority figures—particularly appealed to young boys.

Dime novels achieved peak popularity during the latter half of the nineteenth century, beginning with the publication of Ann Sophia Stephens' *Malaeska: The Indian Wife of the White Hunter* in June 1860. *Malaeska* was the first publication of Beadle and Company (later, Beadle and Adams), the indisputable leader in the field. The firm—which produced many series, including "American Novels"; "American Sixpenny Library"; "American Tales"; "Boy's Library of Sport, Story and Adventure"; "Dime Library"; "Frontier Series"; "Half-Dime Library"; "New Dime Novels"; "Pocket Library"; "Pocket Novels"; and "20 Cent Novels"—underwent three distinct phases: (1) the production of "yellow backs," pamphlets of varying sizes (e.g., 4" × 6 1/4", 6" × 9 1/4") wrapped in a saffron paper cover; (2) the issuing of little paper-covered books of varied colors; and (3) a change to a rather unattractive magazine format necessitated by the institutions of more restrictive postal rates for books. The company's chief competitors (e.g., George Munro and Company, Robert DeWitt, Street and Smith, Nickel Library Company) were also very successful during the boom years between 1870-1890.

The fortunes of Beadle and Adams entered into a severe decline during the 1890s, brought on by the retirement of longtime head,

Erastas Beadle, in 1891; competition from other mass media such as nickel libraries and boy's weeklies (i.e., the pulps, themselves dime novels in slightly altered form), juvenile series books (e.g., Frank Merriwell, the Rover Boys, Tom Swift), yellow journalism and the cinema; and the continued attacks of moralists and literary critics. Standing on the brink of bankruptcy, Beadle and Adams was purchased by M.J. Ivers and Company in 1889, who continued to use the famous imprint in the production of inexpensive publications until the late 1930s.

Ironically, while the sensationalism and violence inherent in dime novels left them open to charges of immorality, they subscribed to the conventional moral patterns of the day and fostered nationalistic pride, emphasizing the democratic vigor and individualism of the American people. Despite the reliance of the medium upon countless hacks, it also gave rise to notable authors and fictional characters, including Edward L. Wheeler, who created "Deadwood Dick," and J.R. Coryell, creator of "Nick Carter."

BIBLIOGRAPHY

"Books—Dime Novels," in: *Official Price Guide to Paper Collectibles*, edited by Thomas E. Hudgeons III. 2nd ed. Orlando, FL: House of Collectibles, 1983, pp. 161-169.

Gehman, R.B. "Blood and Thunder," *Collier's*. 124 (October 15, 1949) 32.

Gehman, R.B. "Deadwood Dick to Superman," *Science Digest*. 25 (June 1949) 52-57.

Johannsen, A. *House of Beadle and Adams and Its Dime and Nickel Novels*. 1980.

Leblanc, Edward T. "Dime Novels," *Antiques & Collecting Hobbies*. 92 (December 1987) 84-87.

Miller, C. "Dime Novels," *Hobbies*. 69 (November 1964) 107.

"On Dime Novels," *Newsweek*. 35 (May 29, 1950) 85-87.

Pearson, Edmund. *Dime Novels*. Port Washington, NY: Kennikat, 1968. Reprinted from the 1929 edition.

"Science Catches Up with Fiction; Dime-Novel Inventions That Have Come True," *Popular Science*. 150 (March 1937) 48-49.

Winterich, J.T. "Adventure for the Tenth Part of a Buck," *Saturday Review of Literature*. 33 (June 10, 1950) 9-10.

Winterich, J.T. "Bonanza Boys from Buffalo; or, The Beadles and Their Books," *Publishers' Weekly*. 157 (May 20, 1950) 2134-2138.

Disco

Although discotheques — clubs which featured dancing to prerecorded music — had existed since the early 1960s, disco did not emerge until the mid-1970s. A reaction to the dearth of danceable rock music during the early 1970s, its initial impetus came from New York's gay male subculture; the deejays serving this group became adept at locating and then promoting little known black pop records via the club setting. When word of mouth enabled some of these songs to become underground hits (e.g., Manu Dibango's "Soul Makossa," Shirley and Company's "Honeybee"), record labels began utilizing the disco scene as an incubator for hits and, in turn, incorporated prolonged instrumental breaks and novelty effects calculated to facilitate the showmanship of the disc jockeys.

The genre went aboveground as pop artists — in an effort to sound contemporary — began grafting the accentuated dance beat onto their own material. The importance of instrumental grooves and the preeminence of recorded performances over live ones led to the rise of the producer as hitmaker and superstar; Italian Giorgio Moroder was a case in point. Many so-called "artists" were faceless studio aggregations, who catapulted into the public's eye with a hit or two, and then disappeared from view. The following list represents an honor roll of one-shot disco careers:

Peter Brown — "Dance With Me" (1978)
Cerrone — "Love in 'C' Minor (Part 1)" (1977)
Disco Tex and The Sex-O-Lettes — "Get Dancin'" (1974-1975)
Gary's Gang — "Keep On Dancin'" (1979)
Gloria Gaynor — "Never Can Say Goodbye" (1975); "I Will Survive" (1979)
M — "Pop Music" (1979)
Van McCoy — "The Hustle" (1975)
George McCrae — "Rock Your Baby" (1974)

Thelma Houston — "Don't Leave Me This Way" (1976)
Evelyn "Champagne" King — "Shame" (1978)
Cheryl Lynn — "Got to Be Real" (1978-1979)
Vicki Sue Robinson — "Turn the Beat Around" (1976)
Salsoul Orchestra — "Tangerine" (1976)
Silver Convention — "Fly Robin, Fly" (1975); "Get Up and Boogie" (1976)
Andrea True Connection — "More, More, More" (1976)
The Trammprs — "Disco Inferno" (1977-1978)
Amii Stewart — "Knock on Wood" (1979)

A few artists managed to enjoy lengthy careers within the disco field, most notably Donna Summer ("Love to Love You Baby," "I Feel Love," "Hot Stuff," "Bad Girl," etc.), KC & The Sunshine Band ("Get Down Tonight," "That's the Way," "Boogie Shoes," etc.), Chic ("Dance, Dance, Dance," "Le Freak," "Good Times," etc.) and Barry White ("Can't Get Enough of Your Love, Baby," "You're the First, the Last, My Everything," etc.). The biggest disco act — also the one most responsible for broadening the genre's following — proved to be The Bee Gees. Following a decade of intermittent success as Beatles clones with a decidedly gothic twist, the group hooked up with veteran rhythm-and-blues producer Arif Mardin and created *Main Course* (which contained "Jive Talkin'"). Released in 1975, that album started The Bee Gees on an unprecedented roll; "You Should Be Dancing," "How Deep Is Your Love," "Stayin' Alive" and "Night Fever," among other number one hits, rendered the group the most dominant force on the pop music charts during the second half of the 1970s. The latter three songs were culled from the soundtrack for the hit film, *Saturday Night Fever*, which sold over twenty million copies (a total unsurpassed until the release of Michael Jackson's *Thriller* in the mid-1980s). The movie removed the stigma once and for all that disco was only for blacks and gays. By the late 1970s, artists as solidly within the FM rock camp as Blondie ("Heart of Glass"), the Rolling Stones ("Miss You") and Rod Stewart ("Do Ya Think I'm Sexy") had flirted with the genre. All-disco radio stations began earning top ratings in many urban areas.

By 1980 disco had peaked as a commercial force. A victim of oversaturation (which — in turn — fostered a strong wave of antidisco agitation, particularly on the part of the blue collar sector), parodies (e.g., the crass exploitation of The Village People, six male hunks who TV lip-synched to middle America while portraying themselves as cartoon homosexual pinups) and the failure of its ephemeral "stars" to make any long-term identification with the public, the genre passed back to the underground. The continued experimentation with its rhythms by rock musicians, particularly techno-pop acts such as Depeche Mode and The Human League, gave rise to yet another wave of dance-oriented hits in the early 1980s. The dance clubs continue to thrive, drawing from traditional disco (now limited to the output of a few independent record labels), British synth-rock and the hip hop and rap emanating from the urban ghettos, all choreographed with state-of-the-art video hardware.

BIBLIOGRAPHY

"Dancing Madness," *Rolling Stone*. n194 (August 28, 1975) 42-64. A collection of features delineating the disco phenomenon.

"Disco," in: *The Rolling Stone Encyclopedia of Rock & Roll*, edited by Jon Pareles and Patricia Romanowski. New York: Rolling Stone Press/Summit Books, 1983, pp. 151-152.

"Disco-Haters to the Barricades," *Newsweek*. (July 23, 1979) 90.

Emerson, K. "Village People: America's Male Ideal?," *Rolling Stone*. (October 5, 1978) 26-27ff.

"Feverish Hustles for Big Disco Profits," *Business Week*. (June 26, 1978) 42.

Goldman, Albert. *Disco*. New York: Hawthorn, 1978.

Joe, Radcliffe A. *This Business of Disco*. New York: Watson-Guptill, 1980.

Perew, T. "Disco Craze Sweeps the Country," *Soul*. 10 (July 7, 1975) 16-17.

Pollack, Bruce. *The Disco Handbook*. New York: Scholastic Book Services, 1979.

Rose, F. "Discophobia: Rock & Roll Fights Back," *Village Voice*. 24 (November 12, 1979) 36-37.

Rosenblum, C. "Discomania," *Human Behavior*. 7 (November 1978) 27.

Sherratt, Brian, and Nalani M. Leong. *Disco Chic*. New York: Harmony, 1979.

Smucker, Tom. "Disco," in: *The Rolling Stone Illustrated History of Rock and Roll*, edited by Jim Miller. 2nd ed. New York: Random House/Rolling Stone Press, 1980, pp. 425-434.

Ward, Ed, Geoffrey Stokes and Ken Tucker. "Outside Art: Disco and Funk," in: *Rock of Ages*. New York: Rolling Stone Press/Summit Books, 1986, pp. 523-536.

Double Feature

During the 1930s the public expected to see two movies for the price of one — a fad that engendered ambivalence. Everyone knew the first feature would be mediocre to bad and the second somewhat better but not necessarily a good film. *Mutiny on the Bounty* might be paired with *Petticoat Fever* or *Tale of Two Cities* with *Dimples*; but more likely the marquee announced *Head Over Heels in Love* with *Pigskin Parade*, all 1930s movies. In between there were drawings for encyclopedias, washing machines, and other prizes; or giveaways of linen, cutlery, tea, costume jewelry, doughnuts, ice cream, candy, coffee, razors, and silk stockings. The public surely got its money's worth then, or did it? What happened was "B" movies inundated the theaters, driving away many patrons, especially cultured ones. The four to six hours required to sit through two features, cartoons, and trailers for forthcoming films dominated a person's time. To take full advantage of the double feature one lost sleep, strained eyesight, and wasted productive hours. The double feature became an opiate and Hollywood found it harder each year to supply more of the mesmerizing drug. Therefore "B" movies only got worse.

The Great Depression bred the trend as many dejected Americans sought solace in the dark confines of movie houses. Unemployed, they whiled away half a day or more for fifteen cents and temporarily forgot their troubles. A paradoxical fad, double features forced Hollywood to overproduce bad movies, theater-owners to lose money in the long run, and the public to think less of the very entertainment they wanted to worship. Excess was ruining the business. At the end of the 1930s Hollywood suffered from another malady, World War II. Europe was in no position to lease American films — a lucrative market gone — which meant domestic sales had to increase, i.e., more double features. Movie mogul, Samuel Goldwyn voiced his lament in a *Saturday Evening Post* article entitled, "Hollywood Is Sick." Goldwyn tells that he hired Dr. George Gallup to survey American preference for the single vs. the double bill. Gallup's preliminary sample disclosed that "three out of every four potential movie patrons do not want double bills." This was self-serving because single feature houses continued to lose business to double feature ones belying Gallup. Goldwyn traces the history of multiple features to Haverhill, Massachusetts in 1916, a place and a year guessed at by someone other than himself. In the early days two-reelers were always shown together to make a program, something very different from running two full-length features back-to-back. Despicable to Goldwyn is the marquee hook, "Free Bake Oven Dishes," "Free Lunch," "Cash Prizes," above a film he labored to produce. Also distressing is the burden to spew out more film:

> Hollywood is now making 600 feature pictures a year. If you brought all the finest writers in the world to Hollywood, there wouldn't be enough of them to create 600 fine stories. As it is, of this 600, I'd say not more than fifty are excellent, with another 150 fair.

Ditto that for actors:

> Share them among 600 pictures, only fifty of which can be rated as fine, and you inevitably have a few good actors in many bad roles.

Goldwyn suggests "we restrict production to 200 pictures a year" and everyone will profit. Would that Goldwyn were still alive today to utter such sane advice.

BIBLIOGRAPHY

Crowther, Bosley. "Double Feature Trouble." *New York Times Magazine* (July 14, 1940): 8, 20.
Goldwyn, Samuel. "Hollywood Is Sick." *Saturday Evening Post* (July 13, 1940): 18-19, 44, 48-49.

Elvis Is Alive

Nearly eleven years after his "death," many Americans appeared obsessed with the notion that Elvis Presley was still alive. The craze appears to have been stimulated by the publication of Gail Brewer-Giorgio's book, *Is Elvis Alive? The Most Incredible Elvis Presley Story Every Told* in July 1988. For $29.95 Giorgio also provided an audiotape on which "Elvis" complained about "a constant battle of growing beards . . . to keep from being recognized." A voice-identification examiner hired by Giorgio indicated that the speaker on the tape might be Presley; however, he noted that the recording can't be accurately dated.

The rash of Elvis sightings reported that summer ranged throughout the U.S. Some indicated that he had lost a considerable amount of weight and looked much like he did as a young man. Others claimed that he was just as plump as he was before he supposedly died. While Giorgio described him as balding, he was also seen sporting a full head of snowy white hair. Settings included a Las Vegas parking lot, a Burger King, a J.C. Penney outlet, supermarkets, sports cars and pick-up trucks.

The basic scenario generally set forth by believers is that Presley faked his death so as to retire from the spotlight—a theme previously employed to explain reported sightings, albeit on a smaller scale, in the early 1980s of Jim Morrison, lead singer of the rock band, The Doors, who died in Paris in 1971. Giorgio reiterated this idea on a string of interviews with the mass media to hype her book during the summer, most notably on television programs such as "The Oprah Winfrey Show," "Larry King Live" and "Nightline." The myth continued to gain momentum among the more gullible Elvis fans despite repeated efforts by members of the late star's inner circle to present hardcore evidence to the contrary. Accordingly, these true believers undoubtedly kept the faith when Presley failed to reveal himself, let alone give a concert, at an annual memorial show in Memphis in mid-August as it was rumored he would do.

Throughout all of this hullabaloo, Graceland—Presley's former home turned museum—received countless letters addressed to Elvis as well as collect phone calls for him. The calls were refused and the mail bore an inscription familiar to Presley devotees: "Return to Sender."

Meanwhile, Tudor Publishing reported orders of one and a half million copies of *Is Elvis Alive?* in its first three weeks on the market. Over that period, 75,000 enquiring minds called 900-999-ELVIS—also run by Tudor—to hear an excerpt from the tape of Presley's voice. Each call cost $2.70 plus tax. In addition, 50,000 people called one of Tudor's two additional 900 numbers—at $1.50 a shot—to vote on whether Presley was alive or not.

BIBLIOGRAPHY

Corliss, Richard, with Elizabeth L. Bland. "The King Is Dead—or Is He? The Elvis Cult Has the Makings of a Rising New Religion," *Time*. (October 10, 1988) 90-91.

"Elvis's Ultimate Comeback," *Newsweek*. 111:23 (June 6, 1988) 66.

Gates, David. "Elvis Statue Found on Mars! (Or, Just Your Average Week on the Elvis Watch)," *Newsweek*. (October 3, 1988) 63.

Leland, John, and Beth Eilers. "Is Elvis Alive?," *Spin*. 4:6 (September 1988) 98.

"People," *Time* (August 22, 1988) 72.

M.C. Escher

Maurits Cornelis Escher (1898-1972) was a Dutch artist who created some of the most visually challenging art of the twentieth century. His best work toys with the viewer's perception of things in such a way that once seen his art is unforgettable. An Escher cannot be mistaken for the work of another artist. As the world awoke to his genius, *Scientific American* published a brief introduction to Escher in 1966. The article got people talking, but then in 1972 when he died and more appreciative notice appeared, mild interest turned into exhilaration. Escher was already well known in parts of Europe before the United States heard of him. During his lifetime Dutch and British mathematicians discussed his creations in class. The mathematical precision of his draftsmanship and the changing field of view he presented fascinated the academics. The many Escher posters that decorated dormitory walls in European universities crossed the Atlantic to America and were just as fervently admired here.

Two of his most popular posters (originally lithographs) were "Reptiles" (1943) and "Drawing Hands" (1948). In "Reptiles" identical lizards parade in a continuous ellipse over a writing desk. If there is a beginning to their perambulation, it is when the head and front right leg of one of the lizards emerges from a two-dimensional drawing on a sheet of paper en route to becoming a three-dimensional creature. The next lizard has emerged even more, and the third fully-formed one climbs over a book. Four more lizards clamber up and over objects on the desk before the fifth one begins to flatten out into a two-dimensional drawing on a sheet of paper. Thus the lizard ellipse is complete. On the sheet of paper, though, there is an interlocking puzzle of replicated lizards, some white, some gray, and some charcoal. Miscellaneous articles on the writing desk bring the whole composition into perfect balance. The second Escher poster, "Drawing Hands," is not as detailed but is just as delightful to look at. A graceful left hand holds a pencil and draws the cuff on the shirt of the right hand which is busy drawing the cuff on the shirt of the left hand. Once again, Escher employed mirror images and continuous motion to arrest the eye of the viewer.

The Mobius strip ("A one-sided surface that can be formed from a rectangular strip by twisting one end 180 degrees and attaching it to the other end" — *Webster's II*) reoccurred in Escher's art. Out of the strips he made human busts that floated in the heavens conjuring up a kind of infinite existence beyond time and space. Such a composition in the faddish '60s also sold well as a poster. Another one of his popular posters depicted a classic Mobius strip completely perforated like film with large ants crawling over it in an endless march. For Escher fans that symbolized a new myth of Sisyphus and illustrated existentialism, both mental states they had to grapple with everyday. The hot-selling poster art and the late discovery of his genius escalated prices for Escher prints. Upon his death the usual $17 to $40 per print rose to $2,000 and higher, leveling off around $15,000. A maverick artist, Escher had been little concerned with moneymaking when alive. The fact that curious mathematicians revered his art and engendered a fad probably would have pleased him, an artist curious about the mathematical symmetry in nature.

BIBLIOGRAPHY

Davis, Douglas. "Teasing the Brain." *Newsweek* 80 (July 31, 1972): 59-60.

Ernst, Bruno. *The Magic Mirror of M.C. Escher*. New York: Random House, 1976.

Gardner, Martin. "Mathematical Games: The Eerie Mathematical Art of Maurits C. Escher." *Scientific American* 214 (April 1966): 110-121.

Hughes, Robert. "n-Dimensional Reality." *Time* 99 (April 17, 1972): 64.

Locher, J.L., ed. *The World of M.C. Escher*. New York: Harry N. Abrams, 1971.

Fantasia

Released in 1940, Walt Disney originally intended this cartoon masterpiece to bolster Mickey Mouse's career. Two of his other cartoon characters, Donald Duck and Goofy, had overshadowed the soft-spoken mouse mainly because of their more distinctive personalities. After Disney had completed "The Sorcerer's Apprentice," based on a musical composition by Dukas and starring Mickey Mouse, he engaged the renowned Leopold Stokowski to conduct it. Stokowski readily agreed and perhaps told Disney that he should expand the cartoon project to a full-length feature. Disney did by animating eight selections of classical music at a cost of over $2,000,000. Whoever had the idea first, when it came to fruition *Fantasia* marked the zenith of animation for a long time to come. The "voyage of discovery into the realms of color, sound, and motion" created a small sensation in 1940 for its novelty. But in 1970 during a major rerelease *Fantasia* scored big and advanced to fad status.

By 1970 the hippie revolution was well entrenched. Young people had dropped out of the mainstream culture into one of their own making. Hippies dressed in beads, leather, paisley shirts, and bell-bottom jeans. They wore their hair long and gave voice to a litany of complaints. And they indulged in mind-altering drugs. It was while on one of these drug-induced "trips" that hippies found *Fantasia* so "mind-blowing." Recalling the eight musical compositions Disney selected and his animation of them will assist in understanding the attraction. In order of appearance they are: Bach's "Toccata and Fugue in D Minor"—kinetic abstractions illustrate "pure" music; Tchaikovsky's "The Nutcracker Suite"—fairies fly and mushrooms dance; Dukas' "The Sorcerer's Apprentice"— Mickey Mouse can't stop brooms from multiplying and dumping pails of water into a dungeon; Stravinsky's "The Rite of Spring"— visualizes the creation of the world; Beethoven's "Pastoral Symphony"—depicts centaurs and satyrs in a classical setting; Ponchielli's "Dance of the Hours"—ostriches, hippos, and crocodiles flutter through a mock ballet; and Mussorgsky's "Night on Bald Mountain" and Schubert's "Ave Maria"—good and evil wage war for domination of the world. With so much color splashed on the screen and great music shifting moods, those in the audience not under the influence of drugs still succumbed to *Fantasia's* spell. But for hippies high on drugs the film was surrealistic and a better acid trip than the real stuff (lysergic acid diethylamide—LSD—capable of producing hallucinations).

Hippies had discovered another Disney film, *Alice in Wonderland*, a few years before. They had liked the hookah-smoking caterpillar and the disappearing Cheshire Cat in particular, and thought that the author, Lewis Carroll, was a "head" (a user of hashish). *Fantasia* promised much more, though, since it wasn't just a story but a mind journey through cosmic space both past and future. Movie theaters close to large congregations of hippies and sympathizers burst at the seams with mellow, peace-loving patrons. They even sat in the aisles to drink in the experience. At first Disney promoters were at a loss to explain the phenomenal success of a rerelease film. Why all of a sudden the tremendous interest in a dated animation project? When they figured it out they began booking *Fantasia* in big-college towns. Walt Disney died in 1966 so was not around to smile at the cultural change. He and Leopold Stokowski had wanted to introduce children to classical music. *Fantasia* was to be a delightful voyage combining sight and sound. Neither man would have guessed that a different set of passengers from the ones they had envisioned would enshrine the film.

BIBLIOGRAPHY

Culhane, John. *Walt Disney's Fantasia*. New York: H.N. Abrams, 1983.
"Tripping on Disney." *Newsweek* (January 19, 1970): 88.
Zinsser, W. "Walt Disney's Psychedelic Fantasia." *Life* (April 3, 1970): 15.

Farrah Fawcett-Majors

The most popular series on television during the 1976-1977 season was "Charlie's Angels." Its stratospheric ratings were largely due to the fact that one of its three starlet-heroines, Farrah Fawcett-Majors, had become America's reigning sex symbol. For a while, it was impossible to pass a newsstand without seeing her face on the cover of a half-dozen magazines. A bathing suit poster set sales records; a doll and Farrah "head" (prompted by the popularity of her coiffure) also sold well. In a 1977 *Ladies Home Journal* survey of 1,000 students from grades 1-12 which asked, "If you could be any famous person living in the world today, who would you be?," Fawcett-Majors received twice as many voters as the runner-up. One analyst attributed this phenomenon to the fact that

> . . . the public had had its fill of exotic Cher . . . is tired of cause-fighters like Jane Fonda and Helen Reddy . . . is sated by the sexuality of Elizabeth Taylor . . . seeks respite from the cerebral drama of Liv Ullmann . . . is frightened by the "off-beatness" of Liza Minnelli and Goldie Hawn. Maybe the public wants a gentle, safe heroine; maybe people want to rest in the cool, outstretched arms of their fantasy-Farrah, with her perfect features and long hair and pretty clothes, want to shut their eyes to art as life and life as art, and then to dream only of things that look nice and seem safe.

In short, as noted by one television critic, she was "safe and transgenerational, but not solemn."

Upon leaving "Charlie's Angels" after one season to join her then husband, Lee Majors, in making films for their own company, her popularity dropped off precipitously. However, roles such as that of rape victim in the TV-movie, "The Burning Bed," have garnered some measure of respect for her acting talents.

BIBLIOGRAPHY

Champlin, C. "Farrah Fawcett-Majors: an Unlikely Sex Symbol," *McCall's*. 104 (April 1977) 28ff.

Grant, James. "Farrah Fawcett," *Life*. 10 (November 1987) 16ff.

Meyer, Karl E. "The Barbie Doll as Sex Symbol," *Saturday Review*. 5 (October 1, 1977) 45.

Miller, Mary Susan. "The Farrah Factor," *Ladies Home Journal*. 94 (June 1977) 34-38, 151.

"General Hospital"

While "General Hospital" achieved only modest success during its early years, it went on to become perhaps the most successful television program of its kind. Premiering on April 1, 1963, the ABC soap opera is credited with stimulating the extraordinary popularity of daytime soaps that began in the late 1970s; this interest was infested in daily newspaper columns carrying the storylines, fan magazines devoted to the daytime serial stars and scholarly interpretations of the genre.

The domination of the daytime ratings race by "General Hospital" was largely due to its effectiveness in attracting teenage viewers (a particularly desirable strategy given the increasing numbers of women — always the core of the soaps-watching audience — entering the work-force), the first soap opera to make an impact within this demographic sector. This was accomplished primarily by relegating the program's central character in the 1960s, Dr. Steve Hardy, and his trademark Dry Knowing Chuckle, into the background in favor of youthful actors and actresses. The key ingredients were Anthony Geary (playing Luke Spencer), Genie Francis (Laura), Tristan Rogers, Emma Samms and rock star Rick Springfield.

Geary, regarded as the first superstar created by exposure only in daytime drama, was a true original; in contrast to the casual, rugged, chiseled-dimple glossiness characterizing most soap-opera heroes, he came across as "a goofball wiseacre with a chicken-like chin, a broad, strong brow, . . . an untamed flare of orange macaroni curls . . . [and] alert, quick eyes which tell you something is going on upstairs." His offbeat romance with Laura overshadowed anything the show's competitors had to offer; their wedding during a fall 1981 episode became something of a national event, with Elizabeth Taylor making several guest appearances in the segments leading up to the nuptials.

In addition, "General Hospital" scored on the strength of its hipness. Perhaps the fleetest-paced TV soap, the program exuded a pronounced playfulness and self-awareness, often at the expense of sacred soap-opera conventions. For example, rather than portraying romance as the first tentative step to matrimony, "General Hospital" indulged in romance for its own sake.

Due to the spread of the VCR — and its time-shifting capabilities — the audience for daytime serials has continued to expand, with "General Hospital" winning a substantial share of these converts. Although many of the program's top young stars have moved on (soaps have yet to shake the minor league stigma), it has continued to top the daytime ratings throughout most of the 1980s.

BIBLIOGRAPHY

Angel, S. "General Hospital," *50 Plus*. 25 (February 1985) 68-71.

Binback, L. "Daze of Our Lives," *Rolling Stone*. (October 1, 1981) 33ff.

Bricker, R., and C. Dykhouse. "Do Skin and Sin on the Soaps Affect Viewers? Social Scientists and the Stars Argue It Out," *People Weekly*. 17 (June 14, 1982) 74-76ff.

Green, M. "A Newly Trim Liz Taylor Joins the Over-50 Movie Queen Rush to the Glamour & Gold of TV Soaps," *People Weekly*. 22 (July 9, 1984) 32-34.

"How ABC Found Happiness in Daytime TV," *Business Week*. (August 24, 1981) 62ff.

Lanen, L. "Why Teens Love Soap Opera," *Seventeen*. 42 (March 1983) 132-133ff.

Lemish, Dafna. "Soap Opera Viewing in College; a Naturalistic Inquiry," *Journal of Broadcasting & Electronic Media*. 29 (Summer 1985) 275-293.

Waters, Harry F., with Janet Huck, George Hackett and Eric Gelman. "Television's Hottest Show," *Newsweek*. (September 28, 1981) 60-66.

Wolcott, James. "Playing It Fast and Loose in Soap-Opera Land," *Vogue*. 171 (November 1981) 222, 252.

Gertie,
the Trained Dinosaur

Gertie, the Trained Dinosaur, created by Winsor McCay, may well be the most famous cartoon short in the entire history of animation. The film was reportedly the result of a bet made between Mc-Cay and another cartoonist, George McManus; to win McCay singlehandedly produced the more than ten thousand drawings that comprised *Gertie*. The artist then took his creation on the vaudeville circuit, where, dressed as a circus lion tamer, he would order his cartoon dinosaur through her paces, even throwing a ball for her to balance on her nose.

Unquestionably the first work of animation art, the film created a sensation with the public; perhaps of greater importance, it encouraged fellow cartoonists to pursue a similar course. McCay himself followed up with a two-minute sequel, *Gertie on Tour* (1916), which was received with decidedly less enthusiasm than the original, thereby stalling the momentum of his career.

Despite the fact that hundreds of articles and books have concerned themselves with the inception, technique and impact of *Gertie, the Trained Dinosaur*, there is uncertainty regarding the date of its inaugural showing. In the past it was generally accepted that the film was released in 1909; recent research, however, has made a strong case for 1914. To add to the confusion, there are two sets of *Gertie* prints in existence: one of the original one-reel cartoon, and the other with live-action sequences of McCay, McManus and their colleagues at the beginning and end.

McCay's son Robert attempted to make the dinosaur into a comic strip called *Dino*; however, it achieved little success. The film continues to gain exposure via art theater showings and the videotape format.

BIBLIOGRAPHY

"Gertie," in: *The World Encyclopedia of Cartoons*, Volume 1, edited by Maurice
   Horn. New York: Gale/Chelsea House, 1980, p. 254.
Wilson, H.W. "McCay Before Disney," *Time*. 31 (January 10, 1938) 4.

Glitter Rock

Glitter rock arose as part of the early 1970s backlash against the 1960s sexual revolution, and revolved around an exaggerated sexual ambiquity and androgyny. Self-consciously decadent, "glam-rockers" adorned themselves with foppish and/or futuristic costumes, lots of makeup and the glitter dust that gave the genre its name. The music was generally a slick variant of hard rock, encompassing everything from the British power pop of Sweet to the art rock anarchy of Roxy Music to the proto-punk thrashing of The New York Dolls.

While glitter rock originated in England and reached its highest degree of popularity there, it made significant inroads into the U.S. charts during 1972-1974 and influenced a host of other styles such as cosmic funk, heavy metal and punk. Classic glitter rock recordings included

David Bowie – The Rise and Fall of Ziggy Stardust and The Spiders from Mars (RCA, 1972)

David Bowie – Aladdin Sane (RCA, 1973)

Gary Glitter – "Rock and Roll – Part II" (Bell, 1972)

Mott the Hoople – All the Young Dudes (Columbia, 1972)

The New York Dolls – The New York Dolls (Columbia, 1973)

The New York Dolls – Too Much Too Soon (Columbia, 1974)

Suzi Quatro – Suzi Quatro (Bell, 1973)

Roxy Music – Roxy Music (Atco, 1972)

Roxy Music – For Your Pleasure (Atco, 1973)

Slade – Slade Alive (Polydor, 1972)

Slade – Slayed (Polydor, 1972)

Sweet – "Little Willy" (Bell, 1973)

T. Rex – Electric Warrior (Reprise, 1971)

T. Rex – Tanx (Reprise, 1973)

By the mid-1970s the genre had played itself out, a victim of its own theatrical excesses and stylistic limitations. Glitter rock's flamboyance in dress was appropriated by disco while its more innovative artists shifted their allegiance to art rock and the avant garde.

BIBLIOGRAPHY

Barnes, Ken. "Teenage Rampage: An Overview of the First Golden Glitter Era," *Bomp!* n18 (March 1978) 29-32, 68.
Cromelin, R. "Kiss It Goodbye," *Cream.* 6 (January 1975) 41.
Edwards, Henry. "Rock and Rouge; Will the Glitter-Rock Phenomenon Take Over the Pop-Music Scene?," *High Fidelity.* 23(October 1973) 95-97.
"Glitter," in: *The Rolling Stone Encyclopedia of Rock & Roll,* edited by Jon Pareles and Patricia Romanowski. New York: Rolling Stone Press/Summit Books, 1983, p. 218.

Bowie, David

Copetas, C. "Beat Godfather Meets Glitter Mainman—William Burroughs, Say Hello to David Bowie," *Rolling Stone.* n155 (February 28, 1974) 24-27.
Ferris, T. "David Bowie in America," *Rolling Stone.* n121 (November 9, 1972) 38ff.
Simels, Steve. "David Bowie: No Honey, Its Not One of Those," *Stereo Review.* 30 (January 1973) 90.

Cooper, Alice

Ferris, T. "Alice Cooper's Beer Bottle Polka," *Rolling Stone.* n125 (January 4, 1973) 18ff.

Glitter, Gary

Knobler, P. "Would You Let This Man Touch You?," *Crawdaddy.* n24 (May 1973) 30.

Slade

Charlesworth, Chris. "America Feels the Noize," *Melody Maker.* 48 (November 3, 1973) 21.
Watts, M. "Amerika Gets Slayed!," *Melody Maker.* 48 (May 5, 1973) 12-13.
Werbin, M. "Slade: Knickers and Rahs at Home; Snickers and a Bra in N.Y.," *Rolling Stone.* n135 (May 24, 1973) 14.

T. Rex

Hodenfield, Chris. "Tyrannosaurus Enters Rock Age," *Rolling Stone.* n91 (September 16, 1971) 25.
Thomas, M. "T. Rex is Gonna Fuck You Into the Mick Jagger Gap," *Rolling Stone.* n104 (March 16, 1972) 32-34.

Betty Grable

Betty Grable was the most popular female star in the film industry during the 1940s. Her best known vehicle, lavish formulaic Technicolor musicals (she made twenty-two, all for 20th Century-Fox, including *Down Argentine Way*, *Coney Island* and *Sweet Rosie O'Grady*), invariably ranked among the most popular films at the box office for their respective years of release.

Grable's main claim to fame, however, lay in her ability to transcend film roles, becoming a phenomenally popular cultural icon during World War II. Her studio worked overtime to cultivate the image of a girl next door, always struggling to make ends meet. A classic pin-up poster first distributed in 1943 — depicting Grable as a leggy blonde in a white bathing suit, coyly peeking over her shoulder — remains her prime legacy. The image she projected was of a woman sexy enough to satisfy the longings of homesick soldiers, yet wholesome enough to placate the more staid elements of the Establishment. In addition, she appeared on the covers of *Time*, *Life*, countless movie magazines and on the sides of bombers and PT boats.

Grable's decline appears to have been the result of changing tastes on the part of moviegoers as well as Fox's decision to abandon her and promote another sex symbol, Marilyn Monroe. Grable then turned to the dinner theater circuit, achieving national attention for a brief time in the late sixties in *Hello Dolly!* While not a fixture on television, she has made numerous commercials, principally for Geritol, appearing on that medium.

BIBLIOGRAPHY

"Grable, Betty," in: *The International Dictionary of Films and Filmmakers: Volume III; Actors and Actresses*, edited by James Vinson. Chicago: St. James, 1986, pp. 273-274.
"Living the Daydream," *Time*. 52 (August 23, 1948) 40-42ff.

Martin, P. "World's Most Popular Blonde," *Saturday Evening Post*. 222 (April 15, 1950) 26-27ff.

Pastos, Spero. *Pin-Up: the Tragedy of Betty Grable*.

"Portrait," *Saturday Review of Literature*. 34 (February 24, 1951) 26.

Rosen, Marjorie. *Popcorn Venus*. New York: 1973.

Warren, Doug. *Betty Grable, The Reluctant Movie Queen*. New York: 1981.

Happenings

Artist Allan Kaprow (1927-) first enunciated the tenets of a happening. In a 1958 article in *Art News* he advocated using perishable materials in creating a work of art that could be "handled and walked around." Both artist and viewer participated in the live event. The idea was to remove art from its static museum surroundings — a painting square on a wall or a sculpture firm on a pedestal — and make it bustle with activity. For one of his first happenings, Kaprow built a collage environment lit by blinking lights which the viewer looked at through slashed curtains. That was the genesis of the movement that gained worldwide momentum in the 1960s, then was rarely heard from again after the mid-1970s.

Along with Allan Kaprow, other American artists produced happenings, most notably Red Grooms, Robert Whitman, Jim Dine, Claes Oldenburg, and Robert Rauschenberg. Robert Whitman's "The American Moon," seen at the Reuben Gallery, New York City, can serve as an example of what a well-conceived happening involved. The audience entered the happening through a series of tunnels that opened onto a central stage. Inside, cloth streamers blew almost straight up in the air and a creature in the shape of a mouth with painted teeth lurked about. A film of haystacks moving through a forest was projected on curtains. The film over and the curtains raised, a pendulum covered with red cloth swung across the stage. The cloth fell off exposing the pendulum as really being a man on a rope. The roof of the tunnels peeled back to reveal to the audience a yellow ceiling rising into the shape of a cone. Back on stage male and female performers rolled around and into each other. Then a plastic balloon inflated until it took up nearly all of the stage. Pieces of torn paper slid down the sides of the monster balloon. The performers walked inside of the balloon and struck poses. A blackout and the balloon deflated. At the invitation of the performers the audience went on stage and huddled there. Overhead a man hung from a trapeze and bizarre faces peered down from the catwalks. An explosion of flashbulbs startled the audience and the happening was over.

When happenings were popular the best place to "experience" them was at the Avant Garde Festival in New York City. Each year a fan could observe a hodgepodge of innovative performance art. Musician Charlotte Moorman organized the first festival in 1963 to present the work of ultramodern musicians. Moorman, herself, participated; for Jim McWilliams' "The Intravenous Feeding of Charlotte Moorman," she played cello while submerged in a tank of water. Over the years the attractions got better and certainly more zany. For example, there was a float of neon sculptures that anyone could ride down Central Park West; there was the bedsheet dance in which spectators were tied up in bedsheets and rolled on the grass; there were inflatable flowers that people could feed to make grow thirty feet high; there was a plexiglass maze for people to flounder in; there were performers who allowed the audience to cut away their clothes; there were singers who sang while their heads were shaved clean; and there was the artist who released white mice in the crowd as he asked, "And how are some of the ways you go upstairs?" Eerie electronic music, balloons, colored lights, and nudity were the staples of the Avant Garde festival. Everyone had more fun than they could have imagined, even if the happenings were faddish. Thankfully absent were stiff people sipping champagne at gallery openings, speaking platitudes about art. It was all very refreshing.

Happenings were not always fun and games. In Europe they took a different course erupting into violence. In the old world happenings turned anarchistic expressing deep-seated dissatisfaction with government policies. European artists staged piano-smashings, car-burnings, street fights, and the like. To protest injustice further they detonated large-scale assemblages full of political and cultural allusions, such as pictures of starving people, the atomic bomb exploding, or a symbolic movie star. European angst affected American artists somewhat since happenings did become an important twentieth century art movement. But in this country most happenings were benign. Either way, like much from the turbulent 1960s, they succumbed to the new winds of conservatism.

BIBLIOGRAPHY

Anderson, Jack. "What Happens at a Happening?" *Dance Magazine* (August 1966): 44-46.

Castle, Frederick. "Occurrences." *Art News* 67, no.4 (Summer 1968): 34-35, 71.

Farrell, Barry. "The Other Culture." *Life* 62 (February 17, 1967): 86-102.

Frank, Peter. "The Avant Garde Festival: And Now, Shea Stadium." *Art in America* (November-December 1974): 102-106.

Kirby, Michael. *Happenings*. New York: E.P. Dutton, 1965.

Squirru, Rafael. "The Happening: Art or Jest?" *Americas* 18, no.6 (June 1966): 27-33.

"Mary Hartman, Mary Hartman"

"Mary Hartman, Mary Hartman" became an unexpected national hit in 1976; the first time a syndicated program became the most talked about series on television. Originally financed by CBS, the program's producer, Norman Lear, failed to obtain the backing of any of the three networks. Therefore, Lear pitched it to the independent, local stations. By the time "Mary Hartman, Mary Hartman" premiered in January 1976, he had recruited fifty-four stations to run the daily half-hour series.

The appeal of "Mary Hartman, Mary Hartman" lay in its merging of the traditional soap opera format with a satirical perspective; the pacing was faster than the usual soaper and the expected plot complications of illicit sex, unbridled ambition, etc., were set slightly but effectively askew by exaggerating both the format and its plot conventions. The program revolved around Louise Lasser's portrayal of a typical middle class housewife and mother, with the exception that she wore a little girl's Pollyanna housedress and pigtails; despite being confronted with a bevy of melodramatic problems—e.g., her husband's impotence, her sister's promiscuity and suicidal tendencies—Mary seemed most concerned with the waxy yellow buildup on her kitchen floor.

While the program failed to duplicate the phenomenal success of its first year, it lasted for two more seasons under the title, "Forever Fernwood." However, the legacy of "Mary Hartman, Mary Hartman" proved to be far more lasting in nature. It showed that worthwhile programming could be successfully sold and promoted without any involvement by the major networks. Lear himself provided two more syndicated ventures in 1977; "All That Glitters" (a humorous soap opera concerned with sexual role reversal) and "Fernwood 2-Nite," a Mary Hartman spinoff/summer substitute that spoofed late night talk shows. Universal Studios and Mobil Oil established Operation Prime Time and Mobil Showcase Network, respectively, ad-hoc networks aiming for a limited but effective penetration of prime time. ABC created its own soap opera spoof for the 1977-1978 season entitled "Soap," which became an immediate top ten hit. The ultimate irony had CBS, the network that had initially rejected "Mary Hartman, Mary Hartman," airing selected reruns of the program as part of its late-night lineup in 1980.

BIBLIOGRAPHY

Brooks, Tim, and Earle Marsh. "Mary Hartman, Mary Hartman," in: *The Complete Directory to Prime Time Network TV Shows, 1946-Present*. New York: Ballantine, 1985, pp. 528-529.

Castleman, Harry, and Walter J. Podrazik. *Watching TV*. New York: McGraw-Hill, 1982.

Javna, John. "Mary Hartman, Mary Hartman," in: *Cult TV*. New York: St. Martin, 1985, pp. 130-133.

Hero-Worship Songs

Some of the men who made America inspired songs about their exploits. As surely as Homer sang about the brave Ulysses and English commoners about Robin Hood, Americans have praised their heroes in words and music. Beginning with the father of our country, George Washington, the Army fife and drum corps played the first Washington March in 1784. Several other marches followed in rapid succession. On April 7, 1786 the *Philadelphia Continental Journal* published a new song adapted to the tune of "God Save the King":

> God save great Washington
> His worth from ev'ry tongue
> Demands applause:
> Ye tuneful powers combine,
> And each true Whig now join
> Whose heart did ne'er resign
> The glorious cause.

If General Washington was the conquering hero before he became president after his inauguration April 30, 1789 his stature grew even more. It seemed that every songwriter in Federalist America fit his name in somewhere. "Ode to Columbia's Favorite Son" was one such tribute:

> Great Washington, the hero's come,
> Each heart exulting bears the sound.
> See! thousands their deliv'rer throng,
> And shout him welcome all around.
> Now in full chorus burst the song,
> And shout the deeds of Washington!

In similar fashion Abraham Lincoln prompted Civil War songs

such as "Old Abe Lincoln Came Out of the Wilderness," "Lincoln and Liberty," "Abraham's Daughter," and "We Fight for Uncle Abe." Confederate tunesmiths viewed Lincoln differently and wrote about the dread "*Abe*-o-lition":

> Jeff Davis rode a dapple gray,
> Lincoln rode a mule
> Jeff Davis is a gentleman
> And Lincoln is a fool.

Assassination ended Lincoln's life but not the making of songs about him. In "Booth Killed Lincoln" the last stanza spoke a blatant untruth that either upset or appealed to people:

> Poor Lincoln then was heard to say,
> And all has gone to rest,
> "Of all the actors in this town,
> I loved Wilkes Booth the best."

The first two decades of the 20th century—a vibrant time for songwriting in general—honored many heroes. Two marches, "Dawn of Peace" and "The Ironmaster" enshrined the industrialist and humanitarian, Andrew Carnegie. After the country's richest man, John D. Rockefeller, and his company Standard Oil of Indiana got into trouble for violating an act forbidding secret railroad rates, a song explained:

> When our good President had seen
> That John D's plans were mighty mean
> This freezing little fellows out
> His "thinker" then began to doubt.

Having to pay a fine of $29,240,000 made Rockefeller a hero to some who admired his stamina under fire. Joining Washington and Lincoln in the triumvirate of our great presidents Woodrow Wilson was also the subject of song. Teenager Blanche Merrill achieved popularity overnight when she wrote, "We Take Our Hats Off to You—Mr. Wilson." The year was 1914, World War I had begun, and President Wilson spoke firmly for isolationism.

Greater than a gladiator, you're the world's big mediator, . . .
We'd trust you in any kind of fuss,
We're glad you belong to us.

Hero-worship songs fill American history uniting people and raising spirits. But the songs are only of the moment and with the exceptions of John F. Kennedy and Martin Luther King, Jr., are noticeably absent in the latter half of this century. Furthermore hero-status changes and in time even a Washington pales.

BIBLIOGRAPHY

Engel, Carl. *Music from the Days of George Washington*. New York: Da Capo Press, 1983.

Levy, Lester S. *Give Me Yesterday: American History in Song, 1890-1920*. Norman: University of Oklahoma Press, 1975.

Silber, Irwin, ed. *Songs of the Civil War*. New York: Columbia University Press, 1960.

Hermann Hesse

A German-born Swiss writer, Hesse (1877-1962), won the Nobel Prize for Literature in 1946. His novels, slowly translated into English, were more forthcoming after the prestigious award. Hesse wrote a shelf full of cerebral fiction culminating in his masterpiece, *The Glass Bead Game*, which the Nobel committee especially praised. Once paperback translations were available in college bookstores the fad of "experiencing" Hesse began. What the 1960s generation in America liked about the foreign writer was his assault on the establishment, his pessimism, and his maverick heroes. Those three things were exactly what heated their blood. The American establishment murderously forced its young people into fighting an illegal war in Vietnam. When they begged authority for change and got none, young Americans suffered the consequences of Freudian malaise which increased their pessimism. And for the young to succeed in the 1960s they had to stand alone and think of themselves as outsiders to avoid hated conformity. Hesse was their mentor because he understood their plight, or at least had the prescience to understand.

In *Steppenwolf*, for instance, the hero despises his middle class upbringing for the mediocrity it imposes. He works to rid himself of society's indoctrination so he can be free. Just the thought of having to imitate his parents doing the same empty things over and again gets him boiling mad. Break away, desert the pack, Steppenwolf howls his displeasure and goes on alone. It is easy to see why this Hesse novel appealed to the 1960s counterculture revolution, and was taken as the name for an ultra-popular rock band. Dog-eared copies of *Steppenwolf*, carried everywhere like a talisman, provided an immediate introduction — "Fantastic, you like Hesse, too" — as did other of his novels: *Demian*, *Narcissus and Goldmund*, and *Siddhartha*. All of these fictional characters rebel against their reigning order and enforced habit patterns to triumph as individuals.

But of the lot, Siddhartha won the greatest following among the flower children.

Set in sixth century B.C. India, the novel tells the story of a young man's search for enlightenment. The son of a Brahman, Siddhartha cannot accept the teachings handed down to him by his father and other holy men. Unanswered questions about the meaning of life and man's place in the universe disturb his peace. He and a friend, Govinda, leave home to pursue self-knowledge. They join the Samanas and like them try purging all sensual desires. This drastic measure proves fruitless. Then they meet Gotama the Buddha, whose tranquil inner spirit impresses them. Govinda stays with the Buddha, but Siddhartha moves on. He realizes god and enlightenment reside in the soul of the individual which no teacher can reveal; the individual must do that for himself. In a turnabout, Siddhartha enters the secular world, delights in a courtesan, Kamala, and prospers as a businessman. He still possesses enough introspection, though, to see that he has become a ruthless, uncaring man and gives it all up. Free of materialism once again, he wanders in a forest where he encounters Vasudeva, a kindhearted ferryman. Siddhartha remains with Vasudeva in the cheerful woods and together they rejoice in the sights and sounds of nature. Kamala reappears with Siddhartha's son. A snake bites her and she dies. Their son, not having had a stable home, runs away. His boyhood friend, Govinda, still searching for wisdom, reunites with Siddhartha and experiences an epiphany. Govinda, who has lived passively at the feet of the Buddha, does not understand Siddhartha's explanation of what life has taught him, but sees in his face a rare divinity. He realizes that Siddhartha is as much a holy man as the Buddha, even though he arrived at his state of bliss by a different path.

No wonder the novel mesmerized young Americans in the 1960s. It combined rebellion, protracted soul-searching, and idealism with Eastern religion. It was as if the author knew their very beings, their trials and tribulations, their distinct longings for a better world. Now Hesse's novels are faddish artifacts except among serious readers who find profit in reflecting on philosophical fiction. Few of today's college students know his name. And the other strange names once heard so often in youthful gatherings across America —

Steppenwolf, Demian, Narcissus and Goldmund, and Siddhartha —
likewise fall on deaf ears.

BIBLIOGRAPHY

Goldman, A. "Fanned by Youth." *Vogue* (January 1, 1970): 82.
Koch, S. "Prophet of Youth." *New Republic* (July 13, 1968): 23-26.
Resnik, Henry S. "How Hermann Hesse Speaks to the College Generation."
    Saturday Review (October 18, 1969); 35-37.
Schott, W. "German Guru Makes the U.S. Scene Again." *Life* (July 12, 1968): 8.

Hippodrome

To be more exact, P.T. Barnum, the impresario of the fantastic, called it the Great Roman Hippodrome. He envisoned a popular entertainment immense in design with not hundreds of performers and animals but with thousands. In 1873 he and his partner, W.C. Coup, took the first step toward realizing their dream. They leased an entire square block between Fourth and Madison avenues in New York City and contracted for an indoor coliseum, 200 feet wide and 426 feet long. The next April the Great Roman Hippodrome opened to the public with every one of its ten thousand seats filled. Here is what the audience saw: a grand procession of gaily decorated, horse-drawn cars carrying one thousand performers dressed as historical monarchs and rulers. The cars circled the arena slowly so the adults could identify the various royalty and tell their kids who they were. The processional having barely disappeared, snorting steeds pulling chariots raced onto the oval track one fifth of a mile long — Ben Hur in New York City! Clouds of dust kicked up as the four-horse teams careened around the rapidly shrinking track. Whips cracked and the horses strained their necks to run faster. The mad dash continued until finally one team nudged out the rest at the finish line. Dust still in the air, tightrope walkers, Japanese acrobats, and clowns ran in, but the track didn't remain idle. Monkey races began and though not as swift as the horses, the furry creatures amused the audience far more. Barnum knew how to keep peaking interest without chancing a lull. Later he added ostrich and giraffe races.

These swirling contests of speed and daring provided breathless entertainment. Barnum by no means invented hippodrama which originated in ancient times and was reprised in the 18th and 19th centuries particularly in England and France. Americans witnessed their first hippodrama in 1773 when the English equestrian Jacob Bates presented "A Burlesque on Horsemanship; or, The Taylor

Riding to Brentford." Bates performed at a ring in Bowery Lane, New York City; his "Brentford" was a proven comedy act straight from London involving different antic characters on horseback. At its crest European hippodrama offered full-scale battles and romantic epics such as *The Blood Red Knight, Uranda, The Enchanter of the Steel Castle*, and the King Arthur tales—anything that employed horses and riders in a spectacle. For all of its vitality Barnum's hippodrome lost momentum for several reasons. His wife, Charity, died the same year the Hippodrome opened leaving him emotionally drained; anytime a show succeeded he wanted to take it on the road which he couldn't do easily with the Hippodrome; and during the 1870s competition among those in the entertainment field was so stiff Barnum felt pressed to try something bigger. The Great Roman Hippodrome held its first race and was on the auction block in the same year. Barnum and Coup sold it but in 1881 Barnum without Coup was back on the grounds again. The short-lived Hippodrome now called Madison Square Garden was the scene for the premier of "The Barnum and Bailey Greatest Show on Earth." All-out chariot, monkey, ostrich, and giraffe races were no more but elements of the hippodrama remained. Acrobatic riders on horseback never left the circus even if pagan chariot races did.

BIBLIOGRAPHY

Saxon, A.H. *Enter Foot and Horse: A History of Hippodrama in England and France*. New Haven and London: Yale University Press, 1968.

Speaight, George. *A History of the Circus*. San Diego and New York: A.S. Barnes, 1980.

Wallace, Irving. *The Fabulous Showman: The Life and Times of P.T. Barnum*. New York: Knopf, 1959.

David Hockney

By the late 1980s the career of British-born artist David Hockney had spanned three decades of success in a variety of media. However, his fiftieth year (1988) was marked by a series of museum showcases — and corresponding journalistic coverage — which have spread an awareness of his work to a far wider audience than had previously existed. The original impetus for this media phenomenon was the decision of the Los Angeles County Museum of Art to organize a retrospective of his prodigious production of paintings, drawings, photographs and photographic collages, prints and illustrated books, as well as examples of his stage designs for such operas as *The Magic Flute*, *Le Sacre du Printemps* and *Tristan und Isolde*. Subsidized by AT&T, the show was also shown at the Metropolitan Museum of Art in New York (June-August 1988) and the Tate Gallery in London (October 1988-January 1989).

Much of Hockney's artistic and commercial success can be ascribed to his close identification with Los Angeles. He first visited the U.S. when twenty-four, making the earliest of many journeys to L.A. two years later. The U.S., especially Los Angeles, represented an enormous and inviting creative terrain for the young artist; as if to herald the impact of his relationship with the country, he dyed his hair blonde. Hockney had actually painted the city before even visiting it. Once he arrived, finding it "just like [he] imagined," it became his subject matter. He later noted,

> It was the first time I'd ever painted a place. In London, I think I was put off by the ghost of Sickert, and I couldn't see properly. In Los Angeles, there were no ghosts. There were no paintings of Los Angeles. People then didn't even know what it looked like. I remember seeing, within the first week, a ramp of freeway going into the air, and I suddenly thought, "My god, this place needs its Piranesi."

Hockney's eclectic style and adventurous spirit, particularly as manifested in his exhilarating photo collages with their fresh reinterpretation of the cubist movement, seemed tailor-made for capturing the spirit of L.A. The light-hearted approach characterizing Hockney's work, combined with Americans' ongoing fascination with southern California and its lifestyle, seem to be responsible for his tremendous vogue in the late 1980s.

BIBLIOGRAPHY

"The Big Splash; A Retrospective Look at the Ever-Fluid, Multifaceted Career of David Hockney," *Horizon*. 31:2 (March 1988) 37-38.

Cothier, P. "Hockney: Hard-Fought Battles and Trivial Pursuits," *Art News*. 87 (April 1988) 161.

Danto, A.C. "David Hockney," *The Nation*. 247 (July 30-August 6, 1988) 104-107.

"David Hockney: Multi-Media Master," *USA Today*. 117 (July 1988) 76-83.

Filler, M. "Tristan by Veri-Lite," *Art in America*. 76 (April 1988) 35ff.

Hockney, David. *Cameraworks*. New York: Knopf, 1984. Includes Lawrence Weschler's essay (with bibliographic references), "True to Life."

Hockney, David. *Pictures*, selected and edited by Nikos Stangos. New York: Abrams, 1979.

Hoy, A.H. "'A Recolution in Seeing,'" *The Courier* (Unesco). 41 (April 1988) 26-29.

Hughes, R. "Giving Success a Good Name," *Time*. 131 (June 20, 1988) 76-77ff.

Larson, K. "The Fine Line," *New York*. 21 (June 20, 1988) 62-63.

Stevens, M. "Painterly Charm," *The New Republic*. 198 (April 18, 1988) 32-34.

Hopalong Cassidy

Hopalong Cassidy was television's earliest cult hero — a cowboy who wore black but represented all things noble and virtuous. The character first appeared in a pulp story, "The Fight at Buckskin," which was sold by its writer, Clarence Edward Mulford (1883-1956), for ninety dollars to *Outing Magazine* and later adapted into a novel, *Bar 20* (1907). The Bar 20 Ranch cowboys formed the basis of a series of black-and-white "B" westerns starring William Boyd; however, the more colorful Cassidy was given top billing over the hero of the novel, Buck Peters. The production schedule for the films included forty-one features for Paramount (1935-1941); thirteen for United Artists (1942-1944); and twelve for Hopalong Cassidy Productions (1946-1948), a joint venture between Boyd and promoter Toby Anguish.

The failure of the latter venture led Anguish to reedit the Paramount and United Artists features for syndication to television. In part due to the fact that no other westerns produced by the major studios were then available on TV, the program was an overnight smash, first on individual stations (1948-1949), and then nationally via NBC (1950-1954). Nielsen surveys ranked *Hopalong Cassidy* consistently within the top three — and briefly at number one — in audience popularity during 1950-1951. Thus encouraged, Boyd contracted with NBC in May 1952 to produce fifty-two new half-hour telefilms to air between 1952 and 1954.

During this period Hopalong Cassidy Enterprises was reaping a merchandising windfall. At the peak of the craze, 108 licensees were manufacturing such items as Hopalong Cassidy bicycles with leather-fringed saddles, handlebars shaped like steer's horns and built-in gun holsters, "Hoppy" roller skate spurs and jewel-studded ankle straps, and pajamas, wallpaper, cookies and peanut butter with an estimated gross of $70 million per annum. *Hopalong Cassidy and the Singing Bandit*, a record album released by Capitol in early 1950, had prerelease sales of 200,000. A comic strip devoted to his exploits—Los Angeles Mirror, 1949-1951/King Features Syndicate, 1951-1955—was carried by more than 150 papers, fifteen million comic books were sold in one year, and KFS circulated an advice column for parents and children called "Happy Talk." King also promoted the Hopalong Cassidy Trooper's Club, which featured its own ten-point creed and a membership of two million, for a time rivalling the Boy Scouts in size. In short, the program stimulated a merchandising phenomenon which remained unsurpassed until the appearance of Walt Disney's "Davy Crockett" series on television.

"Hopalong Cassidy" last aired at prime time on January 16, 1954, a victim of overexposure (by the time NBC began showing the program in 1950 many in the TV audience had already seen each of the reedited features four or five times) and strong competition (e.g., "The Lone Ranger," which benefitted from the introduction of fresh new adventures specifically produced for TV). The "Hoppy" films continued to be shown as re-runs and during two aborted attempts by KTLA-Los Angeles to revive the series in prime time. Since Boyd's death in 1972 the films have not been seen on television due to copyright litigation introduced by the Mulford estate. A limited number of titles are available on videotape in their original Hollywood form.

BIBLIOGRAPHY

"Boyd, William," in: *Current Biography*, 1950, edited by Charles Moritz. 11th ed. New York: Wilson, 1950.

"Hoppy's Re-Deal," *Newsweek*. 37 (January 8, 1951) 52.

Jenson, O. "Hopalong Hits the Jackpot," *Life*. 28 (June 12, 1950) 63-68ff.

"Kiddies in the Old Corral," *Time*. 56 (November 27, 1950) 18-20.

"Life Goes on Tour with Hopalong Cassidy," *Life*. 27 (September 12, 1949) 150-152ff.

"Tall in the Saddle," *Time*. 55 (May 22, 1950) 42ff.

"Tax-Ridden Hoppy to Unsaddle Enterprises," *Business Week*. (January 19, 1952) 151.

Whitney, D. "Inside Story of Hopalong Cassidy," *Coronet*. 29 (December 1950) 87-93.

Woolery, George W. "Hopalong Cassidy," in: *Children's Television; The First Thirty-Five Years, 1946-1981; Part II: Live, Film, and Tape Series*. Metuchen, NJ: Scarecrow, 1985, pp. 223-227.

Howdy Doody

One of the earliest network children's series, "Howdy Doody" became the symbolic program of the first American generation nurtured on television. The show featured Buffalo Bob Smith, its host and creator; Howdy Doody, a four-foot puppet dressed in western duds and possessing an unforgettable face — i.e., red hair, freckles, blue eyes and an enormous snaggle-toothed grin; and Clarabell, a clown whose voice consisted of two horns (a sweet one to indicate "yes," a sour horn for "no").

"Howdy Doody" premiered live on NBC on December 27, 1947, as a one-hour Saturday program and remained on the air until 1960; 2,343 performances in all, until then more than any other show in the network's history. The program survived a rocky beginning — e.g., a period in 1948 without Howdy Doody as a result of legal entanglements, and strong competition from "Pixie Playtime," developed by Frank Paris, creator of the first Howdy Doody marionette — to become the top-rated children's TV offering by April 1950. It was estimated to be a daily national pastime for 6.5 million viewers, largely between the ages two to eight, in 1951.

In addition to its colorful characters, the show's success resulted from an engaging blend of nonsense of pure fantasy, with no pretense to educational value. Still, "Howdy Doody" had a positive social message. Buffalo Bob provided his "peanut gallery" (the fifty boisterous youths who comprised the in-studio audience) and TV audience with advice such as "never pick a fight," "be kind to animals" and "don't cross the street with your feet but with your eyes," a national American Automobile Association campaign slogan. Buffalo Bob also contributed original songs on manners and cleanliness as well as encouraging youngsters to go to their places of worship.

During the peak of its popularity, "Howdy Doody" provided the impetus for a merchandising bonanza. George Woolery notes,

One Howdy Doody premium offer in the early fifties drew over 750,000 letters. At Doodymania's height, well over one hundred products, ranging from earmuffs, suspenders, and T-shirts to comic books, record albums and a rock chair that played "It's Howdy Doody Time," were licensed by Kagran.

The program's decline began on June 16, 1956, when it was rescheduled on Saturday mornings (previously Monday-Friday afternoons) as "The Howdy Doody Show" featuring a new episodic format. Thereafter, it resembled puppet-and-live fairy tales more than the rambling madcap goings-on which had previously been its forté.

After a decade spent in retirement, Buffalo Bob joined the nostalgia circuit in 1970-1971, reviving the program via his kinescope films and visiting college campuses with great success. In response to the clamor for Howdy Doody novelties, NBC Domestic Enterprises licensed an RCA album of songs, T-shirts and other sundries, and PIP Records released original cast recordings of several shows. In 1975, some of the later TV videotapes were syndicated, prompting Smith to resurrect the series as "The New Howdy Doody Show" in 1976; however, it was unsuccessful and soon terminated.

BIBLIOGRAPHY

"Howdy Doody," in: *Children's Television: The First Thirty-Five Years, 1946-1981; Part II: Live, Film, and Tape Series*, by George W. Woolery. Metuchen, NJ: Scarecrow, 1985, pp. 231-236.
"Howdy Doody Show to Introduce Books," *Library Journal*. 85 (March 15, 1960) 1290.
"It's Howdy Doody Time, Again," *Life*. 70 (May 7, 1971) 90-92.
"Little People's Choice," *American Magazine*. 146 (September 1948) 106-107.
"Six-Foot Baby-Sitter; Howdy Doody Show," *Time*. 55 (March 27, 1950) 62-64.

Keystone Kops

Between 1912 and 1917 Mack Sennett made around four hundred Keystone (the name of the film company) comedies for the silent screen. This output earned him the title, "The King of Comedy." Among his stars were Charlie Chaplin, Roscoe "Fatty" Arbuckle, Mabel Normand, Chester Conklin, Ben Turpin, and Gloria Swanson. All superb talents who became legends, but the one undiminished image of Sennett's creativity was then and still is today—his Keystone Kops. The public began laughing the moment the first Kop appeared. *The Bangville Police* (1913) featured a patrol car racing to a farm in response to a burglary call. The farmer's daughter had set off the bumbling police who almost broke their necks getting there, only to discover that the so-called burglars had delivered a present for her. It was a calf from her father. The Bangville police wore street clothes and the patrol car was an exhaust belching rattletrap with "Police" and the number "13" painted on its hood. The Chief looked more like an unemployed railroad worker than an officer of the law. The more familiar uniformed Kops brandishing nightsticks led by a chief in gold braid were yet to come.

Sennett employed his Kops in several ways. New Keystone players served their apprenticeship on the force, learning how to mug and pratfall before moving on to more central roles. Few of his comedies focused entirely on the Kops, but when a surefire laugh was needed in an unrelated story they dashed in pell-mell after the suspect. These surprise entrances alerted the audience to expect the hapless Kops at anytime. The guessing game was a great source of amusement. The Kops also quick-changed into the Keystone Firefighters who in "The Alarm" (1914) and "Cinders of Love" (1916) ran into one another in an uproarious clash of interests. All for laughs, Sennett portrayed police irreverently. Keystone Kops slept on park benches, strolled by fruit stands helping themselves, flirted with married women, and for the most part neglected their duty. The Chief, perhaps a jot smarter than his men, seemed to have them well trained until a call for help came in. Then the antics began. The Kops were all mismotion; they scampered one way, then the next, getting their legs entangled. Usually grouped together they fell on the ground like rows of leaning dominoes. Pursuit was no easier crammed in the patrol car. They always drove in the wrong direction while some of them tumbled or blew out of the car. Sennett loved his Kops and in the early comedies played one himself. Sticking a foot-long handlebar mustache under his nose and pinning an authoritarian badge on his chest limbered him up for fun. Because audiences eagerly anticipated the Keystone Kops, not sure when they would stumble in, faddish interest in them escalated. Certainly, Keystone's biggest stars like Charlie Chaplin and Roscoe "Fatty" Arbuckle brought prominence to the film company, but the crazy Kops who never starred were just as popular.

Before leaving Mack Sennett two other of his innovations that achieved fad status deserve mention. For pure decoration he embellished many of his comedies with bathing beauties. Of course, they were gratuitous adding nothing to the story. The audience got to see bare arms, a little thigh, and knees. Other filmmakers avoided the ploy maintaining that character and story were all important. Sennett agreed with them but knew that a pretty face and form also sold tickets. Lots of beauties in bathing suits walked through his comedies to keep the public remarking, "Hey, have you seen Sennett's latest girls?" Another Keystone trademark was the pie-in-the-face. Sennett didn't originate the comic bit but he surely promoted its usage. Incidentally, the kind of pie pressed in the face or launched across a room wasn't custard as often thought. Custard, light in color, didn't show up on film as well as a dark berry pie topped with whipped cream. The mess was much more glorious that way. Until they lapsed into clichés Sennett Kops, bathing beauties, and pies fixed a smile on American faces.

BIBLIOGRAPHY

Lahue, Kalton C., and Terry Brewer. *Kops and Custards: The Legend of Keystone Films*. Norman: University of Oklahoma Press, 1972.

———. *Mack Sennett's Keystone: The Man, the Myth, and the Comedies*. South Brunswick and New York: A.S. Barnes and Company, 1971.

Emerging from a cascade of streamers, these Mack Sennett girls teased the viewer, as did a bevy of other beauties in Sennett film comedies. Girls, girls, and more girls, especially on the beach, was his formula for mesmerizing an audience. But Sennett's lasting fame came from his Keystone Kops, a band of hapless law enforcement officers whose kinetic energy brought roars of laughter.

155

Freddy Krueger

While slasher films have long been a favorite of American youth, none have approached the popularity of New Line Cinema's *A Nightmare on Elm Street* series. The first three installments grossed more than $100 million at theater box offices, with each sequel out-grossing its predecessor; in addition, they had sold more than half a million videocassettes as of September 1988. *A Nightmare on Elm Street 4: The Dream Master* (1988) earned $12.8 million in its first three days of release — the biggest opening weekend ever tallied by an independently released film — and elevated the series' central character, Freddy Krueger (played by Robert Englund), to cult status.

Freddy — whose raison d'être is to stalk teenagers in their dreams — cuts a striking figure with his moldy black felt hat, scalded face, red-and-green-striped sweater and right-hand glove equipped with steel finger-knives. An improbable culture hero; yet, by late summer of 1988, signs of Freddymania were everywhere. Sales of tie-in merchandise (e.g., Freddy dolls, the trademark sweater, a glove with plastic finger-knives) had surpassed $15 million; the Freddy mask and hat outsold all other Halloween costumes in 1987. Two *Nightmare* books, five record albums and a board game were also hot selling items. A number of rock artists released take-offs of the craze, including The Fat Boys ("Are You Ready For Freddy") and D.J. Jazzy Jeff and The Fresh Prince (whose video clip of "A Nightmare on My Street" was pulled from TV rotation due to legal pressure from New Line Cinema). He had a fan club, a 900 chat line and was featured in an MTV special. In October, a syndicated television series, "Freddy's Nightmares," had its debut on more than 160 stations.

The phenomenon appeared to owe much to the comparative style and intelligence of the *Nightmare* films. In a genre known for its excesses and blatant commercial exploitation, they provided, according to Richard Corliss, sharp humor, a hint of the B-movie aura and the eerie simplicity of a child's counting rhyme, tapping profound adolescent fears, then exorcising them. However, it was Freddy who provided the series with its energy and dramatic impact. Wes Craven, the writer and producer of the films, has noted that "Freddy is the most ruthless primal father. The adult who wants to slash down the next generation."

At the time this volume went to press, Freddy remained a hot commodity. Further installments of the series are an inevitability. After all, at the climax of *A Nightmare on Elm Street 4*, everyone cheers when Freddy declares, "I am eternal!"

BIBLIOGRAPHY

Corliss, Richard. "Did You Ever See a Dream Stalking?," *Time*. 132 (September 5, 1988) 66-67.

"'Elm' Scares Up Reported $5-mil from CBS-Fox for O'Seas Rights," *Variety*. 331 (June 8, 1988) 67.

"'Elm Street 3' Sets Indie B.O. Record; National Biz Lively," *Variety*. 326 (March 4, 1987) 3ff.

Farber, J. "Blood, Sweat, and Fears: Why are Horror Movies Such a Slashing Success?," *Seventeen*. 46 (July 1987) 108-109ff.

Gilmore, Mikal. "Fab Freddy," *Rolling Stone*. n536 (October 6, 1988) 91-95.

Yarbrough, Jeff. "Hold the Cutting Words, Please, for Robert Englund, the Friendly Cuss Who Plays Elm Street's Nightmare Stalker," *People Weekly*. 27 (March 23, 1987) 42-43.

Jenny Lind

Jenny Lind, the "Swedish Nightingale," was the first singer whose name has remained a household word, particularly in the United States as a result of her visit in the early 1850s and the hysteria orchestrated by promotional genius P.T. Barnum. Based upon her unparalleled reputation as a concert vocalist, she was invited by Barnum in 1850 to tour America. With an eye to optimizing his potential earnings, the showman staged a mob scene in New York to greet her arrival in the U.S. in the fall of 1850; a parade up Broadway, serenades and speeches followed. From New York Lind and her entourage went on the road; according to Barnum, ninety-five concerts in eight months grossed $712,161.34, of which the singer received $176,675. The country was seized by Lind-fever; many concerts resembled a madhouse, due in part to Barnum's penchant for hype and the heightened demand for tickets.

Lind finally broke the contract in June 1851, paying Barnum a forfeit of $25,000, allegedly as a result of her disgust over the vulgarity and show business atmosphere that Barnum represented. She then married pianist/composer Otto Goldschmidt, nine years her junior, in early 1852. Her farewell American concert took place in New York on May 25, 1852; the couple then returned to London and lived a quiet life.

Lind's popularity was based — first and foremost — upon her vocal prowess; she had total command of the most incredible coloratura technique, including a trill held to be unparalleled in the annals of singing. As noted by Harold Schoberg, her success also owed much to the confluence of her particular outlook and the spirit of the times.

> She was the very symbol of the Victorian age . . . She would never sing in France because she disapproved of French morality . . . She was always going to church. She gave a considerable part of her considerable earnings to charity. Her

private life was beyond reproach. Women liked her because she seemed simple and unspoiled, not flamboyant or glamorous, not even pretty, and thus no threat to them or their husbands.

BIBLIOGRAPHY

Bulman, Joan. *Jenny Lind*. London: 1956.

Hume, R. "Jenny Lind Was a Flop as Her Own Tour Manager," *Variety*. 289 (January 4, 1978) 56.

Kirk, E.K. "Nightingales at the White House," *Opera News*. 45 (November 1, 1980) 18.

Schonberg, Harold C. "Jenny Lind: The Moral Lady," in: *The Glorious Ones*. New York: Times Books, 1985, pp. 139-154.

Schultz, Gladys Denny. *Jenny Lind – The Swedish Nightingale*. Philadelphia: Lippincott, 1962.

Turner, M.C., and G.B. Turner. "Dolls for Remembrance; Jenny Lind Dolls," *Hobbies*. 67 (November 1962) 38ff.

Ware, W.P., T.C. Lockard. *P.T. Barnum Presents Jenny Lind: the American Tour of the Swedish Nightingale*. Baton Rouge: Louisiana State University Press, 1980.

P.T. Barnum's promotion of Jenny Lind's first American concert created near panic among those who thought they might not get a ticket. Her voice was billed as the loveliest ever heard on earth or, for that matter, in heaven. The monkey in the tree in "The Second Deluge" cartoon is none other than the master of humbug himself, P.T. Barnum.

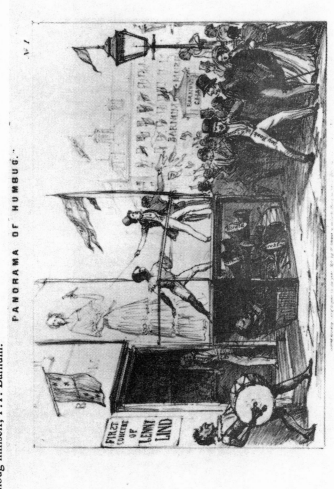

FANORAMA OF HUMBUG.

Showman_"Walk up, Ladies & Gentlemen and see the greatest wonder of the age —
the real Swedish Nightingale, the only specimen in the country"

161

THE SECOND DELUGE.

First appearance of Jenny Lind in America

162

Peter Max

Peter Max's art epitomized the spirit of the flower power generation. During the 1960s, Victor Zurbel, art director for the New York ad agency, Doyle Dane Bernbach, prophesied that Max would be "the Walt Disney of the next generation." Another contemporary, Ken Deardoff, the art director of the now defunct leftist magazine, *Evergreen Review*, predicted that he would "become the first artist since Norman Rockwell in the '40s to be known by the American public at large." While Max never quite attained such heights, he made a sizeable impact upon American culture in the late 1960s.

Max had a cosmopolitan upbringing, he was born in Berlin and raised in Shanghai and Israel. After studying at New York's Art Students League for five years, he opened an art studio in 1962. By 1965, the Daly-Max Studio had worked for almost every notable Madison Avenue advertising agency and had won sixty-two design awards. He then quit the studio and experimented on his own for the next two years, hoping to link his name directly to the merchandising process.

In 1967 Max started designing posters for local stores. When his printing firm, Security Printing Co., began receiving vast numbers of requests from individuals who wanted personal copies of the posters, Max instituted Peter Max Posters. Within eighteen months 2.5 million posters had been sold; by spring of 1969 Max's work had appeared on more than forty products (e.g., china, linen, belts, decals, tattoos, puzzles, ashtrays, stationery) as well as boutiques and restaurants. The Beatles' animated film classic, *Yellow Submarine* (1968), blatantly aped his style. In addition, he found success in 1969 with a new medium, "Transit Art," which entailed placing his posters on vehicles such as buses, subways and trolleys in ten major U.S. cities in order to bring attention to the space Metro Transit Advertising had to sell.

Despite his strong business sense, the psychedelic borrowings of

Max's work had rendered him something of a hippie hero. While often expressing the mind-expanding experiences of the drug culture through swirling, kaleidoscopic patterns and vivid Day-Glo color; i.e., appropriately, at various times, pop, op, camp, art nouveau and mainstream sentimentality. Max's ingratiating creations did meet with occasional resistance. In 1968 General Electric doubted for a time whether his psychedelic clocks—because they had no numbers—would sell. Max responded at the time, "I want people to get hung up on design not time. What does '3:15 and time to go' mean to a kid? He'd rather say it's half past a daisy and quarter to a nose."

In the early 1970s the Max craze disappeared almost as quickly as it had initially captured the public fancy. By then his witty and whimsical work seemed as dated as the summer of love. Max, however, has continued to produce paintings of a more personal, "serious" bent; while his later work has generated considerably less fanfare than was the case with his 1960s output, it has proven to be financially lucrative.

BIBLIOGRAPHY

"Commercial Graffiti," *Time*. 91 (June 7, 1968) 74-75.

Denvir, B. "London Arts Gallery; Exhibit," *Art International*. 16 (November 1970) 76.

"Exhibition at Zierler Gallery," *Art News*. 68 (May 1969) 69.

"Hot Mod Artist Gets in Commercial Groove," *Business Week*. (March 16, 1968) 78-82.

Kraner, M.R. "Peter Max, the Ubiquitous Designer and His Book Publishing Debut," *Publishers' Weekly*. 197 (April 27, 1970) 70-71.

"Man in Motion," *Newsweek*. 73 (April 14, 1969) 112-113.

Meisal, A.R. "Traveling Exhibition Called 'The World of Peter Max'," *Craft Horizons*. 30 (May 1970) 66.

"Peter Max: the Wizard of Ahs Paints a Vivid Self-Portrait," *Seventeen*. 29 (April 1970) 236.

"We Talk To: Interview by Mademoiselle Guest Editors," *Mademoiselle*. 67 (August 1968) 366.

Paul McCartney Is Dead

The death rumor surrounding then-Beatle Paul McCartney seems to have originated in the September 23, 1969 issue of *Northern Star*, the student newspaper at the University of Illinois. It quickly spread to WKNR-FM (Detroit), WMCA (New York) and other radio stations. Articles appeared in the *Michigan Daily*, Bill Gavin's influential trade newsletter, *Top Forty*, and countless local newspapers. A television special devoted to the topic was aired which featured lawyer F. Lee Bailey weighing the evidence.

The rumor was based upon a number of supposed clues, particularly those deciphered from Beatles songs and album covers. These included:

1. The *Abbey Road* cover, on which Paul appears barefoot (like a corpse) and out of step with the others. Paul, who is left-handed, holds his cigarette in his right hand. John is dressed as a minister, Ringo as an undertaker and George as a gravedigger. The VW shown in the picture has a license plate reading 28IF, the age Paul would've been if he'd lived.
2. The *Sgt. Pepper* cover reveals a hand held above Paul's head, allegedly a symbol of death.
3. Dr. Henry Truby of the University of Miami's language laboratory, who conducted "voiceprint" experiments of Beatles recordings (dated before and after November 1966—the date of Paul's "death"), concluded that while the other Beatles each had a distinctive voiceprint, Paul had three different voiceprints.

The core of the story, according to McCartney biographer Chet Flippo, went as follows:

Paul had been killed on November 9, 1966, after an argument with the others at the Abbey Road Studio. He left in his Aston-Martin in a fury and was involved in a car wreck in which he was decapitated. The ever-shrewd Brian Epstein could not let the Beatles die, so he found a double for Paul. After plastic surgery this Paul look-alike filled in admirably. He even sounded like Paul and was a better songwriter. That explains Paul's sudden domination of the group, beginning with Sgt. Pepper.

While there was no evidence that either the Beatles or the group's various business concerns encouraged the rumor, Capitol Records had its biggest month ever (up to that point) in terms of Beatles' sales. McCartney finally felt compelled to call a press conference in London where he allowed himself to be photographed and stated "Reports of my death are greatly exaggerated. If I were dead, I'd be the last to know . . . It's all a drag . . . We can't control what people read into our music."

BIBLIOGRAPHY

Bashe, Phil. "Dateline: Rock & Roll: November 1969; Paul is Dead," *Circus*. n273 (November 30, 1982) 31.

Brown, Peter, and Steven Gaines. *The Love You Make: An Insider's Story of the Beatles*. New York: McGraw-Hill, 1983.

Burks, J. "A Pile of Money on Paul's 'Death'," *Rolling Stone*. n46 (November 15, 1969) 6.

"'Dead' Beatlemania Mounts," *Melody Maker*. 44 (November 22, 1969) 1ff.

Flippo, Chet. *Yesterday: the Unauthorized Biography of Paul McCartney*. New York: Doubleday, 1988.

Hamilton, Alan. *Paul McCartney*. London: Hamish Hamilton, 1983.

"Kids' New Macabre Game: Is Paul McCartney Dead?," *Variety*. 256 (October 22, 1969) 1ff.

"McCartney 'Death' Gets 'Disk Coverage' Dearth," *Billboard*. 81 (November 8, 1969) 3.

Salewicz, Chris. *McCartney*. New York: St. Martin, 1986.

Tremlett, George. *The Paul McCartney Story*. London: Future, 1975.

Welch, Chris. *Paul McCartney: The Definitive Biography*. London: Proteus, 1984.

Rod McKuen

Rod McKuen's message was tailor-made for the 1960s: "don't fear to bare your emotions. *Be* sentimental. Be natural, not hip. Don't stay cool, stay warm." Termed the "King of Kitsch" by *Newsweek*, McKuen's popularity cut across mass media. His books stimulated the sale of his recordings, which in turn enhanced his draw in nightclubs and concerts, which further triggered book sales, and so forth. By the time his popularity peaked in 1968, McKuen had sung, performed and wrote his prose-poetry; he'd produced instrumental albums of his music for other companies; he'd created and arranged scores for TV specials and feature films; he'd composed English lyrics for tunes written by Jacques Brel and Gilbert Becaud; he'd dashed off an occasional lyric on demand; and wrote a children's book. In 1968, alone, McKuen earned $2 million from these varied projects. He attributed his success to the fact that he tried to "say something about people's inability to communicate with each other."

Born in 1933, McKuen's career began as a singer-songwriter in the San Francisco area and progressed to acting work in beachball-bikini films. From there McKuen tried rock singing in New York. He developed the sand-and-gravel baritone he is known for as a result of the strain from an eight-week, eighty-performance tour of the nation's bowling alleys promoting his first album, *Oliver Twist*. A trip to France and his exposure to the French-style chansonniers — Brel, Becaud, Charles Aznavour, George Brassens — opened his eyes to the dramatic possibilities of the most mundane material — the sea, the view from a window, a statue in the park — provided it was infused with feeling. He found himself in sympathy with French artists, "their ability to be man enough to say how they feel, something the American singer and performer [didn't] do."

When he returned to the U.S., his poems and songs gradually began to catch on. In one month during 1965, seventy-nine of his songs were recorded by artists such as Eddy Arnold, The Kingston

Trio, The Limelighters and Jimmie Rodgers. "Stanyan Street," which made a hit in Glenn Yarbrough's album of McKuen songs, *The Lonely Things*, in 1966, accidentally launched his publishing career. In order to protect the talk in the song, McKuen told the record company that it was culled from a book of his poetry called *Stanyan Street and Other Sorrows*. He then went home and wrote the book in his spare time. When letters asking where the book could be bought started arriving at the office of Stanyan Music (the basement of his home), McKuen decided to publish it himself; within a year it has sold some 60,000 copies. Random House gave him a contract for a book, *Listen to the Warm*. His popularity was now snowballing. His collection of poems, *Lonesome Cities* (Random House, 1968) had a staggering first printing of 190,000 copies. By the end of 1968 the three volumes had sold about one million copies.

His work in the music field was also very popular during this period. Three albums of his material by the San Sebastian Strings — *The Sea*, *The Earth*, *The Sky* — hit the upper reaches of the pop charts in 1967-1968 and his own *Live at Carnegie Hall* was equally successful in early 1964.

As both a songwriter and poet McKuen thought of himself as an "anti-poet." He answered the outdated modes of poetry with a verse that drawled in country cadences from one shapeless line to the next, carrying the rusticated innocence of a Carl Sandburg thickened by the treacle of a man who preferred to prettify the world before he described it. The disillusionment which imbued American society by the end of the 1960s (e.g., growing unrest over the Vietnam War, the repressive social agenda of the Nixon administration) appears to have been responsible for the defection of his audience. To the present day, McKuen persists in following the same road, confident that we're on the verge of another Romantic era.

FIGURE 2. Example of a Rod McKuen Poem

Bengie

I was wrong to invade your little world
of museums and kites and pigeons flying.
I have deceived you.
Not by meeting other peoples' eyes

or knowing arms that were not yours
but by pretending to be young at heart
and invading your stuffed-animal world

I should have stood aside when your kite
                          came
              sailing
          down
but I had to run and help

BIBLIOGRAPHY

Coxe, L. "Money in Art," *New Republic*. 162 (January 3, 1970) 32-33.
Edelstein, Andrew J. "The Pop Poet — Rod McKuen," in: *The Pop Sixties*. New York: World Almanac Publications, 1985, p. 207.
Fincher, Jack. "What? A Best-Selling Poet?," *Life*. (February 9, 1068) 35-37.
"King of Kitsch," *Newsweek*. (November 4, 1968) 111, 114.
"Loner," *Time*. 93 (May 16, 1969) 98.
Miller, E., ed. "Pop Personality," *Seventeen*. 28 (August 1969) 408ff.

Vaughn Meader

A former $45-a-week stand-up comedian, Vaughn Meader achieved overnight stardom in the fall of 1962 with the release of *The First Family* (Cadence), a record album which provided a humorous look at John F. Kennedy, his family and associates. The LP was a fixture on the national bestseller charts for forty-nine weeks, remaining at number one for three months; it ultimately sold more than five million copies. A sequel, *The First Family—Vol. 2* (Cadence) also reached the Top Five in early 1963. Americans were intrigued by the fact that Meader, then a twenty-six-year-old from New England, sounded very much like (and even vaguely resembled) the President.

Whatever potential existed for mining the Camelot lode evaporated a year after Meader's initial rise to fame with the assassination of JFK. He has stated, "Nobody wanted to hear from me. I was as dead as the president." Meader's career has been decidedly flat since that time. He became heavily involved in drug use in the late 1960s and subsequently went broke in the 1970s. He then got involved in the Jesus movement (a 1972 album about Christ, *The Second Coming*, bombed) and later worked as counselor in a Louisville drug-rehab clinic. He has also found work as a film and stage actor and country singer.

BIBLIOGRAPHY

Bunzel, Peter. "Kennedy Spoof Full of Vigah; The First Family," *Life*. 53 (December 14, 1962) 83-84ff.

Edelstein, Andrew J. "A Rogue's Gallery of '60s Celebs: Vaughn Meader," in: *The Pop Sixties*. New York: World Almanac Publications, 1985, pp. 228-229.

"Fate of the Myna Bird," *Time*. 83 (January 10, 1964) 78.

"First Family," *Time*. 80 (November 30, 1962) 20.

Medicine Shows

In operation from 1870 to 1930 throughout the United States medicine shows brought in a lot of money. Their proprietors got rich hawking fradulent pick-me-ups and cure-alls for every type of ailment. The standard routine was for as few as two performers and as many as forty to draw a crowd of people to watch their show. The entertainers might parade a boa constrictor before the crowd to grab attention, or set up a stage and present variety acts. But in the end it was all the same—a pretext to sell worthless elixirs to gullible people. Customers tried one after another of the "magic" elixirs hoping for a cure for whatever ailed them. Usually they got nothing more than an alcoholic high. To try each new product they had to follow the shows and depending on the pitchman's skill take or forgo the ballyhooed elixir. One pitchman might come to town and find that his competition had already "medicated" the citizens. Then his job was to discredit the counterfeit stuff and offer real medicine—his.

Besides the revolving product line with one elixir leading for a time before losing out to a better concoction, the pitches changed to suit the occasion. There were appeals to mortality: "How long can you expect to live without this medicine?"; to sexual potency, "Men, you don't want to become infirm, do you?"; and to mental acuity, "Why not wake up every morning with a clear head ready for work?" Whatever the pitch the liquid in the bottles was the same old stuff. Hadacol, created by Louisiana State senator Dudley J. LeBlanc in 1943, became so popular that it inspired a song. "The Hadacol Boogie" celebrated renewed sexual prowess. Ventriloquism, jokes, magic, banjo playing, singers, performing monkeys, and scaly reptiles primed the crowd for Hadacol or whatever was up for sale. Jars of animal tapeworms passed for human parasites and other cautionary medical displays worked equally well. Mental wizardry, acts of daring (such as setting oneself on fire), pseudo-anatomy lessons, anything to stop people in their tracks. But the surefire way to gather a crowd was with an Indian show.

The American Indian whom the white man had all but eliminated wasn't an object of pity in these shows. Great strength in both body and nerve was the pitch; the Indian grows robust, lives off the land, and reaches ripe old age without aches and pains. He does so by using natural medicine which has been his secret alone until now! Wearing an Indian headdress along with a regular vested suit, the pitchman looked deceitful. The big Indian shows strived for more authenticity and had white men in full costume beating drums and dancing Indian-style. The faddish entertainment over, greedy hands reached for bottles of Kickapoo, Sagwah, Awaga, Old Indian Liver and Kidney Tonic, and Ka-Ton-Ka. Then there was Dr. Ranell's complete line of products: Indian Herb Tablets, Pain-Expeller, Rattle Snake Oil, Indian Corn Remover, Worm Eradicator, and Tape-Worm Expeller.

BIBLIOGRAPHY

Freeman, Graydon L. *The Medicine Showman*. Watkins Glen, NY: Century House, 1957.
McNamara, Brooks. *Step Right Up*. Garden City, NY: Doubleday & Co., 1976.

Mickey Mouse

According to legend, Walt Disney created Mickey Mouse on a 1927 train ride back to Hollywood from New York City, where he had been forced to turn his *Oswald the Rabbit* series over to Charles Mintz. Retaining overall direction, Disney delegated the actual drawing to his talented assistant, Ub Iwerks. The success of *The Jazz Singer* and other early talkies at the time convinced Disney to utilize sound with his new character. Therefore, with the help of a pickup band, a crudely devised score of his invention and a couple of sound effects men, he recorded a synchronized soundtrack (supplying Mickey's voice himself, as he would for more than twenty years) to go with the animated short, "Steamboat Willie."

The completed cartoon premiered at the Colony Theater in New York on September 19, 1928; it was an overnight sensation. The following year saw the release of *Plane Crazy, Gallopin' Gaucho, Karnival Kid, The Jazz Fool!* (a spoof of *The Jazz Singer*) and *The Opry House*. With Mickey now an established star, the Disney fantasy factory began cranking out Mickey Mouse shorts at a dizzying pace; the studio placed him in a wide variety of roles (e.g., bandleader, train engineer, suitor, explorer, cowboy) and settings (e.g., Arabia, the Sahara, the South Pacific and, of course, Hollywood).

During the 1930s Mickey's persona took on mythical proportions. He was adapted to a comic strip in 1930, and to comic books shortly thereafter. His familiar likeness could be found on countless products — toys, watches, glasses, clothing, soap, etc. Soviet film director Sergei Eisenstein pronounced him "America's most original contribution to culture."

With the appearance of Donald Duck in 1934, however, Mickey Mouse was ousted from the top spot in the cartoonland popularity sweepstakes. By the late 1930s Mickey was largely confined to the role of master of ceremonies. Despite Disney's efforts at reviving this popularity — e.g., being cast as the Sorcerer's Apprentice in

Fantasia (1940), a starring role in *Fun and Fancy Free* (1947) — the Mouse's impact on the film medium continued on the wane. Ultimately, Mickey found his niche in other enterprises. He became an icon on the "Mickey Mouse Show" which became a fixture of children's television programming in the 1950s. The opening of Disneyland — as well as a new wave of merchandising ventures — further solidified his role as a cultural ambassador of the first magnitude bridging the gap between generations and nationalities.

BIBLIOGRAPHY

Bragdon, C. "Mickey Mouse and What He Means," *Scribner's Magazine*. 96 (July 1934) 40-43.

Burnet, D. "Rise of Donald Duck, Mickey Mouse's Enemy," *Pictorial Review*. 37 (October 1935) 19ff.

"But is it Art? Walt Disney Parlayed a Mouse and an Idea into a $7,000,000 Plant," *Business Weekly*. (February 10, 1945) 72ff.

Mann, A. "Mickey Mouse's Financial career," *Harper's Magazine*, 168 (May 1934) 714-721.

"Mickey Mouse," in: *The World Encyclopedia of Cartoons*, Volume 1, edited by Maurice Horn. New York: Gale/Chelsea House, 1980, pp. 399-389.

Nugent, Frank S. "That Million-Dollar Mouse," *New York Times Magazine*. (September 21, 1947) 22ff.

Wallace, Irving. "Mickey Mouse, and How He Grew," *Collier's*. 123 (April 9, 1949) 20-24.

Minstrel Shows

The minstrel show evolved during the generation of cultural ferment immediately following the War of 1812 when the masses demanded entertainment that they could understand and enjoy, such as inexpensive popular books and folksy weeklies, menageries, acrobatic troupers and equestrian shows. Built upon a close interaction between performers and the vocal audiences that they sought to please, minstrelsy combined the folkways of early American culture with a P.T. Barnum flair for promotion and added a compelling new ingredient — the black man. Robert Toll addressed the conditions behind the medium's rise in the following passage:

> By addressing themselves to race in the decades when white Americans first had to come to grips with what the position of blacks would be in America, while at the same time producing captivating, unique entertainment, blackfaced performers quickly established the minstrel show as a national institution . . . White men in blackface had portrayed Negro characters since well before the American Revolution. But until the War of 1812, Negro characters in popular songs were either comic buffoons or romanticized Noble Savages. Both types used dialects that owed more to Englishmen than to Afro-Americans. After the War of 1812, when the quest for a distinctly American culture dominated the arts, however, blackfaced characters became increasingly Afro-American . . . By the late 1820s, blackfaced white American performers like George Nichols, Bob Farrell, George Washington Dixon, J.W. Sweeney, John N. Smith, and Thomas D. Rice toured the nation, performed alleged Negro songs and dances in circuses and between the acts of plays.

The pivotal event in the evolution of minstrelsy took place in February 1843, when four blackfaced white men performed an entire evening of the "oddities, peculiarities, eccentricities and comicalities of That Able Genus of Humanity" on a New York stage. Billed as the Virginia Minstrels, their success inspired public demand as well as a bevy of imitators. While the phenomenon swept the nation in the mid-1840s, the Midwest and South — the birthplace of blackface entertainment — as well as the Far West had to make do with provincial minstrel troupes. The most famous companies (e.g., Wood's Minstrels, Ordway's Aeolians, Hooley's Minstrels, E.P. Christy's Minstrels, Sanford's Minstrels) — born and nurtured in the large cities of the Northeast — remained close to home due to the great success they enjoyed; it was not uncommon for them to have consecutive runs of one decade.

By 1860 minstrelsy, in response to the demands of its audience, transformed itself from unorganized individual acts to a structured entertainment form, consisting of three basic sections. In the first part, the entire company appeared in a semicircle and followed a standard pattern that included jokes and comic songs interspersed between "serious" songs and dances performed by individuals with the cast often singing the choruses. The second portion — the variety section, or alio — offered a wide range of entertainment (e.g., song-and-dance men, acrobats, men playing combs, porcupine quills or glasses) to the audience and allowed time to put up the closing act's set behind the curtain. Its most distinctive feature was the stump speech, a discourse meant to illustrate the kind of oration that a pompous black, better stocked with words than judgment, might give. The show concluded with a one-act skit, usually heavily pervaded by slapstick humor (e.g., cream pies, fireworks explosions).

Faced with strong competition from other staid entertainment forms (e.g., variety shows, musical comedies) during the post-Civil War era, minstrelsy assimilated their successful features such as exotic attractions (e.g., giants, stuntmen), scantily clad female performers and female impersonators. Once the exclusive domain of men, the medium now attempted to expand its audience by appealing to the entire family. The concern with providing "clean, bright, amusement" led to the last step in the evolution of the minstrel form. In the early 1880s, the highly influential company, Thatcher, Primrose and West's Minstrels, in an effort to further the image of refinement, deleted all vestiges of low comedy from their show. They focused on lavish song-and-dance productions delineating contemporary fads such as lawn tennis, baseball, bicycle riding and polo on skates. The desire of some of its audience for the older minstrel formulas inspired nostalgic revivals in the latter years of the century under billings like "histories of minstrelsy" and "Ethiopian Renaissances."

By the turn of the twentieth century, the popularity of the minstrel show had entered a decline, retreating back to its Southern and rural base. Tin Pan Alley, musical comedies and vaudeville became the major vehicles for minstrels—the only means by which they could reach a mass audience. The popularity of the minstrel show had coincided with public curiosity regarding plantation life and Southern blacks; when this waned, minstrelsy was doomed. The medium's prime legacy, according to Toll, consisted of providing

> . . . a nonthreatening way for vast numbers of white Americans to work out their ambivalence about race at a time when that issue was paramount. Consistent with their nationalism, egalitarianism, and commitment to the status of whites, minstrels ultimately evolved a rationalization of racial caste as a benevolent fulfillment of, not a contradiction to, the American Creed. If Negroes were to share in America's bounty of happiness, minstrels asserted, they needed whites to take care of them. To confirm this, minstrels created and repeatedly portrayed the contrasting caricatures of inept, ludicrous Northern blacks and contented, fulfilled Southern Negroes. Besides providing "living" proof that whites need not feel guilty about racial caste, the minstrel plantation also furnished romanticized images of a simpler, happier time when society was properly ordered and the loving bonds of home and family were completely secure. Minstrelsy, in short, was one of the few comforting and reassuring experiences that nineteenth-century white Americans shared.

BIBLIOGRAPHY

Davidson, Frank C. "The Rise, Development, Decline, and Influence of the American Minstrel Show," Ph.D. dissertation, New York University, 1952.

Green, Alan W.C. "'Jim Crow,' 'Zip Coon': The Northern Origins of Negro Minstrelsy," *Massachusetts Review.* (1970) 385-397.

Nathan, Hans. *Dan Emmett and the Rise of Early Negro Minstrelsy*. Norman, OK: 1962.
Paskman, Dailey, and Sigmund Spaeth. *Gentlemen Be Seated! A Parade of the Old Time Minstrels*. New York: 1928.
Rice, Edward LeRoy. *Monarchs of Minstrelsy*. New York: 1911.
Toll, Robert C. *Blacking Up; The Minstrel Show in Nineteenth-Century America*. New York: Oxford University Press, 1974.
Wittke, Carl. *Tambo and Bones*. Durham, NC: 1930.

ORIGINAL GEORGIA MINSTRELS ARE COMING.

Either composed of black performers or white actors in blackface, minstrel shows were extremely popular beginning in the early 19th century. They sang songs, told jokes, and did many antic things which made them court jesters of their day.

181

The Monkees

In an era when one mass medium can propel an artist to super-stardom, The Monkees benefitted from the high visibility afforded by several — television, radio, the concert hall, sound recordings and later, motion pictures. The desire of producers Bert Schneider and Bob Rafelson to combine the zaniness of The Beatles' *A Hard Day's Night* with the Marx Brothers in a TV sitcom provided the impetus for the formation of the group. After briefly considering The Lovin' Spoonful for the role, they placed an advertisement in the entertainment trade paper, *Daily Variety*. The headline read, "Madness!! Auditions," followed by a request for "Folk and Rock Musicians-Singers for Acting Roles in a New TV Series. Running parts for four insane boys, ages 17-21."

It is alleged that 437 applicants materialized, including Danny Hutton, later a member of Three Dog Night; songwriter Paul Williams; former star of "The Donna Reed Show," Paul Peterson; and Stephen Stills. The individuals chosen for the group had had differing degrees of involvement in show business up to that time. Mickey Dolenz had acted both as a regular ("Circus Boy") and guest performer ("Mr. Novak," "Peyton Place") in television. He learned to play the drums only after being assigned to the instrument by Schneider and Rafelson. Davy Jones had logged time in the Broadway production of *Oliver* as well as recording some (then unreleased) tracks for Colpix Records. Michael Nesmith drifted through the folk scenes in San Antonio and Los Angeles, recording briefly for Colpix under the name of Michael Blessing. Peter Tork had been a folk music accompanist in Greenwich Village prior to checking out the L.A. scene. The foursome proved to have a remarkable chemistry onscreen; first telecast on September 12, 1966, the free-form, youth-oriented series featured surrealistic film techniques (fast and slow motion, distorted focus, comic film inserts), one-liners, non sequiturs, etc., all delivered at a rapid-fire pace. The basic premise had the lads cast as a rock band that got into a multitude of bizarre scrapes as they rescued maidens, ran afoul of dastardly villains and generally perpetrated pranks on unsuspecting bystanders.

Although rock critics universally despised the quartet because they were "manufactured" and had not played any instruments on their first two albums, The Monkees enjoyed an equally successful recording career. Among their many hits, "Last Train to Clarksville," "I'm A Believer" and "Daydream Believer" all reached number one on the pop charts during 1966-1967. During this run the band enjoyed heavy promotion via the inclusion of a couple of songs per TV episode as well as access to material from Don Kirshner's roster of Brill Building songwriters, including Gerry Goffin-Carole King, Neil Diamond, Neil Sedaka, David Gates, Barry Mann-Cynthia Weil and Tommy Boyce-Bobby Hart. The group's recording career stalled in the face of progressive rock and the cancellation of the TV series by NBC effective August 19, 1968. The film scripted by Rafelson and Jack Nicholson, *Head*, was a critical success but a commercial failure, confusing The Monkees' younger fans. An NBC special broadcast on April 14, 1969, "'33 1/3 Revolutions Per Monkee," failed to reverse the band's decline and The Monkees ground to a halt in 1970.

"The Monkees" continued to live on in Saturday morning re-runs on CBS from September 1969 to September 1973. Dolenz and Jones briefly reformed the band in 1975 as Dolenz, Jones, Boyce and Hart. The 1980s have witnessed an explosion of interest in the group as part of a general nostalgia for the 1960s via cable TV re-runs on MTV, Nikelodeon and other channels. Amidst the healthy sales of videotapes of the old TV series and compact discs of old recordings, The Monkees have reformed again (sans Nesmith) as a recording and touring entity. Pegging this renaissance as largely a baby boomer phenomenon, television executives created The New Monkees for those too young to remember the real thing.

BIBLIOGRAPHY

Baker, Glenn A., with Tom Czarnota & Peter Hogan. *Monkeemania: The True Story of The Monkees*. New York: St. Martin, 1986.

Bronson, Fred. "Last Train to Clarksville (by) The Monkees"; "I'm a Believer (by) The Monkees"; "Daydream Believer (by) The Monkees," in: *The Bill-*

board Book of Number One Hits. New York: Billboard Publications, 1985, pp. 211, 216, 233.

Cohn, Nik. "The Monkees," in: *Rock; From the Beginning*. New York: Stein & Day, 1969, pp. 228-231.

DiMartino, Dave. "Harold Bronson, Co-Founder of Rhino Records, Discusses the Label's Success," *Billboard*. 99 (December 12, 1987) 17.

DiMauro, Phil. "Sixties are Reborn on New Disks, Second Coming of The Monkees," *Variety*. 324 (August 20, 1986) 77ff.

Edmondson, Brad. "Hey, Hey, We're Your Parents," *American Demographics*. 9 (October 1987) 18.

Lovece, Frank. "Old TV Shows Make a Comeback—On Tape," *Billboard*. 99 (February 28, 1987) 17ff.

Morris, Chris. "Monkeemania Reaps $$ for Rhino Tour, IV Reruns Spur Reissues Sales," *Billboard*. 99 (July 12, 1986) 46.

Puterbaugh, Parke. "Monkee Business Revisited," *Rolling Stone*. (September 25, 1986) 36ff.

Tamarkin, Jeff. "Tork Talk: Confessions of a Former Monkee," *Goldmine*. n72 (May 1982) 10-13.

Theroux, Gary, and Bob Gilbert. "Last Train to Clarksville; The Monkees," in: *The Top Ten*. New York: Simon & Schuster, 1982, p. 125.

Marilyn Monroe

More has been written about Marilyn Monroe than any other film star and probably more than any other woman who has ever lived. Her legendary status derives from her beauty, her talent, her sexuality, her private life, her mercurial troubled personality and the mystery surrounding her untimely death. Monroe's prime legacy was that of the quintessential dumb blonde; yet she longed to be taken seriously as an actress. However, the most notable aspects of her cinematic appeal—i.e., her physical attributes and a certain luminous quality (described by Lee Strasberg as "a combination of wistfulness, radiance, yearning that set her apart and made everyone wish to be part of it, to share in the childish naiveté which was at once so shy and yet so vibrant")—served to undermine public recognition of Monroe's studious efforts at developing her craft.

Following a disturbed childhood (e.g., orphaned by her father's desertion and mother's insanity, a marriage at sixteen which soon ended in divorce), Monroe's early film career featured a succession of bit parts and leading roles in "B" pictures which provided little hint of either the mass adulation or accomplished artistry still to come. Her first starring role came in *Niagara* (1953), which propelled her to the ranks of the top box office attractions. Solid parts—almost exclusively in a comic vein—then followed in rapid succession; e.g., *Gentlemen Prefer Blondes* (1953), *How to Marry a Millionaire* (1953), *The Seven Year Itch* (1955).

Still considered an actress of modest ability at this point in time, Monroe studied one year at Lee Strasberg's Actors Studio, learning to tap her own emotional experience so as to grasp the essence of a character. Monroe's next film, *Bus Stop* (1956), proved once and for all that she was a genuinely gifted actress. The success of *Some Like It Hot* (1959) and *The Misfits* (1961) reinforced this impression. Unfortunately, personal problems—as manifested by Monroe's chronic lateness on the job and addiction to alcohol and pills—led to her removal from a subsequent film, *Something's Got to Give* (1962) and, ultimately, it is believed, to her premature death at thirty-six from a drug overdose.

The Monroe mystique, however, has continued to attract a strong, almost cultlike, following, particularly among youth born after her death. A vast array of memorabilia such as posters, wigs and clothing continues to sell well in boutiques, record stores and nostalgia shops. All of the films in which she starred are available on video (hyped by 1988 promotional offers from CBS/Fox including a portrait poster, mini-theatrical posters, a mug and Gloria Steinem's bestselling book, *Marilyn*), and have been distributed through discount department store chains as well as the more traditional sources.

BIBLIOGRAPHY

Conway, Michael, and Mark Ricci, editors. *The Films of Marilyn Monroe*. New York: 1964.
Guiles, Fred. *Norma Jean: The Life of Marilyn Monroe*. New York: 1969.
Hoyt, Edwin. *Marilyn: The Tragic Years*. New York: 1965.
Kobac, John. *Marilyn Monroe: A Life on Film*. New York: 1974.
Mailer, Norman. *Marilyn*. New York: 1973.
"Monroe, Marilyn," in: *The International Dictionary of Films and Filmmakers: Volume III; Actors and Actresses*, edited by James Vinson. Chicago: St. James, 1986, pp. 446-447.
Murray, Eunice, with Rose Shade. *Marilyn: The Last Months*. New York: 1975.
Pepitone, Lena, and William Stadiem. *Marilyn Monroe Confidential: An Intimate Personal Account*. New York: 1979.
Sciacca, Tony. *Who Killed Marilyn?* New York: 1976.
Spada, James, and George Zeno. *Monroe: Her Life in Pictures*. New York: 1982.
Summers, Anthony. *Goddess: The Secret Lives of Marilyn Monroe*. New York: 1985.
Wagenknecht, Edward. *Marilyn Monroe: A Composite View*. Philadelphia: 1969.
Weatherby, W.J. *Conversations with Marilyn*. New York: 1976.

Monster Movies

Science fiction devotees consider the 1950s the "popular years." Some of the best space yarns and monster movies were made then — and some of the worst. On June 24, 1947 near Mt. Rainier, Washington private pilot Kenneth Arnold sighted a group of glistening, moving objects that sliced through the air almost without resistance. For the media Arnold could think of only one way to describe the mysterious objects; they resembled "saucers when skipped over water." Soon everyone talked about "flying saucers" scouting the United States for possible invasion. Hollywood took notice also and started production on a full slate of science fiction movies to mirror public interest. UFO sightings, swift advances in space technology and other branches of science prepared Americans to believe anything was possible. So primed for science-based fiction not far from fact, alert to a future of wonder, anxious for entertainment that explored the unknown, what Americans got were monster movies.

It seemed that radiation caused horrid cells to multiply like mosquitoes and create monsters. Photographs from Hiroshima and Nagasaki clearly exhibited the ravages of atomic warfare. Radiation distorted human form and was a new, invisible, and insidious evil that humankind had inflicted on itself. Most of the 1950s monster movies used radiation as the progenitor of its freaks. No telling what an overdose of angry nuclear particles could do. But now back to the beginning. Released in 1933, *King Kong*, was the first monster movie winner at the box office. It was a beauty and beast fable about a gargantuan ape who became infatuated with a beautiful, blonde woman and carried her off, only to fall to his death from the top of the Empire State Building after a plane attack, as most every movie buff knows. Reissued in 1938, 1942, 1952, and 1956 *King Kong* did equally well. However another ape movie, *Mighty Joe*

Young (1949), failed to match Kong's appeal. Still, credit *King Kong* with initiating the genre.

The 1950s introduced movie audiences to these fabulous monsters:

Cat-Women of the Moon
Killer Ape
The Creature from the Black Lagoon
Monster from the Ocean Floor
Gog
Them!
The Snow Creature
Revenge of the Creature
King Dinosaur
It Came from Beneath the Sea
Tarantula
Beast with a Million Eyes
It Conquered the World
Godzilla, King of the Monsters
Beast of Hollow Mountain
The Mole People
Man Beast
Attack of the Crab Monsters
Kronos
The Deadly Mantis
The Monster that Challenged the World
The Cyclops
From Hell It Came
Rodan
The Abominable Snowman of the Himalayas
The Black Scorpion
The Monolith Monsters

The standout in this bizarre menagerie is Godzilla who was incorrectly likened to King Kong. The 400-foot amphibious dinosaur with radioactive breath is no lover of women and destroys without provocation. In fact the pituitary lizard delights in toppling buildings whereas King Kong was merely homesick for Skull Island and lovesick for Ann Redman (Fay Wray). No matter the two clashed in a Japanese film, *King Kong vs. Godzilla* (1962), gnashing teeth for an international audience. Among the lesser monsters Gog was one of the first evil nonanthropomorphic robots who with his accomplice, Magog, murder their scientist-inventors. *Them!* were giant ants who ate constantly to survive. The *Beast with a Million Eyes* was an invisible space alien who used mind control to force other creatures to do its bidding. Probably the most wildly preposterous monster movie of the 1950s was *It Came From Hell*. Here is the plot: On the South Pacific island of Kalai, the hateful Korey testifies against her husband, Kimo (supposedly he had visited black plague on the island). On the strength of her testimony the tribal chief condemns Kimo to death. Stabbed in the heart with a skull-headed sacrificial knife, Kimo before he dies pleads innocence and swears revenge. Shortly thereafter from his grave a queer stump grows which the locals recognize as a vindictive spirit called a Tabanga. American scientists on Kalai treating the natives for radiation burns caused by atomic bomb testing, take the stump pierced by a knife to their lab. There they discover it lives! The stump has a heartbeat! So they inject it with something "powerful" to see what will happen next. The scientists led by Dr. Arnold don't have to wait long. The invigorated stump takes off on its stubby legs, finds Korey and the tribal chief, and kills them both. Bloodthirsty, the stump heads for the scientists who had befriended it. Nothing can stop the vicious stump until Dr. Arnold fires a bullet hitting the knife handle squarely driving it deeper. Off balance, the stump falls into a quicksand bog where it sinks forevermore. Remember the Tabanga curse was not at fault (what nonsense!), radiation was the villain.

BIBLIOGRAPHY

Johnson, William, ed. *Focus on the Science Fiction Film*. Englewood, NJ: Prentice-Hall, Inc., 1972.

Warren, Bill. *Keep Watching the Skies! American Science Fiction Movies of the Fifties*. 2 vols. Jefferson & London: McFarland, 1985.

Movie Palaces

Once there were in America the most fanciful architectural creations designed solely for housing the imagination. The fledgling movie industry in the 1910s and 1920s touched off the fad of making movie theaters resemble palaces that never were. Baroque and rococo exteriors only hinted at the profusion of opulence on the inside. Plaster of Paris formed Greek and Roman deities, mythological creatures, ancient temples, and walls full of festoons, friezes, and filigree. The idea was to give the public a total entertainment package — something to gape at before and after the movie, something to remain in memory forevermore.

In 1927 Samuel Lionel Rothafel built one of the grandest, the Roxy (his nickname) at Fifty-First Street and Seventh Avenue, New York City. He told a reporter that his "big baby" was "Roman, with a quick journey into Africa or Spanish Renaissance." And he was quick to add, "I'll make a bet that in my time or yours you are never going to see this theatre equaled." The Roxy cost $10,000,000 to construct. It seated 6,200 patrons. Besides a 110 man orchestra it had a great organ with three consoles and twenty-one chimes 110 feet high. Any shade of colored light could be beamed from the largest switchboard in the world. The Roxy also contained a music library of over 50,000 orchestral scores, expansive washroom facilities, a hospital, and a private health club. *The Love of Sunya* starring Gloria Swanson was the opening night attraction (March 11, 1927), attended by Swanson and the Marquis de la Falaise de la Condraye, Charlie Chaplin, Irving Berlin, and other luminaries.

While the Roxy may have been the grandest and best known of the movie palaces it was not the most imaginative. At the time other impresarios were at work realizing their dreams of Xanadu. On the West Coast in Los Angeles, Sid Grauman already had a head start. The son of a minstrel show owner, he opened his first movie palace,

193

The Million Dollar, in 1917. So named for its cost it appeared to be Spanish in motif but on closer inspection other decorative styles emerged even the latest fad—cubist decoration. Ancient warriors and pagan gods struck poses throughout the interior. Next Grauman conceived the Rialto, an Egyptian theater which upon entering transported the movie-goer to King Tut's tomb. Still intrigued with antiquity, his next venture, the Metropolitan, imitated an ancient temple complete with atmospheric frescos and an incongruous black chandelier. But Grauman's most popular confection was his Chinese Theatre, an authentic pagoda palace boasting a sixty-foot sculpture of silver dragons affixed to the ceiling. The Chinese Theatre opened in 1927 the same year as Rothafel's Roxy and included a unique feature that people thought then was faddish—the walk of stars. During construction of the theater Norma Talmadge accidentally stepped in wet concrete and Grauman who was at her side seized the moment. He asked her to sign the footprint and the usual prank of mischievous children became a Hollywood institution as other stars followed suit.

The heyday of building movie palaces (1927-1931) was for too brief a time, though the craze spread rapidly and most large cities could brag of having one in its midst. No doubt the palaces were expensive to build and maintain. When first opened lights illuminated their interiors so people could walk around and point at the wonders. As movies got better—sound, acting, technical advances, and the like—the palace itself receded into the background. Sadly, workers demolished the Roxy in 1960 but glad to say Grauman's Chinese Theatre still stands today. It is impossible to describe in words the grandeur or grandioseness of the old movie palaces. No contemporary account ever adequately captured the experience. The closest one can come to visualizing them is to look at photographs and then guess at the perspective in Ave Pildas' *Movie Palaces: Survivors of an Elegant Era*.

BIBLIOGRAPHY

Morrison, A. Craig, and Lucy Pope Wheeler, eds. *Nickelodeon to Movie Palace: Ten Twentieth Century Theatres 1910-1931*. Washington, D.C.: Historic American Buildings Survey, U.S. Department of the Interior, 1978.

Naylor, David. *Great American Movie Theaters*. Washington, D.C.: The Preservation Press, 1987.

Pildas, Ave, and Lucinda Smith. *Movie Palaces: Survivors of an Elegant Era.*
New York: Clarkson N. Potter, Inc., 1980.
Sharp, Dennis. *The Picture Palace and Other Buildings for the Movies.* New
York: Praeger, 1969.

Grauman's Chinese Theater the year it opened in 1929. Not the most lavish movie palace, but certainly one of the more exotic — it still stands today unlike most of its other kindred confections.

Movie Serials

A form of film entertainment divided into chapters that relied on "cliff-hangers" at the end of each episode to "keep'em comin' back," The Edison Company released the first movie serial, *What Happened to Mary?*, in 1912; Columbia Pictures produced the last one, *Blazing the Overland Trail*, in 1956. Few of the actors and actresses who played in the movie serials achieved stardom, although some did. During the silent film era such serial queens as Pearl White and Ruth Roland overshadowed their male counterparts. The reverse occurred when sound arrived, then the males got the lion's share of attention — Johnny Mack Brown, Buster Crabbe, Ray "Crash" Corrigan, and Buck Jones. There was no uniform number of episodes in the silent serials; *The Hazards of Helen* maintained its weekly pace through 119 episodes and wore out two leading ladies before it was done, but with sound, twelve episodes comprised a basic serial. Each coming installment sent shivers up your spine: "The Desert of Torture," "The Tressle of Horrors," "The Dragon's Den," "The Missing Finger," "The Noose of Death," and "Written in Blood." What movie-goer wouldn't want to return to learn the secret of "The Flaming Menace" or "Human Rats"?

Hollywood insured the longevity of movie serials by presenting harrowing action as fad dictated. At first heroines in danger were popular: *The Adventures of Kathlyn* (1913), *The Active Life of Dolly of the Dailies* (1914), *The Exploits of Elaine* (1914), and *The Perils of Pauline* (1914). Then enigma sparked interest: *The Million Dollar Mystery* (1914), *The Black Box* (1915), and *The Crimson Stain Mystery* (1916). After which, serials centered around a male hero emerged with: *Daredevil Jack* (1920), *Elmo, The Fearless* (1920), and *The Adventures of Tarzan* (1921). What was the rage once was tried again so that heroines in danger enjoyed a reprise as did enigmas and manly heroes. Like the protagonists in the episodes these story types just couldn't be killed off. Given sound the serials moved in other narrative directions. Westerns, jungle stories, science fiction, and comic book super heroes began to fill the screen. Tarzan was still around and in 1934 *The Perils of Pauline* was remade, but the serials were evolving from an entertainment for all ages to one predominantly for kids. The new plots concentrated on presenting the most exciting action ever seen on film — the dust never settled, the jungle never quieted, and outer space never lacked for bug-headed creatures. In a kid's mind the movie serials were the only reason for living from one Saturday to the next.

Television wrote the final episode for the movie serials. The new medium could broadcast continuous series with much greater ease. But it wasn't the same. Hollywood by leaving the hero or heroine dangling at the end of each episode about to be crushed between two moving walls of stone, or devoured by ravenous tigers, or dropped into a pit of vipers, originated thrill entertainment. None of which was lost on today's top Hollywood director, Steven Spielberg, who has appropriated the old movie serials for his feature films, notably the Indiana Jones series.

BIBLIOGRAPHY

Lahue, Kalton C. *Continued Next Week: A History of the Moving Picture Serials.* Norman: University of Oklahoma Press, 1964.

Stedman, Raymond W. *The Serials: Suspense and Drama by Installment.* Norman: University of Oklahoma Press, 1971.

Weiss, Ken, and Ed Goodgold. *To Be Continued* . . . New York: Crown Publishers, Inc., 1972.

Murder Ballads

Blood spilling and crimes of passion fascinate us. Throughout our history ballads, the most entertaining of verse forms, have been written to celebrate crimson deeds and with a macabre twist delight us at the same time. Folklorist Olive Wooley Burt explains the attraction:

> They (the ballads) relate murders committed from all sorts of motives. There are only two things common to them all — each song tells of an actual murder committed in this country, and each is, so far as I have been able to learn, the work of a humble minstrel. As such they are the voice of the people, speaking authoritatively upon one of the tragic but very real aspects of our civilization.

Lizzie Borden who took an axe and gave her mother forty whacks and Frankie who shot her man, Johnny, because he done her wrong are two of our most fabled murderers. But the reason they are etched in our minds is that some "humble minstrel" wrote verse about them and not someone else. There have always been plenty of murderers to choose from: even axe murderers and shooting an unfaithful lover happens everyday. In the case of Lizzie Borden, a religious spinster of 32 from Fall River, Massachusetts, she was tried and acquitted of brutally killing her stepmother and father in 1892. She had rotted in jail for one solid year before the favorable verdict set her free. On release she and her sister, Emma, inherited their parents' $500,000 estate and began to live graciously. In the meantime Bordenmania had swept the country. Versifiers had a field day with the supposed murderess.

Lizzie Borden took an axe
And gave her mother forty whacks;
When she saw what she had done
She gave her father forty-one.

Lizzie Borden took an axe
And gave her mother forty whacks.
Then she stood behind the door
And gave her father forty more.

Andrew Borden, he is dead;
Lizzie hit him on the head.
Lizzie killed her mother, too—
What a horrid thing for Liz to do!

There's no evidence of guilt,
          Lizzie Borden,
That should make your spirit wilt,
          Lizzie Borden.
Many do not think that you
Chopped your father's head in two,
It's so hard a thing to do,
          Lizzie Borden.

These versions and others cropped up across America, the first three assumed guilt, the last bemused innocence. Borden's defense attorney won the case by repeatedly pointing out that a frail little woman could not possibly have had the strength to wield an axe with so much force. So the last verse, in anticipation of the court's verdict, was the accurate one. The forty and forty-one whacks were grim poetic license; according to the trial records whoever murdered the Bordens inflicted only nineteen axe blows to the head of Mrs. Borden and only ten to Mr. Borden.

The familiar Frankie ballad is actually one of many and her lover was Albert before Johnny. Frankie had other names such as Josie, Sadie, Lillie, and Annie but were all the same femme fatale, or from the woman's perspective, femme juste. Laborers in the 1880s loved to sing the Frankie songs and could easily substitute male and female names to suit their company. Although the ballads varied in name, setting, and minor details, the story was still the same.

Frankie "saw her lovin' Johnny a-lovin' up Alice Bly" so "Three times she pulled the forty-four gun a rooty-toot-toot-toot-toot."

> Now it was not murder in the second degree
> and it was not murder in the third,
> The woman simply dropped her man,
> like a hunter drops a bird.
> He was her man but he done her wrong, so wrong.

Folklorists have searched in vain for the real Frankie and Johnny. A couple of claimants have been discovered, though most likely the Frankie ballads memorialize the eternal man-woman-adultery dilemma rather than one ardent couple.

Today Americans don't sing jingles about murderers like they did in yesteryear. A Lizzie Borden might catch headlines in the morning but by evening she would have to make way for other sensational murder cases. And a Frankie now is odds-on favorite to go free instead of hang as in some of the ballad versions. Perhaps the 20th century has witnessed too much international and domestic carnage to delight in singing about it.

BIBLIOGRAPHY

Burt, Olive Wooley. *American Murder Ballads and Their Stories*. New York: Oxford University Press, 1958.

Sandburg, Carl. *The American Songbag*. New York: Harcourt, Brace & World, Inc., 1927.

Nickelodeons

Literally "nickel," the cost of admittance plus the Greek word for theater, "odeon," they were the first moving-picture theaters in America. Nickelodeons presented a number of silent short screen programs (each one about twenty minutes long) accompanied by piano music. The owners obtained moving-pictures from such outlets as the American Mutoscope & Biograph Company whose 1902 catalogue ran 248 pages long with nearly 2,500 listings – all of which had been filmed in a short time to meet the demand. Extremely popular from the start showing moving-pictures in nickelodeons spawned one of the most amazing American success stories in this century. For the proper exhibition hall owners converted merchandise stores by removing their fronts. Then they erected a new front some distance back from the sidewalk to provide space for a lobby, a ticket booth, and an attractive new entrance. Inside these makeshift theaters were essentially unadorned. Material as mundane as linen served for a screen. Rows of folding or kitchen chairs, often fewer than a hundred, gave patrons a place to sit down. Soon standing room only became a common inconvenience. But outside adornment caught the eye. The recessed theater front sported bright paint, posters, and electric lights. Names like "Dreamland," "Majestic," and "Bijou" (a small, exquisitely crafted trinket), towered above the entrance. Naturally, some of the nickelodeons were fancier than others depending on owner taste and finances.

Many film historians credit John P. Harris and his brother-in-law, Harry Davis, with originating the nickelodeon. Harris coined the term to describe their Pittsburgh theater that opened on Thanksgiving Day, 1905. A critic who disputes this is Kenneth Macgowan. He traces the origin of the store-front theater to Major Woodville Latham and his sons. They started showing films in New York City in 1895; and the next year "Pop" Rock and a partner stood proudly outside their New Orleans Vitascope Hall also predating Harris and Davis. Q. David Bowers insists that Thomas L. Tally's Electric Theater in Los Angeles was the first commercial enterprise (1902). Whatever the case, John P. Harris added a new word to America's vocabulary.

Nickelodeons caught on like wildfire for close to a decade. Eight to ten thousand of them had opened by 1910. A film like *The Great Train Robbery* (1903) certainly helped to accelerate expansion. It thrilled audiences beyond anything they had seen yet and accomplished the feat in less than twelve minutes of film. A band of desperadoes rob a train and its passengers killing several on board. To avenge the deed a posse chases them across the prairie and eventually catches and kill them. Camera shots from the moving train and break-away scenes to show two sets of action pleased the public. It was all too wonderful. But the last scene really awed them—the only desperado left turns, aims his pistol dead at the audience, and fires a bullet. What ended the nickelodeons were better movies—thus costing more than a nickel to see—and a simultaneous move to more spacious theaters. The nickelodeon craze had tested whether the public would sit in a dark hall for a couple of hours and watch moving-pictures in the company of every type of person. The answer was a resounding, yes.

BIBLIOGRAPHY

Bowers, Q. David. *Nickelodeon Theatres*. Vestal, NY: Vestal Press, Ltd., 1986.
Hampton, Benjamin B. *A History of the Movies*. New York: Covici Friede, 1931.
Macgowan, Kenneth. *Behind the Screen: The History and Techniques of the Motion Picture*. New York: Delacorte Press Book, 1965.

Two nickelodeons. Just after the turn the century (c. 1905-1910) audiences came to love pictures that moved and would watch any entertainment from a man sneezing to a running horse. But when action and story were wed, the fascination intensified. Soon the primitive nickelodeons that were only curiosities and diverting gave way to a full-blow industry.

"The Night Before Christmas"

Clement C. Moore's "The Night Before Christmas" represents that rare fad which has gone on to attain institutional status. The poem came into being on Christmas Eve in 1822. Dr. Moore, then a Professor of Hebrew and Greek Literature in New York's Protestant Episcopal Seminary, wrote it after promising his six-year-old daughter Charity a very special Christmas gift.

The poem appears to have been greatly influenced by the literature and mood of that era. Moore had read the story of St. Nicholas which appeared in Washington Irving's *Knickerbocker History* (1809), and probably was familiar with a little booklet, *The Children's Friends* (New York, 1821), which is believed to have contained the first mention of Santa's reindeer and sleigh as we know them today. It is thought that his St. Nick was inspired by the caretaker of the Moore home, a jolly fat man who typified the prosperous Dutch burgers settling in New York in the seventeenth century. The names of the reindeer were also a Moore invention.

Although the entire family loved the poem, it probably would have remained unknown had it not been heard several months later by Harriet Butler, daughter of the nearby Episcopalian rector. Upon hearing a recitation by Charity, Butler shared the verses with her Sunday School class and sent it to the editor of the Troy (New York) *Sentinel*, which published it under the title, "A Visit from St. Nicholas," on Christmas Eve 1823, its author anonymous.

Within a few years the poem began to appear in periodicals everywhere; the first illustrated version was published by the *Sentinel* in the early 1830s. However, it was not until 1837, when it appeared with a collection of local poetry in book form, that Moore — who considered it beneath his dignity as a scholar and Professor of Divinity — reluctantly acknowledged authorship. Since then, it has been included in countless anthologies while many artists have provided their own interpretations of the verses. T.C. Boyd, a wood engraver, introduced the flavor of Dutch New York whereas cartoonist Thomas Nast and children's illustrator Arthur Rackham produced images which continue to be associated with the poem to the present day.

Over the years the poem has been the stimulus for a merchandizing bonanza; its words as well as visual interpretations have adorned a vast array of toys and other consumer items. In addition, Moore's verses have been adapted to many cinematic (and later, video) and recorded sound works. Each year at Christmas since 1954, in Newport, Rhode Island—where Moore lived during the latter stage of his life—a dramatic re-enactment of the poem has been given; its organizer, Jimmy Van Alen (who has written a sequel of seventeen couplets to the poem) has pushed to make Moore's old farmhouse a historic shrine and Christmas Museum.

It is perhaps ironic that Moore, a writer of many poems and light prose works as well as the compiler of the monumental *Hebrew and English Lexicon*, is remembered almost exclusively for this one brief poem. However, his legacy has done far more than render his name immortal; it has established the Santa Claus tradition as was then current in New York in addition to providing a version of the St. Nicholas story (sans the crude and barbaric elements characterizing medieval folklore) which would prove to be universally popular with children.

BIBLIOGRAPHY

Del Re, Gerard and Patricia. "Santa Claus and the Three Men Who Gave Him Birth"; " A Visit from St. Nicholas," in: *The Christmas Almanack*. Garden City, New York: Doubleday, 1979, pp. 138-140; 280-282.
Hervey, Thomas K. *The Book of Christmas*. Gordon: 1977.
Hottes, Alfred Carl. "The Visit of St. Nicholas," in: *1001 Christmas Facts and Fancies*. New York: A.T. De La Mare, 1954, pp. 40-41.
"Moore, Clement Clarke," in: *Dictionary of American Biography*, edited by Dumas Malone. Volume VIII. New York: Scribner's, 1934, pp. 118-119.
Moran, Hugh A. *The Story of Santa Claus*. Palo Alto, CA: Pacific, 1952.
Patterson, S.W. *The Poet of Christmas Eve*. 1956.

Ninja Movies

It took fifteen years for the Ninja craze to reach American shores from Japan, where the legend had originated during feudal times. In the mid-1960s the Japanese couldn't get enough of Ninja feats of glory. They read lurid Ninja novels, watched action-packed Ninja television and movies, and tolerated their children skulking around in Ninja costume. By the 1980s "the stealers-in" (Ninja in translation) had invaded America and catlike were ready to pounce on every spare entertainment dollar. What did the Ninja offer that American cowboys and cops couldn't? Simple, more mystery and a nifty assortment of killing devices.

The Ninja of Japanese legend practice Ninjutsu, or the art of invisibility. As persecuted Buddhists, they have to maintain secrecy or face certain death. So they dress in black from head to toe, leaving only an opening for the eyes. That way from out of the shadow they strike back at their enemies and avoid detection. Their favorite weapon is the shuriken which are razor-sharp metal disks they stack in their hands to throw in rapid succession. Unmatched at guerrilla warfare, a Ninja can swim great distances underwater while breathing through a bamboo tube; can leap from floor to ceiling as if on springs; and can survive for long periods of time by eating concentrated food pills. The craze grew to such proportions that a menacing Ninja appeared on boxes of Kellogg's Corn Flakes, and toy stores sold as much Ninja paraphernalia as they could stock.

That was in Japan. In America Hollywood dubbed them "chop socky" films which includes all the martial arts. *Variety* for March 25, 1981 chronicled the high point of American plans to capitalize on the Ninja craze. The trade magazine reported that "at least fourteen such entertainments" were in preparation. Zanuck-Brown Productions will start work soon on "The Ninja"; Sterling Siliphant is busy writing "The Masters"; CBS Theatrical Films has signed Scott Glenn and Toshiro Mifune for "The Equals"; American Cinema's "Force: Five" is about ready; the Cannon Group has officially begun "Enter the Ninja" starring Franco Nero and Susan George; "The Naked Fist" by New World Pictures will star a lady kung fu artist; and so on for the other titled ventures, "Kill and Kill Again," "An Eye for an Eye," "The Protector," "The Young Dragons," "Kill the Dragon," and "The Falcon Claw." American moviemakers already knew the potential of the martial arts film; in 1973 "Enter the Dragon," starring Bruce Lee, earned Fred Weintraub and Raymond Chow $100,000,000 worldwide. Of that amount $11,000,000 came from U.S. sales, indicating the market was really overseas. Like the Oriental Bruce Lee, the Caucasian Chuck Norris attained celebrity in "chop socky" films. But these two superstars were not Ninjas, just Ninja-like. They thrilled audiences with their superb hand-and-foot coordination, subduing a whole gang of thugs in one whirlwind action. Unlike the Ninja, they conquered with physical dexterity rather than with flesh-ripping shuriken. Hard to believe, but the Japanese have always preferred more violence than Americans which explains their wild enthusiasm for the sadistic Ninja. Also, in Japan the Ninja is a lusty lover who indulges in sex with the same raw nerves he exhibits in warfare. This added trait tantalized adults broadening the pool of admirers. So far in America the Ninja wears himself out leaping around and grunting to strengthen his resolve.

The American Ninja craze roller-coastered in the 1980s. Hollywood's big plans to cash in fell short; not all of the above movies were made. The ones that were released didn't quite excite audiences as expected. For a number of Halloweens kids dressed up in Ninja costumes, and on Saturday mornings watched foreign-made Ninja films. The same kids bought plastic shuriken and threw them at one another. Bruce Lee and Chuck Norris were still their favorites even though diehard Ninja fans knew that Lee and Norris were weaklings compared to the real thing. Then in 1988 "Teenage Mutant Ninja Turtles" captivated a new set of television viewers. The premise of this cartoon show is that four normal turtles fall down a sewer into some radioactive slime. Thickly coated with the ooze, they develop super-reptile strength. Splinter, who is a rat and a Japanese Ninja, assumes the duty of educating the four. First, Splinter names them for his favorite Renaissance artists: Raphael,

Michelangelo, Leonardo, and Donatello. Then he gets down to the serious business of teaching them Ninjutsu. Shredder, a bad Ninja master, is their principal enemy. So they must know more tricks than Shredder to survive. When not on a mission the turtles fill up on banana-sausage pizza. How long this cartoon show will parody and perpetuate the Ninja craze is anyone's guess.

BIBLIOGRAPHY

Maloney, Lane. "'Chop Socky' Still Very Alive as 14 Pend, Three at Major Plants." *Variety* (March 25, 1981): 22.
"Japan: A Good Cocktail." *Newsweek* (August 3, 1964): 31, 34.

On the Road

On the Road — written over a three week period in 1951 but not published until 1957 — established Jack Kerouac (1922-1969) as the standard-bearer and leading novelist of the "beat generation." Utilizing a spontaneous form of composition which captured the emotions and personalities of his years (1943-1950) spent roaming through the United States and Mexico, the book was viewed as a counterpoint to the self-conscious formalism of much of America's university-based writing. According to Kerouac, the word "beat," which originated with his friend Herbert Huncke, "meant being poor, like sleeping in the subways, like Huncke used to do, and yet having illuminated ideas about apocalypse and all that . . ."

While it made only a small dent in the best-seller lists, *On the Road* sold 20,000 copies in hardcover and 500,000 in softcover within two years after its first appearance. The work was followed in short order by additional novels — written during the lean years in the 1950s when Kerouac couldn't find a suitable publisher — including *The Dharma Bums* (1958), *The Subterraneans* (1958), *Doctor Sax* (1959) and *Maggie Cassidy* (1959). Due largely to Kerouac's novels, many young Americans adopted the beat message of revolt against the material values of adults, thereby transforming a cult into something of a national movement. In the 1960s, however, Kerouac would denounce the role he had played in the movement, arguing that the original vision had been distorted and corrupted by the suffocating embrace of his disciples.

BIBLIOGRAPHY

Aksyonov, Vassily. "Beatniks and Bolsheviks: Rebels Without (and with) a Cause," *New Republic*. 197 (November 30, 1987) 28ff.

Ciardi, John. "Book Burners & Sweet Sixteen," *Saturday Review*. 42 (June 27, 1959) 22ff.

Ciardi, John. "In Loving Memory of Myself," *Saturday Review*. 42 (July 25, 1959) 22-23.

Conroad, B. "Barefoot Boy with Dreams of Zen," *Saturday Review*. 42 (May 2, 1959) 23-24.

"End of the Road," *Time*. 94 (October 31, 1969) 10.

Gilbert, E. "He Went on the Road," *Life*. 52 (June 29, 1962) 22-25.

Ginsberg, Allen, and Gregory Corso. "Ten Angry Men," *Esquire*. 105 (June 1986) 260ff.

Hill, Richard. "Kerouac at the End of the Road," *The New York Times Book Review*. (May 29, 1988) 1.

"In the Ring," *Atlantic*. 221 (March 1968) 110-111.

"Kerouac, Jack," in: *Current Biography, 1959*, edited by Charles Moritz. New York: Wilson, 1959, pp. 226-227.

"Lions & Cubs," *Time*. 80 (September 14, 1962) 106.

McNally, Dennis. *Desolate Angel: Jack Kerouac, the Beat Generation, and America*. New York: Random, 1979.

Nicosia, Gerald. *Memory Babe: a Critical Biography of Jack Kerouac*. New York: Grove, 1983.

"Roaming Beatniks," *Holiday*. 26 (October 1959) 82-87.

"Sanity of Kerouac," *Time*. 91 (February 23, 1968) 96.

Tytell, John. *Naked Angels; the Lives and Literature of the Beat Generation*. New York: McGraw-Hill, 1976.

Wakefield, D. "J.K. Comes Home," *Atlantic*. 216 (July 1965) 69-72.

Will, George F. "'Daddy, Who Was Kerouac?' Respectability is the Cruel Fate of Yesterday's Radicals, Especially in the '80s," *Newsweek*. 112 (July 4, 1988) 64.

Optical Toys

All distant relatives of the movies, optical toys gained in kinship as they became more sophisticated. The Thaumatrope devised by Dr. John Ayrton Paris in 1825 was one of the first of these exciting new playthings. It was a paper disc with a different image on each side such as an empty gallows on front and a rope tied around the neck of a man on back. When spun the images made one lifelike picture of a hanging man jerking in the wind. Children begged their parents to bring them whole boxes full of thaumatropes. In 1833 the Phenakisticope, the brain child of Plateau of Ghent, anticipated the Strotoscope invented by Stampfer of Vienna. Both of these toys utilized rotating cogs and wheels to give the illusion of movement. English equivalents were called the Tantascope, Phantascope, Phantamascope, Magic Disc or Kaleidorama, and other names depending on the manufacturer. Through trade or imitation American children soon delighted in peering at these magic motion machines.

Another optical toy, the Zoetrope, gave evidence of bigger things to come. W.H. Horn of Bristol demonstrated the principle of the Daedalum or Wheel of Life in 1832. But it was a Frenchman in 1860 who patented the Zoetrope. Seven years later Milton Bradley marketed the first American version. The Zoetrope consisted of a revolving metal drum pierced by thin slots. Paper strips showing figures in various stages of movement were placed inside the drum. When spun on its axis like a globe and viewed through the slots the once still figures came to life. Bradley, not wanting his prize toy to be just another passing fad, leased the rights for its use to the Ray and Taylor Manufacturing Company of Springfield. The men's haberdashery firm then sold a collar box containing men's shirt collars and pictures for the Zoetrope. The round box containing them converted into the optical toy so that father and the whole family got something from the purchase. However, not everyone picked up the zoetrope just for a moment's pleasure. Edward Muybridge used it to analyze still photographs he had taken of a horse's movement—an experiment on the road to modern cinematography. Before that the popularity of optical toys had hastened the invention of the camera.

The Praxinoscope bettered the Zoetrope by having still scenery behind the revolving drum, so when looked at the figures moved against a backdrop. A mirror reflected both images bringing them together as if in a real theater. The Tachyscope also copied the Zoetrope but used photographs instead of hand-drawn pictures in its revolving drum. The Chromatrope worked by twisting colored discs in a viewer. Brightly colored images merged and dissolved like in a kaleidoscope. Later, Chromatopes employed the cog-wheel principle with slides to show brief scenic movement such as a butterfly fluttering around a garden. But of all these wonderful optical toys the Magic Lantern enjoyed the greatest success.

Its exact origin and inventor are matters of dispute. There is evidence that as early as the 18th century Magic Lanterns aided teaching in aristocratic families. By mid-19th century the device was prevalent not only in Europe but also in America, having been manufactured for a mass market. What distinguishes the magic lantern from other optical toys is that it could "project" entertainment for an audience. Its body was in the shape of either a box or cylinder with a chimney on top and a cylinder nose to direct the picture onto a screen. Early models were tin inside to reflect light from a candle. A concave mirror between the body and the nose threw the images on a glass slide placed upside down in front of the mirror. Flickering candlelight enlivened the projected images. Improvements came rapidly: addition of a paraffin lamp allowed the light source to remain at one level for uniform projection (candles got shorter as they burned), wheels on the base of the Lantern provided backward and forward movement to adjust the size of the picture, superimposed slides of characters could be triggered to give the illusion of action, and a set of different lens permitted sharper projections or full-scale ones. To make the Magic Lantern show even more wonderous the projectionist stood behind the screen and thus was invisible. Not quite the ultimate optical toy, the Panoptical Panorama did things the Magic Lantern couldn't. By altering the angle of the plate being viewed the picture changed dramatically. The Panoptical apparatus could turn a scene of a daytime railroad station into a train puffing through the night. This gave the appearance that the train was speeding along to stay on schedule.

Three other simpler optical toys from the 19th century deserve mention. They were less expensive and therefore more accessible to the public. The Anamorphosis came with a set of distorted pictures and a reflective metal cylinder. The viewer placed the cylinder on a circle marked on the picture card and the distortion disappeared to reveal a famous personality or fictional character. Next, stencil silhouettes gained popularity because all one needed to view them with was a light source. Like cave dwellers gathered before a fire making animal heads flash on rock, the same type of amusement seemed novel again. Holding a precisely cut paper silhouette in front of a candle to enlarge it on the living room wall brought smiles all around. The last optical toy and one that people loved to show off was the pocket cinematograph. It consisted of a small album of successive still photographs, each one showing an action advanced slightly from the one before it. When flipped through, the people in the album became animated; they boxed, fenced, chased each other, whatever.

BIBLIOGRAPHY

Fraser, Antonia. *A History of Toys*. New York: Delacorte Press, 1966.
Remise, Jac, and Jean Fondin. *The Golden Age of Toys*. Greenwich,CT: New York Graphic Society, 1967.

The Original Dixieland Jazz Band

The Original Dixieland Jass (Jazz) Band, whose five members—Nick LaRocca, cornet; Eddie Edwards, trombone; Henry Ragas, piano; Larry Shields, clarinet; Tony Spargo, drums—all hailed from New Orleans, created a sensation by playing jazz at New York City's Reisenweber's Restaurant beginning in January 1917. Later in the year, the group made the first ever jazz phonograph recordings; "Livery Stable Blues" (1917), "Tiger Rag" (1918) and "Sensation Rag" (1918), among others, were runaway bestsellers. Their sound particularly appealed to young dancers, who welcomed the opportunity to break free from the rigidly formal dance steps of the World War I era.

Due to the unfamiliarity of Northerners with the newly emerging genre, the ODJB achieved a degree of eminence considered by experts to be out of proportion to their musical skills; no member was particularly notable as an improviser, and the band's phrasing was rhythmically stilted. As black jazz bands began to record more and more regularly the shortcomings of the ODJB became obvious and their popularity waned accordingly.

When the vogue for jazz dancing temporarily subsided in the mid-1920s, the ODJB disbanded. The group reunited in 1936; however, the stint was brief in duration and only moderately successful.

BIBLIOGRAPHY

Brunn, H.O. *The Story of the Original Dixieland Jazz Band*. Baton Rouge, LA: Louisiana State University Press, 1960. Reprinted by Da Capo Press in 1977.
"Original Dixieland Jazz [Jass] Band," in: *The New Grove Dictionary of American Music*, edited by H. Wiley Hitchcock and Stanley Sadie. Volume Three, L-Q. London: Macmillan, 1986. pp. 450-451.
Second Line. VI:9-10 (1955). Entire issue devoted to the ODJB.

Pantomime

From the Greek, "pantomimos," for "one who does everything by imitation," this form of entertainment seesawed in popularity. *The Adventures of Harlequin and Scaramouch* is considered to be the first documented pantomime in America. It was performed as an afterpiece to a play in Charleston, S.C. on February 4, 1735. Thereafter at least a dozen more pantomimes were presented in Colonial America between 1750 and the Revolution. Imported from England these early pantomimes were purely English products, not having been altered to suit American taste. But upon winning independence from England the demand for indigenous entertainment motivated American composers to write music and librettos for pantomimes. Some of their compositions survive while others since lost are mentioned in advertisements of the day to give proof that the art form made headway for a couple of decades. By 1810 American pantomime was on its last leg; farcical comedy and other theatrical arts supplanted it. Pantomime reappeared sporadically during the 19th century, and when performed by a master of the art attracted large, if ephemeral, audiences. Now gone as a distinct type of theater, its last vestiges were seen in vaudeville and today survives in circus clown acts.

During pantomime's rosy era in America a production most often included harlequinade characters, music, choreographed dancing, and elaborate stage design. The star of the show dressed like the famous English Harlequin, James Byrne. He wore a form-fitting costume covered with different colored patches, the material of which was silk to catch light as he danced. A red patch denoted fire or temper; blue, water or love; yellow, air or jealousy; and brown, earth or constancy. Harlequin's mask was all important—when worn it meant he was invisible and could caper around without being seen. Much of the fun of pantomime derived from Harlequin's foolish antics while invisible. Other symbols of his prowess were two bumps on his mask signifying knowledge and thought, a hare's foot in his cap for luck, and devices on his shoes indicating flight and speed. To be sure Harlequin had many adventures and carried with him either a slapstick (a harmless paddle made of two pieces of wood that slapped together to produce a loud whack when the paddle struck someone) or a magic sword which rendered him safe from defeat as long as he held on to it. Harlequin mimicked everything and danced sprightly. He was Pan and satyr, lover and fool. The role called for an athletic actor and comic, skilled in dancing, with boundless energy. John Durang (1768-1822) was the most famous American Harlequin. He excelled in the demanding part and can be credited with establishing the art form during his career.

Pantomimes not based on the Harlequinade featured children's tales such as *Mother Goose, Cinderella, Dick Whittington,* and *Humpty Dumpty.* Also centered around vivacious dancing and gorgeous costumes, these dumb shows were more appropriate for family viewing. Like other evolving theater in America pantomime consisted of music, dialogue, and sung text in a pastiche taken from many sources. Nearly always patriotic diversions were added to invigorate the audience. When Durang danced as Harlequin, everyone raved about his adroitness; but when pantomime degenerated into a cacophony of slapstick whacks it bored the crowd.

BIBLIOGRAPHY

Beaumont, Cyril W. *The History of Harlequin.* New York: Benjamin Blom, Inc., 1967.

Broadbent, R.J. *A History of Pantomine.* New York: Benjamin Blom, Inc., 1964.

Rankin, Hugh F. *The Theater in Colonial America.* Chapel Hill: University of North Carolina Press, 1960.

Wilson, A.E. *King Panto: The Story of Pantomine.* New York: E.P. Dutton, 1935.

Maxfield Parrish

"Daybreak," Parrish's most popular work, sold in the millions. Originally oil on panel, art publishers Reinthal and Newman who reproduced it couldn't keep up with the public demand. Copies of "Daybreak" sold to college students, to people who gave one as a wedding gift, to hotels for decorating their lobbies, to housewives for placing over the mantle, and so on. In 1923 after only a few months on the market, "Daybreak" earned Parrish $25,000; in 1925 he banked $75,000. Here is what it looked like: a naked child leans forward, her hands on her knees. At her feet is another child lounging on a stone portico. To counterpoint the first child's nudity, she is dressed in a tunic. Both girls smile at one another. Two thick stone columns divide the picture and frame the two children. Just behind the columns still in the foreground are hanging branches in bloom. Rugged mountains, a limpid lake, and a diffuse sky fill the background. What was so special about "Daybreak" was Parrish's use of what became known as Parrish blue and the lighting of the picture. Following the time-honored technique of glazing the artist obtained a transparent pure blue effect. So pure was Parrish blue that the painting radiated turquoise. To gently warm the chill turquoise, Parrish added touches of golden yellow to represent the fingers of dawn.

Unlike other artists unsure of their public appeal, Maxfield Parrish (1870-1966) lived to a ripe old age and knew exactly where he stood. His father had been a successful painter in Philadelphia, and had shaped his son by introducing him to art schools and art galleries both here and in Europe. At the Pennsylvania Academy of Fine Arts and the Drexel Institute Parrish studied with only the best teachers. By 1895 he had already illustrated a cover for *Harper's Weekly* which led to numerous commissions for book illustrations. In addition, during his prolific career he painted murals and a series of landscapes, executed many other magazine covers, and did ad-

vertising artwork that practically sold the products alone. Before the
"Daybreak" rage, Parrish reproductions had done extremely well.
In 1904 *The Ladies' Home Journal* offered its readers a color reproduction of "Air Castles" for ten cents. The picture showed a male
youth, naked from the waist up, blowing bubbles. He sits on the
edge of a stone wall overlooking azure blue water under an azure
blue sky. The bubbles, as large as the youth's head, hang in the air
in front of a faintly visible castle in the distance. Other Parrish art
caused a sensation especially the "Dinkey-Bird" painted for
Eugene Field's *Poems of Childhood*. This time a naked male youth
propels himself higher in a swing. Exhilarated, he tosses his head
back and thrusts his legs straight out to gain more height. In the
background there is a castle surrounded by clouds. As usual in Parrish's most fashionable work transparent pure blue predominates in a
scene of sheer beauty, populated by happy, supple youth.

As popular as these three paintings were in reproduction, it was
his advertising art that really skyrocketed his fame. For Crane's
Chocolates (1917) he painted perhaps the loveliest Cleopatra yet
seen, reclining in her barge rowed by brawny slaves. For Jell-O
(1921) he grouped together a King, a Queen, and a servant—all
three bent forward looking in delight at a bowlful of gelatin. An
unfurled banner inscribed with the word Jell-O connects their mag-
nificent throne chairs. The picture having said it all, the advertisement underneath read simply, "The King and Queen Might Eat
Thereof and Noblemen Besides." Parrish also helped sell Hires'
Root Beer, Swift's Premium Ham, General Electric Mazda Lamps,
and Fisk Tires. He enchanted people with his advertising art and
they responded by displaying it in their homes. The empty boxes of
Crane's Chocolates—also decorated with scenes from the *Rubaiyat
of Omar Khayyam* and *The Garden of Allah* (a bestselling 1904
novel)—became jewelry or nick-nack boxes; and the magazine advertisements were clipped and framed. So plentiful were his images
then that today Parrish art can be found in almost any junk or low-
end antique store.

Few of Parrish's admiring public knew how he achieved the intense colors they loved. He didn't invent the technique of glazing
which had been a favorite method of Leonardo da Vinci's, but he
certainly capitalized on it. Parrish started with the whitest board he

could obtain, then applied only pure, unmixed colors in thin layers to enliven his composition. Each layer of color had to dry thoroughly before a thin coat of varnish was brushed over it as a sealant. Built-up, the varnished layers of color reflected light like a gemstone, or in Parrish's case, like a sapphire or aquamarine or lapis lazuli. The painstaking method of glazing required weeks to complete, but in the end produced a breathtaking painting.

BIBLIOGRAPHY

Brinton, Christian. "A Matter of Make-Believe." *Century Magazine LXXXIV*, no.4 (July 1912): 340-352.
Jullian, Philippe. *Dreamers of Decadence*. New York: Praeger Publishers, 1971.
Ludwig, Coy. *Maxfield Parrish*. New York: Watson-Guptill Publications, 1973.
Wisehart, M.K. "Maxfield Parrish Tells Why the First Forty Years Are the Hardest." *American Magazine CIV*, no.5 (May 1930): 28-31.

This Maxfield Parrish (1870-1966) masterpiece was actually done to fulfill a commission for Crane's Chocolates. Cleopatra reclining in her barge graced a box of sweets — all too lovely to throw away when the contents were eaten. So many Americans reused the box for storing jewelry, love letters, and the like. Other Parrish creations likewise captivated the public and found a permanent place in their homes.

Pasticcio

From the Italian for "hodgepodge," the pasticcio was a theatrical work popular for a brief time in the late eighteenth century that borrowed all or most all of its music and songs from various composers. Prior to pasticcio in America, the English ballad opera was in vogue. It consisted of spoken dialogue interspersed with songs set to familiar tunes of the day. Its intent was to be humorous or satirical or both while poking fun at Italian opera. John Gay's *The Beggar's Opera* (1728), which had a long run in England and America, exemplifies the genre. During the American Revolution (1775-1783) theatrical entertainments were forbidden — at least on the American side; the British, however, staged their own entertainments to lessen the tedium of fighting upstarts. Partly to sever ties with England and partly to provide native theater after the Revolution, American pasticcio was born. Most of the early examples of this "hodgepodge" art have been lost; yet from contemporary notices it can be determined that pasticcio flourished. Having won independence, Americans wanted to celebrate their freedom though in some cities they had to wait a few years before the theater ban was lifted (such as in Boston — not until 1792).

One of the first pasticcio operas of interest to have survived was *The Blockheads; or, The Fortunate Contractor* (1782), author unknown, with music borrowed from many eminent composers. It satirized *The Blockade of Boston*, an entertainment written by the British General "Gentleman Johnny" Burgoyne, and was performed while he occupied that city. American patriots despised Burgoyne for his conceit which in all probablity doubled their enjoyment of *The Blockheads* — if they ever saw it. As stated the opera survives but there is no record of it having been performed. Perhaps *The Blockheads* circulated among subscribers to published works, as was common at the time, and read from the page. The reverse happened to Royall Tyler's *May Day in Town; or, New York in an*

Uproar (1787). It is on record as having been performed but the two-act libretto no longer exists. Tracing pasticcio becomes easier when reviewing the career of William Dunlap, considered the "Father of the American Stage." As a young man, Dunlap studied painting in London with the master, Benjamin West, before returning to America to devote himself to the theater. Like other industrious creative spirits after the Revolution he put his mind to the task of writing plays because the opportunity was there. Native theatrical entertainments were in short supply while the demand for them was great. For his pasticcio, *Darby's Return* (1789), Dunlap wrote the text entirely in verse but appropriated songs from folk sources. He continued to create pasticcios in this manner for a number of years; and since he also managed two New York theaters he had to adapt hurriedly and borrow whatever he could from wherever he could. When Dunlap did write his own work he signed the piece proudly, "By an American and a Citizen of New York."

What made the pasticcio unique was the inclusion at odd times of patriotic songs and popular melodies, i.e., "Yankee Doodle Dandy" and Irish ballads. These musical diversions either were slightly related to or had little to do with the action of the drama or the opera, but just sounded good and got the audience humming. A true pasticcio then amounted to what today would be called a greatest hits compilation. The beginning of the 19th century marked the demise of American experimentation with ballad opera and pasticcio, both faddish inventions on the road to legitimate opera. After that, opera in which a single composer wrote the majority of the music became the standard, and bel canto or beautiful singing was all the rage. Satirizing Italian opera was definitely out, and purloining popular songs instead of writing new ones was done less often.

BIBLIOGRAPHY

Bordman, Gerald. *American Musical Theatre: A Chronicle*. New York: Oxford University Press, 1978.

Dunlap, William. *History of the American Theatre and Anecdotes of the Principal Actors*. New York: Burt Franklin, 1963.

Mates, Julian. *The American Musical Stage Before 1800*. New Brunswick: Rutgers University Press, 1962.

Sonneck, O.G. *Early Opera in America*. New York: Benjamin Blom, Inc., 1963.

Peanuts

It somehow seems apt that the comic strip, *Peanuts*, became wildly successful in the 1960s; Charlie Brown's favorite saying, "How can we lose if we're so sincere?," succinctly summed up the dashed hopes and aspirations of the counterculture during that era. The strip first appeared in 1947 in the weekly, *St. Paul Pioneer Press*, under the title, "Lil Folks." Initially, it gave little indication that it was destined for huge success. When its creator, Charles Schulz, began syndicating the strip in 1950, only seven newspapers became subscribers. During the 1950s, *Peanuts* grew steadily in popularity with the assistance of a series of paperbacks which reprinted Schulz's best work. In 1960, the Peanuts gang made further inroads into the national consciousness by appearing in ads for the subcompact Ford Falcon.

By 1962 the *Peanuts* boom had begun in earnest. A San Francisco businesswoman, Connie Boucher of Determined Productions, initiated a substantial merchandising campaign, commencing with *Happiness Is a Warm Puppy*, a collection of witticisms accompanied by Schulz illustrations, which remained on the *New York Times* bestseller list for forty-five weeks in 1962-1963. Follow-up titles included *Security Is a Thumb and Blanket, A Friend Is Someone Who Likes You, Peanuts Projects Book* and *The Peanuts Calendar-Date Book*. Her non-book products included stuffed pillows, pocket dolls, sweatshirts, Snoopy wristwatches and sleepwear. Additional firms soon went after a piece of the action. Hallmark developed a line of greeting cards and stationery and Wilson Sporting Goods put out a Charlie Brown baseball. By 1969, *Business Week* pegged the *Peanuts* merchandising phenomenon to be generating approximately $50 million annually.

By the end of the decade the strip remained a national obsession. Newspaper circulation had grown from 650 in 1961 to 1000 in 1969. The characters turned up regularly on a series of TV specials:

"A Charlie Brown Christmas" (1965); "Charlie Brown's All Stars" (1966); "It's the Great Pumpkin, Charlie Brown" (1966); "You're in Love, Charlie Brown" (1967); "He's Your Dog, Charlie Brown" (1968); and "It Was a Short Summer, Charlie Brown" (1969). The strip was also represented on film (*A Boy Named Charlie Brown*, 1967) and stage (the musical, *You're a Good Man, Charlie Brown*, opened in New York in 1967 and ran for four years). A rock group, The Royal Guardsmen, had three hit singles based on the Snoopy-Red Baron confrontation ("Snoopy vs. the Red Baron," "The Return of the Red Baron" and "Snoopy's Christmas"). NASA adopted Snoopy as a promotional device; various personnel wore Snoopy pins and emblems and the astronauts of Apollo X in 1969 used the code names "Snoopy" and "Charlie Brown" to designate the command ship and lunar modules.

The appeal of the strip appears to have cut across all demographic boundaries. While Schulz claimed that *Peanuts* was "just about all the dumb things I did when I was little," it was scrutinized by psychologists, argued about by professors and quoted by theologians. Robert Short, in his book, *The Gospel According to Peanuts* (1965), stated that the strip "makes parables about the basic Christian belief in blind faith and love." Schulz himself noted that it "deals in intelligent things — things that people have been afraid of. Charlie Brown represents the insecurity in all of us, our desire to be liked."

Peanuts continues to thrive to the present day, albeit with less visibility via merchandising tie-ins. As of 1985, more than 2,000 newspapers worldwide carried the strip. The TV specials continue to be rerun and have been released in the various video formats.

BIBLIOGRAPHY

Conrad, B. "You're a Good Man, Charlie Schulz," *New York Times Magazine*. (April 16, 1967) 32-35ff. Reprinted in abridged form in the July 1967 issue of *Readers' Digest* (Volume 91; pages 168-172).

Edelstein, Andrew J. "Charles Schulz's 'Peanuts,'" in: *The Pop Sixties*. New York: World Almanac Publications, 1985, pp. 193-197.

"Good Grief; Curly Hair; Peanuts," *Newsweek*. 57 (March 6, 1961) 68ff.

"Good Grief: Peanuts," *Time*. 85 (April 9, 1965) 80-84.

Jennings, C.R. "Good Grief, Charlie Schulz!," *Saturday Evening Post*. 237 (April 25, 1964) 26-27.

Schulz, Charles M. "New Peanuts Happiness Book; Excerpt," *McCalls*. 95 (October 1967) 90-91.

Short, R. "Peanuts & the Bible," *Americas*. 16 (April 1964) 16-20.

Tebbel, J., and Charles M. Schulz. "Not-So Peanut World of Charles M. Schulz," *Saturday Evening Post*. 52 (April 12, 1969) 72-74ff.

Weales, G. "Good Grief, More Peanuts!," *Reporter*. 20 (April 30, 1959) 45-46.

"Woes of a Peanut Manager; Charlie Brown," *Sports Illustrated*. 24 (June 20, 1966) 46-50.

"You're an Adman's Dream, Charlie Brown," *Business Week*. (December 20, 1969) 44-46.

Pete Smith Specialties

These movie shorts covered a wide range of topics from the serious to the zany. Not only did they introduce the public to novel filmmaking but they also chronicled the fads of the day (1931-1955). Their creator, Pete Smith, started out as a press agent for Metro-Goldwyn-Mayer Studios, became head of the publicity department, and then entered the advertising branch. To help out temporarily he took on the additional job of writing and narrating factual short subjects. Invigorated by the challenge he soon ceased all other activity to work on them alone. In 1935 MGM gave Smith carte blanche to produce ten to eighteen shorts per year. He could choose the subject matter, the players, the length, as long as he kept within his yearly budget. Shorts were the hors d'oeuvres before the main feature to whet the appetite. For the next twenty years Smith served up a bountiful selection.

Among his close to three hundred movie shorts some were pedestrian and some outstanding (Smith won two Academy Awards). Three of his best were *Audioscopiks* (1935), *New Audioscopiks* (1938), and *Third-Dimensional Murder* (1941). The trio featured three-dimensional photography. In *Audioscopiks* a man seemingly pitches a baseball into the audience, a trombone player pokes everyone in the eye with his slide, and seltzer squirts all the way to the back row. More of the same in the sequel; but *Murder* presented a cloak-and-dagger tale filmed in green sequences that literally gripped the audience as the murderer reached out toward them. When 3-D really came into vogue in the 1950s MGM released a composite of the three called *Metroscopiks* and earned a bundle. Other Smith shorts offered instruction and might have bored viewers who cared little or nothing about the subject. Except that Smith narrated them in a mock-serious style and usually avoided any stuffiness. One such short was *Vital Victuals* (1934), a droll cooking lesson for the ladies; another one was *Let's Dance* (1936), a lighthearted demonstration of tap and ballroom steps. Sports and the unusual comprised a second category. *Donkey Baseball* (1935) chronicled a 1930s fad, that of playing baseball while riding a donkey. *Dare-Deviltry* (1936) filmed aerialists, flagpole sitters, and high divers in action. Just about anything of interest Smith concocted a short around: beauty contests, audience-participation quizzes, nature stories, and many others. *Water Bugs* (1941) documented water sports fads; *Fala* (1943) and *Fala at Hyde Park* (1946) presented a day in the life of President Roosevelt's Scottie dog from the viewpoint of the dog.

Also under contract at MGM Dave O'Brien collaborated with Smith on their unforgettable pests series. *Movie Pests* (1944) depicted self-centered members of a movie audience: a lady wearing an immense hat, a guy noisily shelling peanuts, a lazy slob sticking a leg out in the aisle for others to trip over, and the like. But what caused the respectful audience to howl with laughter was the revenge scene at the end. Then the poor victims of the movie pests got even. The person sitting behind the lady wearing the hat cut it in shreds, people close to the guy eating peanuts threw the shells at him, and instead of tripping over the slob's foot the entering patron stomped it. *Bus Pests* (1945), *Guest Pests* (1945), and *Neighbor Pests* (1948) likewise fractured funny bones. For a while they were the talk of movie-goers everywhere. Faddish appeal was evident in all of these movie shorts as people proclaimed their wit and ingenuity. Pete Smith possessed a rare personality that found humor and delight in everything. He was especially adept at exhibiting faddish and idiosyncratic human behavior on film. If all of his movie shorts were readily available now for viewing they would furnish us with a history of popular culture that few books reveal.

BIBLIOGRAPHY

Maltin, Leonard. *The Great Movie Shorts*. New York: Crown Publishers, Inc., 1972.

Mary Pickford

At the peak of her career, Mary Pickford was the most popular of all film stars, and probably the best-known woman in the world. Following the notable career as a child actress on the stage, she made her film debut as an extra in *Her First Biscuits* in 1909. During her stint with D.W. Griffith's Biograph (1909-1912) she essentially re-defined film acting. As she later noted, "I refused to exaggerate in my performance . . . Nobody ever directed me, not even Mr. Griffith."

While contracted to Adolphe Zukor's Famous Players between 1913-1918, she became Hollywood's top female star, headlining such films as *Tess of the Storm Country* (1914), *The Poor Little Rich Girl* (1917) and *Rebecca of Sunnybrook Farm* (1917). Known as "Little Mary" and "America's Sweetheart," the public adored her long golden curls and her embodiment of the eternal child/woman: loveable, spirited, whimsical and pure. In actuality, however, Pickford was also a shrewd businesswoman. By 1916 she had negotiated a contract guaranteeing her $10,000 per week and was choosing her own scripts, cameraman and director. Along with Charlie Chaplin, D.W. Griffith and her second husband, Douglas Fairbanks, she founded United Artists in 1919 in order to control the production and distribution of their films.

Pickford remained a top draw throughout the 1920s. She was an accomplished and versatile actress, as revealed in her work in *Stella Maris* (1918), *The Hoodlum* (1919), *Sparrows* (1926) and *The Turning of the Shrew* (1929). Her earliest sound film, *Coquette* (1929), won her an Oscar for best actress. The public wanted "little Mary," however, and Pickford relished wealth and fame too much to veer far from her carefully constructed image. As a result, she was forced to retire from filmmaking in the early 1930s when the appeal of her stereotyped roles waned.

BIBLIOGRAPHY

Carey, Gary. *Doug and Mary: A Biography of Douglas Fairbanks and Mary Pickford*. New York: 1977.

Cushman, Robert. *Tribute to Mary Pickford*. Washington, D.C.: 1970.

Lee, Raymond. *The Films of Mary Pickford*. South Brunswick, NJ: 1970.

Niver, Kemp. *Mary Pickford: Comedienne*. Los Angeles: 1970.

"Pickford, Mary," in: *The International Dictionary of Films and Filmmakers: Volume III; Actors and Actresses*, edited by James Vinson. Chicago: St. James, 1986, pp. 500-501.

Windelen, Robert. *Sweetheart: The Story of Mary Pickford*. London: 1973.

Play-Party

Imagine America's frontier days and isolation far from the amusements of city life. Then picture young people of marriageable age in those far-flung rural communities trying to entertain themselves. One way they did was to have play-parties in which they engaged in singing and dancing games enlivened by music and dramatic action. A band (or solo performer) played accompaniment to songs that told a story and could be acted out. Too old for children's games and too young for "intimate" dancing, the unmarried youth had to settle for something in between. Church restrictions limited forms of dancing that involved repeated physical contact. In public a young man couldn't wrap his arm around the waist of his sweetheart until after they were married. But as young people are wont to do, touching one another was on their minds and the play-party — where some touching couldn't be avoided — was their only recourse outside of open defiance.

The waist-swing was the real problem and kept parents ever watchful. Some frontier girls, due to their strict upbringing, believed it a sin to dance at all, but not to go to a play-party. Next to the waist-swing fiddle-playing was just as bad. The lively music caused a girl to dance faster and perhaps lose her inhibitions. Hot and excited she might fall in the arms of her partner and later on end up doing something foolish. Occasionally a song like "Buffalo Girls" energized the evening:

> Buffalo boys are coming out to-night,
> Coming out to-night, coming out to-night,
> Buffalo boys are coming out to-night,
> To dance by the light of the moon.
>
> Dance all night till broad daylight,
> Till broad daylight, till broad daylight,

Dance all night till broad daylight
Go home with the girls in the morning.

In the parlance of the times this was known as a "devil's ditty" whereas "song-ballets" formed the basis of the entertainment. Examples are "The Bear Went Over the Mountain," "Frog In the Middle," "The Muffin Man," "The Old Gray Goose Is Dead," and "Pop Goes the Weasel." These innocent song-ballets suggest an extended childhood rather than an initiation into adulthood. The play-party gained momentum and wherever frontier youths toiled on the land to help their parents, they thought about the next social get-together with delight. Singing lines like these bolstered their spirits:

Cream and peaches twice a week,
Kiss her on the other cheek.

Apples fried and apples dried,
Kiss her on the other side.

Irish potatoes tops and all
Kiss her now or not at all.

Consequences flowing free,
Come, my love, and go with me.

I am too young, I cannot go,
Because I love my mother so.

Old enough and plenty of good,
You could leave her if you would.

Compared to today's sexually-explicit rock music these lyrics seem very innocent indeed—even if the intent is somewhat the same. Recalling America's frontier days and a roomful of apple-cheeked youths wanting to know one another better without much touching is sweet. Yet perhaps the "devil's ditty" held sway over the "song-ballet" and old times were no different than now.

BIBLIOGRAPHY

Botkin, Benjamin A. *The American Play-Party Song*. New York: Frederick Ungar Publishing Co., 1937.

Pop Art

Pop art generally involved the depiction of the common, everyday aspects of modern life in a realistic manner. This realism was indebted to the commercial art of the era in subject as well as method of working. The media most involved with the style — painting, prints and sculpture — dealt with commonplace objects that had become so ubiquitous in our culture that they were usually looked at without being noticed. Among the other frequently employed characteristics of the style were bright colors, repeated images, large scale and simplicity of theme.

Philosophically, the pop artists rejected the elitist nature of fine art that, especially during the late 1940s and throughout the 1950s, seemed withdrawn from the real world. The forms of expressionism — at that time the dominant movement in elitist circles — sprang entirely from the soul of the artist, and the highly personal, introspective results represented an escape from reality. Pop artists sought ways to bring the real world and all its complexities closer to fine art, to make living and art synonymous, with as little of their own selves being injected into the work as possible.

Although pop art is generally considered to be an American phenomenon, it actually had its genesis in England in the mid-1950s. The term has been attributed to English critic Lawrence Alloway who, along with a number of young painters, sculptors, architects and critics, formed the Independent Group late in 1952. Meeting in London at the Institute of Contemporary Art, discussions focused on popular culture — e.g., western movies, science fiction, billboards, machines — and its implications; in short, those aspects of the contemporary scene considered to be anti-aesthetic. These meetings provided the impetus for seminal works which established much of the vocabulary and attitude of subsequent pop art. Richard Hamilton's collage, *Just What Is It That Makes Today's Homes So Different, So Appealing?* (1956) is representative of this period. It shows a modern apartment decorated with a haughty female nude and her mate, a muscle man in a Charles Atlas pose. The setting includes mass culture products; e.g., a television, a tape recorder, an enlarged comic book cover, a Ford emblem and an advertisement for a vacuum cleaner. Through the window can be seen a movie marquee announcing *The Jazz Singer* featuring Al Jolson.

In that many of the images used by the British pop artists during the later 1950s derived from American artifacts, it was perhaps inevitable that the style would realize its fullest expression in the United States during the 1960s. Because English artists viewed the products of American industrial and commercial development from afar, they frequently instilled their work with romantic, sentimental overtones. The American pop artists, however, once they realized the tremendous possibilities of their everyday environment, tended to imbue their efforts with a bolder, more aggressive treatment of the subject matter. Their work found a receptive audience among both intellectuals and lay persons tired of the traditional rules and values associated with serious art.

Robert Rauschenberg and Jasper Johns were early pioneers in the American pop art movement during the late 1950s. In the 1960s, they were joined by Roy Lichtenstein, Tom Wesselmann, James Rosenquist and Claes Oldenburg. However, the artist who more than any other has come to represent pop art in the public mind, through his paintings, objects, underground movies and personal life, is Andy Warhol. Like many of his peers, he was initially a commercial artist. He first attracted attention by means of his depiction of standard brands and supermarket products — e.g., Coca-Cola bottles, Campbell's soup cans, Brillo cartons — filtered through the repetition motif (a literal representation of store shelves). Warhol then turned to the examination of the contemporary folk hero (e.g., Marilyn Monroe, Elvis Presley, Elizabeth Taylor). By the end of the decade he was concentrating on films. For experimental work, they were substantial financial successes. Much of the work by mainstream popular artists and musicians, most notably Peter Max and John Lennon/Yoko Ono, was directly influenced by his output.

When the socio-political climate of the U.S. turned decidedly to the right in the late 1960s, Warhol and other pop artists continued to explore their artistic capabilities, albeit to a considerably smaller audience. Consequently, some excellent works in the style have been created in the 1970s and 1980s.

BIBLIOGRAPHY

Alloway, Lawrence. *American Pop Art*. New York: Collier, 1974.

Arnason, H.H. "British Pop Art and Offshoots"; "U.S. Pop Art and Offshoots," in: *History of Modern Art*. 2nd ed. Englewood Cliffs, NJ: Abrams, 1977, pp. 613-645.

Lippard, Lucy. *Pop Art*. New York: Praeger, 1966.

Patrick, Darryl. "Pop Art," in: *Popular Culture and Libraries*, by Frank W. Hoffmann. Hamden, CT: Library Professional Publications, 1984, pp. 191-205.

Pierre, Jose. *Pop Art: An Illustrated Dictionary*. London: Methuen, 1977.

Elvis Presley

The Elvis Presley story began on a Saturday afternoon in late summer 1953. Presley stopped by Sam Phillips' Memphis Recording Service (also the office of Sun Records) to make an acetate of two songs to give to his mother as a present. Remembering Phillips' statement, "If I could find a white boy who could sing like a Negro, I could make a million dollars," Marion Keisker made a tape recording of the session for her boss.

Although Phillips was not initially impressed with Presley's voice, he eventually invited the eighteen-year-old in for a recording session on July 5, 1954. The resulting single, "That's All Right, Mama"/"Blue Moon of Kentucky" (the former a rhythm and blues hit penned by Arthur Crudup, and the latter a country and western standard) was a regional hit. While none of Presley's five Sun releases made the pop music charts, the final two ("Baby Let's Play House"/"I'm Left, You're Right, She's Gone" and "Mystery Train"/"I Forgot to Remember to Forget") reached number ten and number one, respectively, on *Billboard's* country and western charts.

Presley's growing success led to the purchase of his contract (along with all Sun Records material) by RCA for the then unprecedented amount of $40,000. Supported by RCA's marketing muscle and the promotional genius of his recently acquired manager, Colonel Tom Parker, the Presley phenomenon swelled to the dimensions of a national mania in short order. His first recording session for RCA took place in Nashville on January 10-11, 1956. One of the songs recorded at that time, "Heartbreak Hotel," shot to the top of the pop charts with the assistance of television appearances on Tommy and Jimmy Dorsey's "Stage Show" and the "Milton Berle Show." The recording, which remained number one for eight weeks and was rated the top single of 1956 by *Billboard*, was followed by a string of number one hits, including "I Want You, I

Need You, I Love You," "Hound Dog"/"Don't Be Cruel," "Love Me Tender," "Too Much," "All Shook Up," "Teddy Bear" and "Jailhouse Rock." Presley's first film, *Love Me Tender*, opened on November 16, 1956; 20th Century-Fox released 550 prints to theaters, more than any other film ever issued up to that point. Presley's dominance of the show business world during 1956 was such that he set standards for rock artists equalled only by The Beatles a decade later. For example, he followed himself into the number one position, occupied the top two positions simultaneously and had both the A- and B-sides of a single occupy the top slot individually.

Presleymania continued at full throttle well into 1958. In the spring of that year "Wear My Ring Around Your Neck" became the first RCA single by Presley to fall short of the top rung of the charts. Parker's decision to stop the flow of product while Presley was fulfilling his military obligations (1958-1960) substantially diminished the intensity of his early wave of popularity. However, his career revived immediately upon the release of his comeback single, "Stuck on You," in March 1960. While the aesthetic quality of his post-army work was uneven at best, his star quality has continued to burn brightly over a decade after his death.

During the 1980s, RCA has continued to release new compilations of old material at regular intervals—a practice begun long before Presley's death. The appearance of new media format such as home video and the compact disc have fueled fan interest. His fan club network may well be the most active of any performer in the twentieth century. And while an abundance of commercially exploitative articles and books have appeared since his death which portray his personal life in less than flattering terms, Presley appears to have achieved the status of a true American institution, impervious to the bad publicity which might pull down mere mortals from grace.

BIBLIOGRAPHY

"Baptist Minister's Sermon vs. Elvis: He'll Hit the Skids," *Variety*. 204 (October 17, 1956) 1ff.

Bronson, Fred. "Heartbreak Hotel (by) Elvis Presley"; "Love Me Tender (by) Elvis Presley," in: *The Billboard Book of Number One Hits*. New York: Billboard Publications, 1985, pp. 10, 15.

Brown, L. "Can Fifty Million Americans Be Wrong?," *Down Beat*. 24 (September 19, 1956) 41.

Carr, Roy, and Mick Farren. *Elvis Presley: The Complete Illustrated Record*. New York: Harmony, 1980.

Cotton, Lee. *Elvis: His Life Story*. Ann Arbor, MI: Pierian, 1980.

English, M. "Presley Invades H'wood with Impact of a Brando," *Down Beat*. 23 (May 30, 1956) 39.

Friedman, J. "Presley Juggernaut Rolls," *Billboard*. 68 (September 29, 1956) 31ff.

Goldman, Albert. *Elvis*. New York: McGraw-Hill, 1981.

Harbinson, W.A. *The Life and Death of Elvis Presley*. London: Michael Joseph, 1978.

Harms, Valerie. *Trying' to Get to You: The Story of Elvis Presley*. New York: Atheneum, 1979.

Hopkins, Jerry. *Elvis: A Biography*. New York: Simon and Schuster, 1971.

Hopkins, Jerry. *Elvis: The Final Years*. New York: St. Martins's, 1980. Excerpted in October 2, 1980 issue of *Rolling Stone* (n327; pp. 10-16).

Kohlmeier, L.M. "Heartbreak, Hound Dogs Put Sales Zip Into Presley Products," *Wall Street Journal*. 148 (December 31, 1956) 1.

Lichter, Paul. *The Boy Who Dared to Rock: The Definitive Elvis*. Garden City, NY: Dolphin, 1978.

Marsh, Dave. *Elvis*. New York: Rolling Stone Press/Times Books, 1982.

Torgoff, Martin, ed. *The Complete Elvis*. New York: Delilah, 1982.

Psychedelic Posters

The rise of psychedelic posters in San Francisco during the late 1960s was, in many respects, an anachronistic development. As noted by Keith Murgatroyd in *Modern Graphics*, some governments and commercial concerns found the poster to be "an ideal instrument of information and propaganda to be directed towards populations which, for the duration of the war at least, were pedestrian. But even before World War II the poster as a means of communication, persuasion and expression had been declining in effectiveness in the United States." The medium was well suited to the Haight-Ashbury scene, however, where a self-contained community continually wandered the neighborhood on foot, in search of the next concert, the next happening, etc.

Levon Mosgofian, whose lithograph firm, Tea Lautrec, printed most of the posters created by San Francisco artists, has attributed their impact to the fact that the concerts they advertised were considered an art form, and it was felt that everything associated with these events should reflect that quality; that's why they became so popular. Artist Alton Kelley has noted that the posters worked because the radio wasn't established yet as a promotional vehicle; they were the only form of communication available.

Between 1966-1971 approximately 550 posters were designed by poster artists to advertise events at the Avalon and Fillmore Ballrooms, the major musical venues in the city at that time. In addition, many other amateur or "one-shot" posters were produced, most of them imitative of the styles of the major artists. These major artists included the aforementioned Kelley, Stanley Miller (a.k.a. Mouse), Victor Moscoso, Wes Wilson, David Singer, Lee Conklin, Randy Tuten, Rick Griffin, Greg Irons, Bonnie Maclean and Bob Fried. The work they produced was dazzling (particularly in its use of dense, bright color), ingenious, surreal and frequently difficult to read. Stimulated by the psychedelic vision conjured up by the rock music of that era, the artists produced work which often defied interpretation. Bill Graham, owner of the Avalon and the Fillmore, recounts having to incessantly remind the artists that the raison d'être for these posters was to tout a commercial venture.

Poster activity declined significantly when Graham closed both of the Fillmores — East (New York) and West — in 1971 and stopped commissioning them. Those mass media possessing a higher profile in American society — e.g., newspapers and radio — became the prime vehicle for announcing concerts. However, special commemorative posters continued to be done for many events; the best examples are fully as striking as anything from the Golden Age; e.g., the "Tumbling Dice" poster heralding The Rolling Stones' 1973 San Francisco appearance, The Who/GratefulDead poster promoting their joint billing at Oakland Stadium in 1976. In recent years the work of the masters has most frequently turned up on record album jackets. A notable example is the Kelley-Mouse winged horse appearing on the cover of Steve Miller's *Book of Dreams* (1976). The image, already in existence as an original painting, was deemed so powerful that it was employed on a wide array of Miller merchandise. The San Francisco band, Journey, has also utilized Kelley and Mouse to develop a style of unified signature graphics (based on the infinity symbol) that, in its instant identifiability, became a highly successful marketing device for the band.

BIBLIOGRAPHY

Borgzinne, J. "Great Poster Wave," *Life*. 63 (September 1, 1967) 36-43.
"Coolest Things; Personality Posters and Psychedelic Posters," *Newsweek*. 69 (March 6, 1967) 8.
McDonough, Jack. "Posters and Visuals," in: *San Francisco Rock: The Illustrated History of San Francisco Rock Music*. San Francisco: Chronicle, 1985, pp. 54-69.
"Nouveau Frisco," *Time*. 89 (April 7, 1967) 66-67ff.

Punch and Judy

This puppet show of European origin first appeared on stage in America at the Park Theatre, New York, September 1828. Immediately popular it continued to be performed both in public arenas and in private for the remainder of the century. In the traditional story Punch batters his own baby to make it stop crying. Then to get peace and quiet he tosses the still screaming child out the window. When Judy returns from shopping and finds out what has happened she attacks Punch with a stick. He grabs the stick and whacks her over the head until he kills her. Variations on the same theme followed with more characters for Punch to bash. *The New York Daily Tribune*, December 25-30, 1843, acknowledged the "charm" of *Punch and Judy* summarizing the plot thusly:

> The mirth and fun which this play produces for the children of all ages is immense. Punch is a real fighter; he beats the Negro, kicks the Doctor out of doors, knocks down the Constable, whips his own dear Judy, hangs the Hangman, and is finally carried off by Old Nick.

Punch looked the part of an unrepentant bully; he had a beak nose and he squawked and strutted. An argumentative fellow, he didn't waste words. Bashing seemed much more effective in every situation. Nature had also failed to bless Judy; her equally beaked nose and abrupt mannerisms labeled her a shrew. As far as charm goes it was more in the comical fury of the couple's actions than in the sordid tale. Formally entitled *The Tragical Comedy or Comical Tragedy of Punch and Judy*, the performance was intended to be a medieval morality play. Old Nick, the Devil, settled accounts with Punch for braining people by dragging him to Hell. But in the early performances the puppeteer deviated from the plot to cash in on laughs. In such instances Punch continued his rampage and even bashed the devil into submission. This ending met with great applause. Punch gone berserk was the main source of hilarity, and whether he had to pay the consequences or not mattered little to children watching his antics. The supple sparring of the puppets on an intimate stage (over the height of an adult so the puppeteer could stand behind a curtain) made the show. When human actors were tried *Punch and Judy* fell flat; flesh and blood characters lacked the frenzy of the puppets which was so stimulating.

But back to the morality issue. J.P. Collier edited the traditional text of the play (1828) that became the one most used in America; George Cruikshank was the illustrator. In his history of Punch and Judy, Collier included this ballad stanza:

> The Devil with his pitch-fork fought,
> While Punch had but a stick, sir,
> But killed the Devil, as he ought,
> Huzza! there's no old Nick, sir.

That sanctioned Punch's bashing the embodiment of evil, or in one version, death. The arcades and dime museums of large cities were free to present such godless fare. But as the play gained a following and begged performance in decent circles a proper ending was called for. Killing the devil after a murder spree was not to be condoned even though besting him at any other time was highly thought of. Audiences hadn't stopped laughing long enough to realize that Punch was the son of the devil and belonged in Hell. Bashing community people was evil enough, but braining one's wife and child despicable. To satisfy Victorian sensibilities the Devil as a set character had to go. The Devil was not to be depicted on stage nor was he to come out on the short end of a fight with a remorseless murderer. The answer was to substitute for Old Nick a crocodile who ate Punch's stick, and then Punch. Another dramatic device was to have Judy return as a ghost to scold Punch for killing her. After one or both of these additions the play could be performed at fraternal picnics, in church, and in the nursery. The original ending with Punch bashing everyone in sight—that had filled early 19th century Americans with glee and started the rage—was discounted as a hateful fad. Children were not to watch glorified evil ever again.

Punch and Judy songs also delighted Americans in the decade after its first stage performance (1828-1838). "Mister Punchinello" cheered Punch's exploits though sympathized with Judy. Another comic song, "The Lost Child," told of a frantic mother who found her sweet little dear watching Punch. With song there must be dance and musicians composed waltzes, galops, and schottisches on the Punch and Judy theme. These diversions played out quickly, though. Finally, before the ending was changed, moralistic primers pointed out Punch's evil influence. In the tale of wicked Oscar Bruce from *The Variety Book For Children*, Oscar learned his wickedness from spending hours enthralled by Punch and Judy. It's a good thing the crocodile came along.

BIBLIOGRAPHY

Leach, Robert. *The Punch & Judy Show: History, Tradition and Meaning*. Athens: University of Georgia Press, 1985.

McPharlin, Paul. *The Puppet Theatre in America: A History*. New York: Harper & Brothers, 1949.

Punk Rock

Punk rock has made a substantial impact upon the public consciousness at two separate times in rock history. First came the aggressively amateurish response of mid-1960s, middle-American garage bands to the retro-rhythm and blues style of the leading proponents of the British Invasion (e.g., The Animals, The Rolling Stones, The Yardbirds). This manifestation left little imprint other than a cache of marvelous hit (or near-hit) singles, including The Standells' "Dirty Water," Shadows of Knight's "Gloria," Count Five's "Psychotic Reaction," ? (Question Mark) and The Mysterians' "96 Tears" and The Seeds' "Pushin' Too Hard."

One decade later a new strain of punk rock arose as a reaction to what a certain cross-section of youth perceived as a corpulent tradition-bound, and essentially irrelevant, rock establishment. The new variant was substantially rawer and cruder than its predecessor, featuring speeded-up rhythms, buzz-saw guitar work and hoarse screaming for vocals. Trailblazing groups (most notably The New York Dolls and The Ramones) first appeared in the New York City area, developing an underground following at clubs like CBGB.

These artists provided the inspiration for a wave of English bands — e.g., The Sex Pistols, The Clash, The Jam, The Buzzcocks, The Damned, The Dead Boys — who infused the genre with a strong socio-political bent; i.e., an expression of postindustrial angst, nihilism and revulsion for the inhumanity of the status quo.

The scene in Great Britain heightened interest in the States for punk music. However, the majority of American fans — enjoying a considerably higher standard of living than their British brethren — shunned the genre's social-political trappings in favor of its musical energy and fashion statements. The musicians typically performed with severely cropped hair (later worn in spikey or mohawk fashion and dyed in rainbow hues), black leather and sadomasochistic bondage gear (e.g., chains, pins stuck in both apparel and flesh, tattered clothing); their audience appropriated the look, while engaging in frenzied slam dancing. Although middle America seemed revolted by the whole affair, punk fashions infiltrated the boutiques and department stores patronized by everyday youth. The dressed-down Madonna look of the 1980s owed much to the punk dress of the mid-1970s.

The greatest impact made by punk rock, however, was musical in nature. The genre was in large part responsible for resurrecting the importance of the single and EP—in decline since the rise of progressive rock in the late 1960s—as art forms. In the late 1970s, the arty wing of the movement (e.g.,Talking Heads, Television, Pere Ubu) metamorphosed into new wave, which essentially represented a merging of the stripped-down underpinnings of punk with the progressive rock ethic. New wave, in turn, engendered a diverse array of subgenres in the 1980s, including techno-pop, the new romantics and dance-oriented rock. The more conservative branch of the punk school founded hardcore, which featured even louder, faster and more abrasive music than that emanating from the parent form. Despite all the extra-musical brouhaha, 1970s punk rock produced many memorable songs and albums, including:

Blondie—*Parallel Lines* (1979)

The Buzzcocks—*Spiral Scratch* (EP, 1976)

The Clash—*The Clash* (1977; import l.p. sold over 100,000 copies in the U.S., making it the biggest selling import of all time)

The Ramones—*The Ramones* (1976), including "Blitzkrieg Bop"; "Sheena Is a Punk Rocker"

The Sex Pistols—*Never Mind the Bollocks, Here's the Sex Pistols* (1977), including "Anarchy in the U.K." and "God Save the Queen"

Patti Smith—*Horses* (1975)

Talking Heads—*More Songs About Buildings and Food* (1978), including "Take Me to the River"

Television—*Marquee Moon* (1977)

BIBLIOGRAPHY

Alfonso, B. "Punk Rock: Played Out or Still Punching?," *Songwriter*. 3 (July 1978) 34-36.

Anscombe, I., and D. Blair. *Punk*. New York: Urizen, 1978.

Bianco, David, compiler & editor. *Who's New Wave in Music; an Illustrated Encyclopedia, 1976-1982 (The First Wave)*. Ann Arbor, MI: Pierian, 1985.

Christgau, Georgia. "Punk Out," *Village Voice*. 23 (June 19, 1978) 50.

Coon, Caroline. "Punk Alphabet," *Melody Maker*. 51 (November 27, 1976) 33.

Coon, Caroline. "Punk Power," *Melody Maker*. 51 (November 27, 1976) 33-35ff.

Freedland, N. "Punk Rock Due to L.A. Whiskey; a 'Gingerly' Club Reopening," *Billboard*. 88 (November 20, 1976) 20.

Jones, A. "But Does Nihilism Constitute Revolt?," *Melody Maker*. 51 (August 7, 1976) 24-25.

Jones, A., and B. Harrigan. "Cindarotten: a Punk Pantomime in Three Acts," *Melody Maker*. 51 (December 18, 1976) 24-25.

Kirby, F. "Punk Called 'Music of '80s,' But Can It Get Started Today?," *Variety*. 290 (March 22, 1978) 1.

Kozak, R. "Punk Rock Grows in N.Y.," *Billboard*. 88 (November 20, 1976) 1ff.

"Pros and Cons of Punk," *Melody Maker*. 51 (December 11, 1976) 17.

"Punk Rock," in: *The Rolling Stone Encyclopedia of Rock & Roll*, edited by Jon Pareles and Patricia Romanowski. New York: Rolling Stone Press/Summit Books, 1983, pp. 449-450.

"Punk Storm Grows," *Melody Maker*. 51 (December 11, 1976) 4-5.

Simels, Steve. "Punk Rock," *Stereo Review*. 41 (October 1978) 94-96ff.

Williams, R. "Let's Have a Generation Gap Again," *Melody Maker*. 51 (August 28, 1976) 14.

Ragtime

In *Green Book Magazine* (1915) Irving Berlin claimed ". . . such songs of mine as 'Alexander's Ragtime Band,' 'That Mysterious Rag,' 'Ragtime Violin,' 'I Want to Be in Dixie,' and 'Take a Little Tip from Father,' virtually started the ragtime mania in America." He did and didn't. Before Berlin ragtime had evolved from American minstrel and vaudeville traditions, specifically from the "coon songs" sung in Negro dialect. At the World's Columbian Exposition in Chicago (1893), attended by more than 20 million people, a group of black musicians performed something new known as syncopated music. Ben Harney, Scott Joplin, Johnny Seamore (or Seymour), and Jesse Pickett were among those innovative musicians. In 1896 Ernest Hogan published a song, "All Coons Look Alike to Me" with a syncopated "Rag" accompaniment and the name stuck. Shortly thereafter other syncopated coon songs appeared and "Rag" moved into the title, the first being "The Mississippi Rag" (1897). Then Thomas M. Turpin and Scott Joplin raised rag to an art form by composing purely instrumental rags for the piano. Playing one of their rags required considerable dexterity and thus drew admiration for its performance. Its characteristic feature was an eccentric, broken rhythm that was a little hard to get used to for those who liked to hum a melody. Instrumental rags peaked in popularity early, whereas vocal ragtime took much longer to fall from public favor.

R.M. Stults, a successful composer of sentimental songs, noted the phenomenon in *Etude* (March 1900):

> The craze for 'coon songs,' as they are familiarly known, began about three years ago, and shows little sign of abatement at the present time. Not content with 'rag-time' songs, marches, two-steps, and even waltzes have been subjected to this syncopated style of treatment, in order to appease the

seemingly insatiable thirst for that peculiar rhythmic effect produced by successive irregular accent.

Just listening to rags was not enough; Americans had to dance them. The cakewalk, march, and two-step in ragtime were the first ballroom rages. But true to their faddish conception, by 1904 the cakewalk had ceased to amuse; by 1908, the march; and by 1911, the two-step. Still, Americans had to dance and ragtime mania produced the turkey trot, the one-step, and the fox-trot. In black communities ragtime dances were more expressive as their names indicate: the cake walk prance, slow drag, clean up dance, Jennie Cooler dance, back step prance, dude walk, stop time, and Seddius walk. After World War I the Jazz Age began and absorbed, not replaced, ragtime. Even in the 1920s musicians spoke of both forms as one-in-the-same. It would take musicologists and a lot of print to distinguish between jazz and ragtime. Irving Berlin may have written some favorite ragtime songs for white consumption but credit American blacks with originating the musical genre.

BIBLIOGRAPHY

Berlin, Edward A. *Ragtime: A Musical and Cultural History*. Berkeley: University of California Press, 1980.

Blesh, R., and H. Janis. *They All Played Ragtime*. New York: Knopf, 1950.

Hasse, John E., ed. *Ragtime: Its History, Composers, and Music*. New York: Macmillan, 1985.

Jasen, David A., and Trebor J. Tichenor. *Rags and Ragtime: A Musical History*. New York: Seabury Press, 1978.

Waldo, Terry. *This Is Ragtime*. New York: Hawthorn Books, 1976.

Rambo:
First Blood, Part II

Rambomania—an American reaction to Sylvester Stallone's film, *Rambo: First Blood, Part II*—manifested itself throughout society during 1985. The movie was outgrossed only by *Back to the Future* for that year, selling $185 million in theater tickets.

Additional signs of success were everywhere. There was a Rambo magazine and a novel based on the film sold approximately one million copies. The fashion fad among youth consisted of closely cropped, marine-style haircuts and camouflaged battle jackets. Rambo knives, with fifteen-inch blades, sold for $760 apiece. A Los Angeles firm claimed to have sold more than 150,000 aluminum replicas of Rambo's bow—which killed fourteen people in the film—at $150 apiece. Other war toys—many of which raised the ire of parental groups—included an action figure doll and a "semiautomatic" squirt gun that could shoot a water stream up to thirty feet. In addition, merchandising tie-ins included bubblegum trading cards, Halloween costumes, bumper stickers (e.g., "Warning: This Vehicle Patrolled by Rambo"), coloring books, greeting cards and keychains.

Perhaps most auspicious of all was President Reagan's comment, made during a microphone test prior to a speech on the freeing of the thirty-nine American hijacking hostages in Beirut, "Boy, after seeing *Rambo* last night, I know what to do next time." It has been estimated that the resulting publicity may have added $50 million to Tri-Star Pictures' coffers.

Rambo's success was in large part a result of its success in reinforcing the widespread feeling among Americans that the U.S. could have won the Vietnam War. The film was merely the most popular of a long string of titles—e.g., *Uncommon Valor* (1983), *Missing in Action* (1984), *Missing in Action II: The Beginning* (1985)—forming a new trend called "Namnesia." In addition to the right-wing revisionist plot, *Rambo* was criticized for being racist in tone and excessively violent. Many felt that it would recruit a whole generation of youth into believing that war is fun and that winning is easy.

The appeal of *Rambo*, however, encompassed more than mere war-mongering. Some observers noted its message of hope that the downtrodden can still win. Joanna Wragg of the *Miami Herald* wrote

> The film is about being fed up with the smug bureaucrats, the prep-school boys who would use a decent working class man—use him up, in fact, and then discard the remains.

Although the public's fascination with the film had subsided by 1986, there were plans for a sequel. In the meantime, heavily promoted pay cable and network showings as well as video tape and disc releases have done extremely well commercially.

BIBLIOGRAPHY

Arkin, William M. "At the Movies," *Bulletin of the Atomic Scientists*. 42 (May 1986) 6ff. Re. the popularity of military action films.

Broeske, Pat H. "Rambo: First Blood Part II," in: *Magill's Cinema Annual 1986*, edited by Frank N. Magill. Pasadena, CA: Salem, 1986, pp. 299-303.

Cockburn, Alexander. "The Age of Rambo," *Nation*. 240 (June 29, 1985) 789.

Edelstein, David. "Somewhere Over the Rambo; Moviegoers Need a Rest from the Latest Trend: Reach Out and Grip Someone," *Rolling Stone*. (December 19, 1985) 101ff.

Ellis, John. "'Rambollocks' is the Order of the Day," *New Statesman*. 110 (November 8, 1985) 15.

Fairley, Ellen. "The U.S. Has Surrendered—Now Rambo is Taking the World by Storm; the Movie is Boffo from Japan to Lebanon—and a Horde of Products is Coming," *Business Week*. (August 26, 1985) 109.

Goldman, Peter. "Rock & Rambo; Love Him or Hate Him, with His Two Hit Movie Series, Sylvester Stallone Has Brought the Hero Back to the Forefront of American Mythology," *Newsweek*. 106 (December 23, 1985) 58-62.

Greenberg, Harvey R. "Dangerous Recuperations; Red Dawn, Rambo, and the New Decaturism," *Journal of Popular Film and Television*. 15 (Summer 1987) 60.

Jewett, Robert. "Zeal Without Understanding: Reflections on Rambo and Oliver North," *Christian Century*. 104 (September 9, 1987) 753.

"Pickets Assail Stallone for 'Rambo' Depictions at Hub Press Briefing," *Variety*. 322 (February 26, 1986) 2ff.

Saltzman, Joe. "North, Goetz, and the American Audience," *USA Today*. 116 (November 1987) 55.

Silverman, Michael. "'Rambo' to Vid Market at $80, Debuts Jan. 22," *Variety*. 320 (August 28, 1985) 1ff.

Simonov, Vladimir. "The 'New Patriotism'," *World Press Review*. 2 (December 1985) 50.

Spillman, Susan. "Action Dolls, Other Tie-Ins Spark Toy War; Rambomania," *Advertising Age*. 56 (August 5, 1985) 3ff.

Van Biema, David H. "With a $100 Million Gross (out), Sly Stallone Fends Off Rambo's Army of Adversaries," *People Weekly*. 24 (July 8, 1985) 34-37.

Zoglin, Richard. "An Outbreak of Rambomania; Sylvester Stallone Starts Hollywood's Summer with a Bang," *Time*. 125 (June 24, 1985) 72-73.

Reviews of the film in:

Life. VIII, August 1985, p. 11.
Los Angeles *Times*. May 22, 1985, VI, p. 1.
Ms. XIV, August 1985, p. 71.
The Nation. CCXL, June 22, 1985, p. 776.
The New Yorker. LXI, June 17, 1985, p. 117.
Newsweek. CV, May 27, 1985, p. 74.
Saturday Review. XI, July 1985, p. 81.
Sight and Sound. LIV, Autumn 1985, p. 300.
Time. CXXV, May 27, 1985, p. 91.
Variety CCCXIX, May 22, 1985, p. 14.

"Rock Around the Clock" and the Birth of Rock 'n' Roll

The song, "(We're Gonna) Rock Around the Clock," created a line of demarcation between popular music that had come before and all that followed. Recorded by Bill Haley and The Comets on April 12, 1954, it ushered in the rock 'n' roll era.

"Rock Around the Clock" was not the first rock 'n' roll recording. Rock historians possess varied opinions regarding what these trailblazing songs were; many point to "Rocket 88," recorded by Jackie Brenston for Chess in 1951 (the record was in reality by the Ike Turner Band, vocalist Brenston being Turner's full-time saxophonist). "Rocket 88" was recorded by Haley later in the year, rendering it the first rock 'n' roll song by a white act.

The term "rock 'n' roll" was coined by disc jockey Alan Freed upon hearing the 1947 rhythm and blues hit, "We're Gonna Rock, We're Gonna Roll," by Wild Bill Moore. The genre represented a blend of black r & b, country and western and Tin Pan Alley pop. Haley's role consisted of bringing rock 'n' roll to the consciousness of America — and the world at large. While he failed to remain a superstar in the face of the Elvis Presley craze, he is now recognized as the "father" of the form.

When first released, "Rock Around the Clock" was only a moderate hit. Haley's next single, a cover version of Joe Turner's "Shake, Rattle and Roll," was the one responsible for propelling him to stardom. However, the song's writer, Jimmy Myers, refused to give up on "Rock Around the Clock." He sent copies to virtually every influential person in Hollywood, hoping for further exposure. His efforts paid off when MGM released the film, *The Blackboard Jungle*, with his song accompanying the opening credits. *The Blackboard Jungle*, which starred Glenn Ford as a high school teacher confronted with the specter of juvenile violence, created a sensation. Teens frequently rioted at theaters where it was showing.

Re-released, Haley's single surged up to number one, remaining atop the charts for eight weeks in July/August 1955. Haley and The Comets became, albeit briefly, the figurehead of a movement and were tapped to star in a movie titled, *Rock Around the Clock*. Although the hits stopped coming for Haley by mid-1957, he and his band continued for years as a top tour attraction. The fame of the song enabled him to enjoy renewed success in the early 1970s via the Richard Nader rock and roll revival circuit. His recording of "Rock Around the Clock" even returned to the top forty in 1974; it continues to rate as one of the all-time favorite oldies among music enthusiasts.

BIBLIOGRAPHY

Bronson, Fred. "(We're Gonna) Rock Around the Clock" (by) Bill Haley and the Comets," in: *The Billboard Book of Number One Hits*. New York: Billboard Publications, 1985, p. 1.

Colman, Stuart. "Bill Haley: Father of Rock 'N' Roll," in: *They Kept on Rockin': The Giants of Rock 'N' Roll*. Poole, Dorset, England: Blandford, 1982, pp. 12-28.

Elliott, Brad, and Denise Gregoire. "A Bill Haley Retrospective," *Goldmine*. n72 (April 1981) 8-10.

Hamm, Charles. "'Rock Around the Clock'; or, The Rise of Rock 'N' Roll, in: *Yesterdays: Popular Song in America*. New York: Norton, 1979, pp. 391-424.

King, Gary. "*The Bill Haley Story*," *Music World*. n85 (May 1981) 46-50.

Swenson, John. *Bill Haley: The Daddy of Rock and Roll*. New York: Stein & Day, 1983.

Whitesell, Rick, with Stan Mayo. "The Brightest Comet of Them All – Bill Haley," *Record Exchanger*. 4:4 (1975) 4-9.

The Rocky Horror Picture Show

Arbiters of taste and parents everywhere only wish that *Rocky Horror* was a fad. Released in 1975 it still haunts the midnight shows across America and has grossed untold millions for its executive producer, Lou Adler. During its lengthy cult life, *Rocky Horror*, has indeed bred several fads and at the same time provoked the interest of scholars. Hardly an award-winning movie, its very lack of polish is its appeal. First conceived by Richard O'Brien for the London stage, *The Rocky Horror Picture Show* (1973) capitalized on the then British rage for glitter rock. Combining the bizarre appearance of its players with histrionics, bisexuality, slapstick, and fantasy — all part of glitter rock — the stage musical attracted both young and gay audiences in throngs. Adler bet the same thing would happen with a movie. But at first it didn't. In the two years it took to prepare the movie glitter rock had become passé, especially in America where it had sparkled less brightly than in England. Adler had a fad movie on his hands and virtually no one to watch it. He had to rethink his distribution strategy or lose a substantial investment of time and money. The only way to reach his target audience was by limiting the film's release, so Adler decided *Rocky Horror* could only be seen at midnight shows. It was a simple solution that repayed big dividends.

Rocky Horror parodies three mainstays of Hollywood: horror films, science fiction films, and musicals; and it satirizes sexual norms. One stormy night two sweet kids, Brad Majors and Janet Weiss, while driving to Dr. Everett Scott's to announce their engagement, have a flat tire. They seek help at a Gothic castle where a wild party is taking place. The owner, Dr. Frank N. Furter, a man of great sexual charisma, invites them in. Before the night is over, Dr. Furter seduces both Brad and Janet, his own creation — Rocky Horror, and just about every guest in the castle. When Dr. Scott arrives looking for his nephew, Eddie, he is also defenseless against

the lascivious maniac. Finally, Dr. Furter's servants, Riff Raff and
Magenta, in a jealous rage kill him (all the sex should have) and
whisk the castle back to its home planet (yes, it was an alien invasion all along).

The midnight hour was the first *Rocky Horror* fad. Young, hip
movie-goers had already established the wee hours as the best time
to view cult films. Nothing new, but *Rocky Horror* greatly increased their attendance and from week to week the movie didn't
have to be changed. Every weekend almost the same audience reappeared with new converts as if programmed to do so. A theater
owner's dream, *Rocky Horror* like "Old Man River" just kept rol-
lin' along. Another fad that started early was audience participation. In any other movie if someone in the audience yelled out the
dialogue, that person would be shown the door—not so in *Rocky
Horror*. Often the whole audience spoke the lines in unison, sang
the songs, and carried on in imitation of the screen characters. The
next faddish steps were unusual but predictable. During the appropriate movie scene the audience threw rice, toilet paper, playing
cards, and hot dogs; lit candles; turned on flashlights; and shot
streams of water from squirtguns. Most theater owners didn't mind
the mess because they were too busy counting the profits. Some
daring audience members wore the same costumes as the characters. Particularly popular were Dr. Frank N. Furter in long gloves,
black frilly corset and garter belt, and Brad and Janet dressed like
nerds. The crowning fad arrived when audience members got up on
stage (of the older theaters) and acted out the movie while casting
shadows on the screen.

Assistant Professor at Rochester Institute of Technology, Bruce
A. Austin studied the cult phenomenon of *Rocky Horror*. After
thorough scientific scrutiny (seven tables of data), he concluded
that:

Further examination of the audiences for cult films is clearly
warranted. . . . Many questions remain to be answered. Why
does audience participation occur? What are the social and
psychological needs of the audience that are being met and
presumably gratified by the *Rocky Horror* experience? How
are these needs met? What factors can be identified that deter-

mine the process of how and why one individual becomes a *Rocky Horror* regular and others do not? . . .

An unscientific answer might be that *Rocky Horror* was so bad it was good. Tim Curry as the frenetic bisexual, Dr. Frank N. Furter, impassioned the audience. Barry Bostwick as Brad Majors and Susan Sarandon as Janet Weiss—the good kids—reminded them of everything they didn't want to be. In some parts of America fans avidly read *Rocky Horror* literature: *The Transylvanian*, *Rocky Horror Official Poster Book*, and the annual *Rocky Horror Picture Show Official Magazine*. But for its biggest devotees there was the yearly *Rocky* convention held in New York City.

BIBLIOGRAPHY

Austin, Bruce A. "Portrait of a Cult Film Audience: The Rocky Horror Picture Show." *Journal of Communication*, 31, no.2 (Spring 1981): 43-54.

Bold, Rudolph. "Rocky Horror: The Newest Cult." *Christian Century* (September 12, 1979): 860-861.

Mano, D. Keith. "The Rocky Horror Cult." *National Review* (November 24, 1978): 1493-1494, 1496.

Sayre, Nora. "Cult Films." *Horizon* (September 1979): 64-69.

Rowan & Martin's "Laugh-In"

Building on the experiments in political satire set forth by "That Was the Week That Was" (1964-1965) and "The Smothers Brothers Comedy Hour" (1967-1969), "Rowan & Martin's Laugh-In" blended a similarly topical approach and new format termed by one author "video vaudeville." The program adapted the latest technological advances of the medium to the time-honored variety show tradition. The result—consisting of one-liners, sight gags, skits, blackouts and celebrity cameos, all edited into a frenetic pastiche— was revolutionary for its time. "Laugh-In" premiered in 1968 on NBC and surged to the top of the ratings; it was the number one program on TV from 1968-1970.

Hosted by two veteran lounge comedians, Dan Rowan and Dick Martin, the show's regulars included Ruth Buzzi, Judy Carne, Henry Gibson, Goldie Hawn, Arte Johnson, Gary Owens and Joanne Worley. Cameo appearances were frequent, including 1968 presidential candidate Richard Nixon, incredulously asking "Sock it to Me?"

"Laugh-In" added other words and phrases to the pop culture lexicon, including "Here come de judge," "bippy" "Look that up in your Funk and Wagnalls," "walnuttos" and the "Fickle Finger of Fate Award." The public was also enthralled by popular features such as the cocktail party and the News of the Future, and memorable characters including Gladys, Tyrone Horneye and Arte Johnson's German soldier.

George Schlatter, producer and one of the creators of the program, attributes its success in large part to the social milieu of the time.

> "Laugh-In" came in 1967 and had a great deal to do with Vietnam, strangely enough. Vietnam had created much of that anger, much of that student unrest, political upheaval. Into that kind of vacuum, that arena of hostility, came this brightly-

271

colored, happy, little lump within which there were very barbed references to the Pentagon and the military-industrial complex . . . [but] "Laugh-In" didn't have any anger; there was no political platform . . . We were not trying to change political views, but to comment humorously on all political views.

Schlatter has said that Nixon had more to do with the decline of the program than anyone else. When the politicians became funnier and more outrageous than jokewriters (e.g., Nixon reciting "I'm not a crook"), "Laugh-In" and its imitators were doomed. The program's legacy included the socially relevant sitcom (e.g., "All in the Family," "Maude") and the snappier kind of punch-line humor utilized by books, commercials, films and Broadway in the 1970s. Although it went off the air in 1973, "Laugh-In" lives on in the 1980s through re-runs on cable channels such as Nickelodeon.

BIBLIOGRAPHY

Barthel, J. "Hilarious, Brash, Flat, Peppery, Repetitious, Topical and in Borderline Taste; Rowan and Martin's Laugh-In," *New York Times Magazine*. (October 6, 1968) 32-33ff.

Dietz, L. "Where TV Comedy is at; Rowan and Martin's Laugh-In," *Saturday Evening Post*. 241 (November 30, 1968) 32-37ff.

Edelstein, Andrew J. "Laughs," in: *The Pop Sixties*. New York: World Almanac Publications, 1985, pp. 100-107.

Ferrer, J.M. "Courage at Last, or Just Bleeps? Smothers Brothers Comedy Hour and Rowan and Martin's Laugh-In," *Life*. 64 (April 12, 1968) 18.

Gordon, S. "Sock it to 'em Judy; Laugh-In World of Rowan and Martin," *Look*. 32 (October 21, 1968) 72-76.

"Laugh-In Dropouts," *Time*. 94 (December 5, 1969) 86.

Porter, G.B. "Sock it to Me; Rowan and Martin Laugh-In," *Newsweek*. 71 (February 26, 1968) 96.

"Put-On is not a Put-Down; Laugh-In," *Time*. 91 (March 8, 1968) 65.

Van Horne, H. "Era of Rowan and Martin? Laugh-In," *McCalls*. 97 (October 1969) 80-81ff.

"Verrry Interesting; But Wild; Laugh-In," *Time*. 92 (October 11, 1968) 50-54ff. Reprinted in the January 1969 issue of *Readers' Digest* (Volume 94; pages 70-74) under the title "Zaniest Team on TV."

The San Francisco Sound

During the Summer of Love in 1967, amidst such slogans as "flower power" and "make love not war," the San Francisco Sound delineated the counterculture attitude ascendant with a substantial portion of American youth. The genre was not defined in musical terms; a wide-ranging array of styles — e.g., folk rock, jazz, blues, country and western, Eastern modalities, the minstrel tradition, classical music — were utilized, much of it amplified at high decibel range and accompanied by mind blowing light shows, all of which attempted to replicate the psychedelic (i.e., hallucinogenic drug taking) experience. The preferred medium for musicians was the live concert — the music they produced was of a spontaneous, free-flowing nature. The structural integrity of a song was extended to its furthest limits; half-hour jams were the norm.

The prime identifying characteristic of the San Francisco Sound may not have been musical but rather sociological; i.e., the communal relationship existing between performer and audience. Various attitudes (most notably, the anti-establishment hippie ethic), fashions and activities (e.g., be-ins, love-ins, drug trips) came to be associated with the music.

Psychedelia or acid rock, as the San Francisco Sound was also called, achieved worldwide coinage during the 1967-1968 period. While few Bay Area artists were commercially successful (this fact was largely due to their suspicions regarding the motives and methods of the major record labels), the style influenced countless other American and English bands enroute to mega-stardom (e.g., The Doors, Pink Floyd, Traffic/Steve Winwood, Jimi Hendrix).

In addition to changing the sound and outlook of rock, the genre is responsible for pioneering changes on virtually every level of the pop music scene. These included:

1. breakthroughs in recording contracts, providing the artist with such amenities as a higher royalty rate and control over the production and artwork of albums;
2. the founding of progressive music formats on radio via FM;
3. the application of full stage production values and theatrical props for rock concerts;
4. the notion of booking a nightclub as if it were a small concert hall;
5 the establishment of a fully computerized and automated recording studio;
6. the perfection of rock poster art and the visual techniques of the modern light show;
7. the utilization of all the marketing techniques that have resulted in the modern record store;
8. the raising of rock journalism to international respectability by *Rolling Stone*;
9. the introduction of new concepts as to how music is taught (e.g., David Rubinson's Fillmore seminars, New Age musical schools such as Blue Bear and Family Light);
10. the production of the first rock opera designed specifically for video, presaging the city's emergence in the forefront of rock-video art;
11. the establishment of the first full-scale municipal rock music archive;
12. acting as the central base of operations for Journey, the first band to endorse a national consumer product as well as the first band to be the subject of home and arcade video games.

The roster of group names generated during the period represented a notable by-product of the San Francisco Sound. These bizarre, often humorous, appelations changed forever the approach to how new bands select stage monikers. The following list of San Francisco acts—a sampling of the roster compiled by journalist Ralph Gleason in 1968—illustrates the creativity applied to this process:

A.B. Skhy Blues Band
A Cid Symphony
The Ace of Cups
Advance Token
Africa Creeps Up and Up
Allman Joy
All Night Apothecary
All Spice Rhythm Band
Amplified Ohm
Ancestral Spirits
Angels Own Social Grace & Deliverance Band
Anonymous Artists of America
The Answer
Asmadius
Aum
Ball Point Banana
The Baytovens
Black Shit Puppy Farm
Blue Crumb Truck Factory
Bronze Hog
Celestial Hysteria
Chocolate Watchband
CIA
Cleanliness & Godliness Skiffle Band
Colossal Pomegranate
Crusader Rabbit
Denver Overland Pony Express
Earth Mother
Edsel Buggy
The Electric Flag
Electric Folk Mind
Evergreen Tangerine
Everpresent Fullness
Father Grumble
Fifty Foot Hose
Fourth Way
Freudian Slips
Frosted Suede

Frumious Bandersnatch
God Mother & Country
Granny Goose and The Soul Chips
Immaculate Contraption
Indian Head Band
Lightening Rod and Circuit Breakers
Little Miss Cornshucks & The Loose Troupe
Magnesium Water Lily
Marble Farm
Moby Grape
Mysore Sugoundhi Dhoop Factory
Mystic Knights of the Sea
New Tweedy Brothers
The Only Alternative and His Other Possibilities
William Penn and His Pals
Pipe Joint Compound
The Psycle
Rhythm Method Blues Band
Harvey Scales & The Seven Sounds
Strawberry Window
Transatlantic Chicken Wicken No. 5
Melvin Q. Watchpocket
Peter Wheat and The Bread Men

BIBLIOGRAPHY

Anthony, Gene. *The Summer of Love*. Millbrae, CA: Celestial Arts, 1980.
Burt, Rob, and Patsy North. "San Francisco Music," in: *West Coast Story*. Secaucus, NJ: Chartwell, 1977, pp. 70-74.
Doukas, James N. *The Electric Tibet: The Rise and Fall of the San Francisco Rock Scene*. North Hollywood, CA: Dominion, 1969.
Edelstein, Andrew J. "The San Francisco Sound," in: *The Pop Sixties*. New York: World Almanac Publications, 1985, pp. 45-47.
Gleason, Ralph J. *The Jefferson Airplane and the San Francisco Sound*. New York: Ballantine, 1969.
McDonough, Jack. *San Francisco Rock: The Illustrated History of San Francisco Rock Music*. San Francisco: Chronicle, 1985.
Perry, Charles. "The Sound of San Francisco," in: *The Rolling Illustrated History of Rock and Roll*, edited by Jim Miller. New York: Random House/Rolling Stone Press, 1976, pp. 265-271.

Scribbling Women

That's how Nathaniel Hawthorne, author of *The Scarlet Letter* and *The House of the Seven Gables*, described his newest competitors in a letter to his publisher (1855). He wrote:

> America is now wholly given over to a d****d mob of scribbling women, and I should have no chance of success while the public taste is occupied with their trash — and should be ashamed of myself if I did succeed. What is the mystery of these innumerable editions of *The Lamplighter*, and other books neither better nor worse? Worse they could not be, and better they need not be, when they sell by the hundred thousand.

Yet a month later Hawthorne sang the praises of Fanny Fern and her novel, *Ruth Hall*: "The woman writes as if the devil was in her; and that is the only condition under which a woman ever writes anything worth reading." Hawthorne shared his ambivalence with other literary men who had dominated fiction-writing up to that time. The impudent women were stealing their thunder not by out writing them, but by supplying the public with sentimental gush. Was serious literature on its last leg? Or were scribbling women transient and meant to fade from the scene quickly? It just had to be a devilish fad.

Like Hawthorne, Maria Susanna Cummins was born in Salem, Massachusetts. She had published several short stories in the *Atlantic Monthly* and other periodicals before her first novel, *The Lamplighter* (1854), delivered her from obscurity. Its plot — what so upset Hawthorne — is as follows: Gerty, an impoverished child, has no real hope for the future until a lamplighter, Trueman Flint, befriends her. The old lamplighter kindly introduces her to the right people before he dies. Upon his death Gerty joins the family of Emily Graham, a rich blind girl, and continues to associate happily with a playmate, Willie. In time Gerty learns that her father is Emily's brother who had accidentally blinded her then left home in shame. That revelation sheds "light" on her own past desertion. Gerty, now grown, marries Willie who has made a fast fortune and she is set for life. *The Lamplighter* sold 70,000 copies in its first year, while Hawthorne's books were bringing in but a pittance.

Fanny Fern, the pen name of Sara Payson (Willis) Parton, was in her forties when *Fern Leaves From Fanny's Portfolio* (light essays) and *Ruth Hall* were published. She had waited practically a lifetime for recognition. On the other hand, Nathaniel Parker Willis, her brother, had achieved notice for his writing talent while still at Yale. A poet, dramatist, and travel writer his collected works appeared in 1846, only to be expanded in 1859 to thirteen volumes. Edgar Allan Poe admired his blank verse play, *Tortesa, or, The Usurer*. Willis engaged in every aspect of literary life – even fighting a duel with one of his more vehement critics. Due to his early and continued success there was every reason for sibling rivalry. Toss in the fact that as a man he had the edge over his sister, and the vituperation of *Ruth Hall* makes perfect sense. In the novel Hyacinth, an established writer who lives in grand style, tells Ruth she has no talent for writing. She should pursue "some unobtrusive employment" and forget authorship altogether. Ruth ignores his advice and after years of struggle eventually succeeds. At last a famous writer, her celebrity eclipses his. Throughout Fern portrays Hyacinth as a fop, a fool, and an egomaniac. In one telling scene Hyacinth impulsively buys a vase for $100 instead of giving Ruth the money for food. Indeed, Fanny Fern did write "as if the devil was in her."

The male literary establishment (except for trend-conscious publishers) hoped that scribbling women would go back to homemaking. What Hawthorne and his tribe failed to realize was that women writers wrote what women wanted to read. The heavy melodrama of *The Lamplighter* was just a woman's cup of tea; and *Ruth Hall* exposed men for what they were – patronizers and subjugators of women. Literary history demarcates the 1850s as the feminine fifties to acknowledge the sudden rise of interest in women writers. An enthusiastic female audience rushed to read these novels because they expressed a woman's desire or wrath as only a woman would know. Male pontificating was absent. Novels like *The Lamp-lighter* (materialism glorified) and *Ruth Hall* (sweet revenge) comprise a much lesser genre than Harriet Beecher Stowe's *Uncle Tom's Cabin* (1852). They were faddish works of fiction that contained neither Stowe's moral indignity nor her purposeful writing.

BIBLIOGRAPHY

Baym, Nina. *Woman's Fiction: A Guide to Novels By and About Women in America, 1820-1870*. Ithaca and London: Cornell University Press, 1978.

Geary, Susan. "The Domestic Novel as a Commercial Commodity: Making a Best Seller in the 1850s." *PBSA* 70 (1976): 365-395.

Pattee, Fred L. *The Feminine Fifties*. New York: D. Appleton-Century Company, 1940.

Smith, Henry Nash. "The Scribbling Women and the Cosmic Success Story." *Critical Inquiry* 1 (1974): 47-70.

Sgt. Pepper's
Lonely Hearts Club Band

On June 2, 1967 — following months of anticipation (fueled by countless articles documenting the recording process) — The Beatles' *Sgt. Pepper's Lonely Hearts Club Band* was released in America by Capitol Records. Although the band had been artistically adventuresome since their initial appearance on the charts, the album managed to take many listeners by surprise. Its commercial success, even given The Beatles' exemplary track record up to that point, was astounding. Entering the *Billboard* album charts on June 24, it rose to number one a week later, remaining there for a total of fifteen weeks. During the summer of 1967, the album was heard everywhere — on the radio, in community centers, at swimming pools, wafting out of homes and dormitory rooms, etc.

In addition, *Sgt. Pepper* became the standard by which all future recordings would be measured. Its influence spanned many areas:

1. Concept albums built around a particular literary and/or sociological theme became the vogue.
2. The psychedelic studio effects contained within its tracks were mirrored in the recordings of virtually every popular artist of that period.
3. Performers took a greater interest in the artwork adorning their album covers. Many sought to achieve a direct correlation between cover illustrations and the nature of their music.
4. Like The Beatles, other artists began spending increased amounts of time in the studio in order to maximize their chances of receiving aesthetic accolades.
5. "Art for art's sake" became the prevailing motto within the rock subculture.
6. The counterculture itself was aped by the music establishment.

It was considered "hip" (even commercially imperative) to be anti-establishment in attitude.

The popularity of *Sgt. Pepper* extended beyond the fabled Summer of Love; it remained on the charts for 113 consecutive weeks. It continually re-entered the charts during the 1970s and 1980s, most notably at the time of John Lennon' assassination. The animated feature, *Yellow Submarine* (1968), employed a sizeable portion of the songs and conceptual ideas from the album.

Another film, *Sgt. Pepper's Lonely Hearts Club Band* (1978), starring Peter Frampton and The Bee Gees, proved to be a bust at the box office (probably due in large part to the absence of The Beatles, save the songs and the skeletal outline of the concept). However, the album was front page news again in 1987 when newspapers, magazines, radio and television stations across the nation marked the twentieth anniversary of its release. The compact disc version of *Sgt. Pepper* — released on June 2, 1987 — swept to the top of *Billboard*'s CD charts. In addition, listings, albeit fanciful, of the greatest LPs of the rock era appear periodically which invariably award *Sgt. Pepper* the top spot (e.g., Paul Gambaccini's *The 200 Greatest Albums of Alltime*; "The Top 100: the Best Albums of the Last Twenty Years," *Rolling Stone*, August 27, 1987, pp. 15ff).

BIBLIOGRAPHY

DeCurtis, Anthony. "'Sgt. Pepper' to Get New Image: Top Directors to Celebrate Twentieth Anniversary with Videos of Each Song," *Rolling Stone*. (July 17, 1986) 15.

Lees, Gene. "Beatles, Op. 15," *High Fidelity*. 17 (August 1967) 94.

Loder, Kurt, and Michael Goldberg. "It was Twenty Years Ago Today . . . The Story Behind the Making of 'Sgt. Pepper,'" *Rolling Stone*. (June 18, 1987) 51ff.

Morris, Chris, and Geoff Mayfield. "'Sgt. Pepper' Leads Major Sales Week," *Billboard*. 99 (June 13, 1987) 1ff.

Pleasants, Henry. "Taking the Beatles Seriously," *Stereo Review*. 19 (November 1967) 52ff.

Poirier, Richard. "Learning from the Beatles," in: *The Age of Rock; Sounds of the American Culture Revolution*, edited by Jonathan Eisen. New York; Random House, 1969, pp. 160-179.

"'Sgt. Pepper' TV Show Planned," *Rolling Stone*. (March 12, 1987) 11.

"'Sgt. Pepper's Beatle Music May 'Pied Piper' Rock Fans to Legit," *Variety*. 276 (October 23, 1974) 93.

Shaw, Arnold. "The Beatles: Raga, Id and Baroque Rock," in: *The Rock Revolution*. London: Crowell-Collier, 1969, pp. 80- 94.

Thompson, Toby. "The New Far-Out Beatles," *Life*. 62 (June 16, 1967) 100-102ff.

Welch, Chris. "Now Let Boring Controversy Begin!," *Melody Maker*. 42 (June 3, 1967) 5.

Compact disc reviews in:

High Fidelity. 37 (November 1987) 97-98.
Rolling Stone. (August 27, 1987) 16.
Stereo Review. 52 (August 1987) 81.

Allan Sherman

In October 1962, after fifteen years as a successful television writer and producer, Allan Sherman achieved overnight fame as a folk singing comedian. While temporarily out of work in early 1962, Sherman approached both Capitol and Warner Brothers about recording some of his musical comedy parodies which had made him a much sought-after guest at Hollywood parties. The latter company expressed an interest, but recommended that he write travesties of folk songs — which are in the public domain — rather than parodying Broadway show tunes, which might involve copyright problems.

His debut album, *My Son, the Folk Singer*, featured folk standards with new lyrics by Sherman satirizing urban Jewish mores. For example, "Frere Jacques: became "Sara Jackman," and "The Battle Hymn of the Republic" was transformed into the saga of a cutter in Irving Roth's garment factory, who stood fast during a catastrophic fire ("trampling through the warehouse where the drapes of Roth are stored . . . Glory, glory Harry Lewis"). The LP became the fastest-selling item in history; over 500,000 copies sold in the first month alone.

Sherman quickly followed with *My Son, the Celebrity* (December 1962) and *My Son, the Nut* (1963), which included his chart topping hit single, "Hello Muddah, Hello Faddah" (cast in the form of a complaining letter from a child in summer camp to his parents, and sung to the music of "Dance of the Hours" from the opera *La Gioconda* by Ponchielli). He also became a top concert draw as well as a frequent guest on television; in August 1963 he replaced vacationing Johnny Carson as host of the *Tonight* show. Additional hit albums were released into the mid-1960s, at which point Sherman's nonsensical brand of humor appeared to have fallen out of step with the public's demands for social relevance from its entertainers.

BIBLIOGRAPHY

"Boychick," *Newsweek*. 66 (November 1, 1965) 96ff.

Knight, A. "Literary Life in Las Vegas," *Saturday Review*. 48 (November 6, 1965) 25.

Kolodin, Irving. "Sherman's Mighty Lyre," *Saturday Review*. 45 (December 8, 1962) 59.

"My Son, the Millionaire," *Time*. 81 (January 4, 1963) 34.

"My Uncle, the Violinist," *Saturday Evening Post*. 238 (September 11, 1965) 16.

"Sherman, Allan," in: *Current Biography*, 1966, edited by Charles Moritz. 27th ed. New York: Wilson, 1966, pp. 371-373.

"Song For Dropouts," *Time*. 83 (April 10, 1964) 76.

Zolotow, M. "Spoofmaster," *Saturday Evening Post*. 236 (April 20, 1963) 26-27.

Silly TV Superheroes

Few television viewers, even the addicts, remember "Captain Nice," "Mr. Terrific," and "Quark." They were ill-conceived from the start and thus guaranteed oblivion. For a few months viewers turned them on just for the whimsy of seeing grown adults look and act foolishly. The episodes weren't plausible nor were they intended to be. This new set of superheroes mocked Superman, Batman, the Green Hornet, and Captain Kirk of "Star Trek," all of whom at least engaged in believable exploits. It was a shot in the dark to try and interest TV audiences in slapstick and high-jinks that children immediately called stupid.

"Captain Nice" on NBC premiered 1/9/67 and was buried 8/28/67. William Daniels played the title role of Carter Nash who transformed into Captain Nice. A police chemist, Nash discovers Super-Juice in the lab which when drunk grants him super powers. His mother, played by Alice Ghostley, knows about the Super-Juice and constantly nags him to get off his duff and go out and save the world. One fanciful episode, "That Thing," begins with a caterpillar drinking the secret formula which turns it into a monster. The Herculean insect stymies Nash until he gives some of the formula to his parakeet Sheldon who promptly has dinner. "Mr. Terrific" on CBS aired from 1/4/67 until 8/28/67. It competed mightily with "Captain Nice," finally surrendering its life on the same day. Stanley Beamish (played by Stephen Strimpell), a gas station owner, pops a secret government pill to become a superhero. He faces two recurring problems: first, each pill is effective for only one hour; and second, he keeps forgetting to take them with him. Beamish also confuses things. In "The Sultan Has Five Wives" he is supposed to exchange phony missile plans with an enemy agent but hands over the real plans instead. History repeated itself when NBC introduced another silly hero, "Quark," on 2/24/78. The comedy series was so bad that it died mercifully on 4/14/78 after only eight episodes. Richard Benjamin portrayed Adam Quark called Commander Quark by his crew. His mates consist of a man-half-plant, a frightened robot, a hemaphrodite, and two beautiful twins. Together they patrol outerspace looking for garbage. Whatever evil force Quark contends with he never loses sight of his primary mission, i.e., to rid the universe of rubbish, refuse, and litter. In "All the Emperor's Quasi-Norms, Parts I & II," Zorgon the Malevolent captures Quark and almost forces him to reveal the location of "It," before the forest people save him. Of course, "Star Trek" and Captain Kirk were already at cult status and vulnerable to parody which "Quark" attempted but botched.

The lesson learned from these faddish burlesques is not to make fun of something that people believe in. True superheroes are popular because they embody the common desire to transcend normal human limitations. In the world of the imagination people would rather do the impossible than laugh at the improbable.

BIBLIOGRAPHY

Brooks, Tim, and Earle Marsh. *The Complete Directory to Prime Time Network TV Shows, 1946-Present.* New York: Ballantine Books, 1985.

Eisner, Joel, and David Krinsky. *Television Comedy Series: An Episode Guide to 153 TV Sitcoms in Syndication.* Jefferson, NC, & London: McFarland & Company, Inc., 1984.

Frank Sinatra

Breaking away from the Tommy Dorsey band after three and a half years as its lead singer — the first of many big band front-men to go on to successful careers as individual artists — Frank Sinatra catapulted to sensational fame and fortune, becoming the idol of the bobby-soxer set. During that period he was regularly mobbed by semi-hysterical audiences, receiving a steady stream of proposals in his fan mail (which averaged 2,500 to 3,000 letters per week). In attempting to explain his success, E. J. Kahn cited high-powered press-agentry and the fact that girls "turned to him as compensation for the absence of their young men."

Sinatra remained a commercial phenomenon throughout much of the 1940s. He was a soloist on the radio program "Your Hit Parade" from 1943 to 1945 and starred in a string of Hollywood musicals including *Higher and Higher* (1943), *Anchors Aweigh* (1945), *Till the Clouds Roll By* (1947), *It Happened in Brooklyn* (1947), *The Kissing Bandit* (1949) and *On the Town* (1949). In the late 1940s, however, Sinatra's record sales slumped, his throat began hemorrhaging, the adulation of his public waned and his film studio, MGM, dropped him from its roster.

In 1953 Sinatra turned his career around with an Oscar winning performance (best supporting actor) in the film, *From Here to Eternity*. By the late 1950s he could write his own contract at almost any night club; his Capitol albums were critical masterpieces and among the most popular recordings ever released; he was a fixture on television (he had his own programs — on CBS from 1950-1952 and ABC from 1957-1958 — as well as guest slots on many shows and specials); and he garnered acclaim as a sensitive, intelligent actor in films such as *Suddenly* (1954), *Young at Heart* (1955), *Not as a Stranger* (1955), *Guys and Dolls* (1955), *The Man with the Golden Arm* (1956), *Pal Joey* (1957) and *The Prize and the Passion* (1957). Despite uneven work as an actor, performer and recording artist since the early 1960s, Sinatra has remained an American institution, widely regarded to be one of the show business giants of the twentieth century.

BIBLIOGRAPHY

Bliven, B. "Voice and the Kids; Phenomenon of Mass Hysteria Seen Only Two or Three Times in a Century," *New Republic*. 111 (November 6, 1944) 592-593. Reprinted in abridged form in the January 1945 issue of *Readers' Digest* (Volume 46; pages 12-14).

Kahn, E.J. *The Voice; Story of an American Phenomenon*. New York:Harper, 1947. An enlargement of the October 26, November 2 and November 9, 1946 issues of *New Yorker*.

Long, J. "Sweet Dreams and Dynamite," *American Magazine*. 136 (September 1943) 41ff.

"Sinatra, Frank," in: *Current Biography, 1943*, edited by Charles Moritz. New York: Wilson, 1943, pp. 700-702.

"Sinatra, Frank," in: *Current Biography, 1960*, edited by Charles Moritz. New York: Wilson, 1960, pp. 384-386.

"Swoon Song," *Newsweek*. 22 (August 16, 1943) 80.

"That Old Sweet Song," *Time*. 42 (July 5, 1943) 76.

"The Voice," *Newsweek*. 22 (December 20, 1943) 94ff.

"The $64,000 Question"

Television's first big-money quiz show — an adaptation of a successful radio program, "Take It or Leave It" (later, "The $64,000 Question") — premiered June 7, 1955 and was a national sensation, making instant celebrities of many of its contestants (e.g., Dr. Joyce Brothers). The primary impetus for the show was the April 1954 Supreme Court ruling that the FCC's 1949 proposal to ban giveaway quiz shows was illegal.

The format consisted of asking contestants to answer a series of increasingly difficult questions in which the cash prize doubled at each step: $1000, $2000, $4000, etc. Each contestant selected a category of questions from a prepared list and, at any point along the way, could stop — retaining the money previously won — or choose to try the next question and risk losing it all. Upon reaching the $8000 level, the contestant was placed inside an isolation booth. While ostensibly done to prevent hearing clues yelled by the audience, the booth's prime purpose was to increase the visual suspense for home viewers. To prolong the suspense, only the $8000 and $16,000 questions were posed the first week; if answered correctly, the contestant was given an additional week to decide whether or not to go on for the $32,000, and yet another week for the $64,000 question.

Within one month of its premiere, the program reached number one in the TV ratings and remained there throughout the 1955-1956 season. The availability of smart but basically average people who happened to have a great deal of specialized knowledge in one particular topic helped the show's popularity enormously because the audience could identify with the contestants, and share vicariously in the decision to "go for the big dough." The program was assisted by the nation's newspapers, which devoted considerable space to the trials and tribulations of the contestants. Almost every variety show did a take-off, and a memorable "Honeymooners" tale had Jackie Gleason going through the agony of mastering music, his chosen topic, only to get stagefright and blank out on the opening question of identifying "Swanee River."

Although spawning many competitors (e.g., "The Big Surprise," hosted by Mike Wallace), including the spinoff, "The $64,000 Challenge." "The $64,000 Question" continued to attract a huge audience until the taint of suspicion emanating from the quiz-show scandals of 1958 forced it off the air. While the scandals primarily surrounded "Twenty-One" and "Dotto," the program was implicated in some of the testimony for questionable practices before a New York grand jury.

The show was revived as "The $128,000 Question" in the fall of 1976 for first-run syndication with the prize money being doubled; however, lackluster ratings resulted in a short-lived run.

BIBLIOGRAPHY

"All Aboard for Rainbow Land! $64,000 Question," *Christian Century*. 72 (September 14, 1955) 1044.

"Big Fix," *Time*. 74 (October 19, 1959) 67-68ff.

Brooks, Tim, and Earle Marsh. "$64,000 Question, The," in: *The Complete Directory to Prime Time Network TV Shows, 1946-Present*. Third Edition. New York: Ballantine, 1985, pp. 767-768.

Brown, Les. "$64,000 Question, The," in: *Les Brown's Encyclopedia of Television*. New York: Zoetrope, 1982, pp. 396-397.

Castleman, Harry, and Walter J. Podrazik. *Watching TV*. New York: McGraw-Hill, 1982.

"Effect of the TV Scandals," *US News and World Report*. 47 (November 16, 1959) 41-45.

"Enormity of it; $64,000 Question," *Time*. 66 (September 19, 1955) 87.

"Finally; $64,000 Question," *Newsweek*. 46 (September 26, 1955) 106ff.

"Fort Knix or Bust? $64,000 Question," *Time*. 66 (August 22, 1955) 47.

Gehman, R. "How to Think Big: $64,000 Question," *Cosmopolitan*. 139 (December 1955) 76-81.

March, H. "Could You Answer the $64,000 Question?," *American Magazine*. 160 (December 1955) 21ff.

Millstein, G. "Its Creator Explains the $64,000 Appeal," *New York Times Magazine*. (August 21, 1955) 30.

"Out of the Backwash of the TV Scandals," *Newsweek*. 54 (November 16, 1959) 66-68.

"Semper Chow; $64,000 Question," *Time*. 66 (September 26, 1955) 17-18.

"$64,000 Question," *Newsweek*. 46 (September 5, 1955) 41-45.

"Tarnished Image," *Time*. 74 (November 16, 1959) 72-74ff.

Soft Sculpture

This type of sculpture utilized flexible material — not traditional stone, metal, or wood — for constructing lifesize or greatly enlarged likenesses of everyday objects. The originator and chief practitioner of the art was a Swedish immigrant, Claes Oldenburg (1929-). Prominent among pop artists in the 1960s, Oldenburg basked in the refulgence of media attention for a full decade. His first major tour de force was "The Store." For that exhibition held in a real merchandise outlet in New York City, he made bread, cake, sausage, soda pop bottles, clothing, and the like out of plaster, muslin, and chicken wire. He splashed the goods with paint to impart a garish look. In commenting about "The Store," Oldenburg expressed his philosophy:

> I am for an art that does something other than sit on its ass in a museum. I am for an art that grows up not knowing it is art at all. . . . I am for an art that involves itself with the everyday crap and still comes out on top. I am for an art that imitates the human, this is comic if necessary, or violent, for whatever is necessary. I am for an art that takes its form from the lines of life . . . and is sweet and stupid as life itself.

The items in "The Store" were soft, but not soft enough. His one-man show at the Green Gallery changed all that. In a room he placed a giant slice of chocolate cake and a giant ice cream cone. Close by were smaller foods, a shirt, a pair of pants, and other personal articles. Their rumpled, rubbery appearance presaged sculpture even softer yet. Oldenburg's discovery of vinyl and canvas was a godsend; with the two materials he could attain a droll poignancy. Kapok became his favorite fill to stuff the vinyl and canvas shells. For a while the art world was all a buzz; everyone agreed Oldenburg's soft sculptures were revolutionary.

Here are some of his creations that made news both inside and outside the artistic ferment of New York City. "Floor-Burger" (1962) measured 52" high × 84" in diameter; "Soft Typewriter" (1963) (9" × 27 1/2" × 26"); "Soft Dormeyer Mixer" (1965) (31 3/8" × 20 1/8" × 12"); "Soft Bathtub" (1966) (30" × 80" × 30"); "Soft Washstand" (1966) (55" × 36" × 28"); and "Soft Drainpipe" (1967) (109 7/8" × 68 7/8" × 15"). He made two versions of his "Giant Soft Fan" (1966-1967). One "Ghost Version" in white canvas filled with foam rubber (120" × 59" × 76") sported a cord and plug 290" long; it is now the property of the Museum of Fine Arts in Houston. The second version in black vinyl filled with foam rubber (120" × 58 7/8" × 61 7/8") tailed a cord and plug 291 1/4" long; the Museum of Modern Art in New York City owns it. Oldenburg also constructed soft scissors, a soft pay-telephone, a soft tea bag, soft shoestring potatoes spilling from a bag, soft light switches, a soft giant drum, and soft giant fag-ends (cigarette butts), among others. All of these sculptures were carbon copies of the real thing except for their size and droopy facade.

Some art critics saw profundity in Oldenburg's soft sculptures. They liked what the sad-looking art said about American consumerism. The larger than life objects were a constant reminder of twentieth century dependence on things, and in the case of food—dependence on fast service and mediocre quality. His mock-heroic homage to the mundane was the glory of his art. Furthermore, each time one of the limp sculptures was moved it assumed another personality. It collapsed or stretched differently so that in a manner of speaking it was also living sculpture. Given that kind of critical acclaim and a public amused by it all, Oldenburg's soft creations triumphed. But when he stopped making them, and having few followers, his art of the moment ceased to exist.

BIBLIOGRAPHY

Johnson, Ellen H. *Claes Oldenburg*. Baltimore: Penguin Books, 1971.
"Master of the Soft Touch." *Life* 67 (November 21, 1969): 58-64A+.
Rose, Barbara. *Claes Oldenburg*. New York: The Museum of Modern Art, New York, 1970.
Sylvester, D. "Soft Machines of Claes Oldenburg." *Vogue* 151 (February 1, 1968): 166-169.
"Venerability of Pop." *Time* 94 (October 10, 1969): 68-69.

Stereoscopy: 3-D

3-D represents a motion picture photographic process — also known as stereoscopy, stereoscopic cinematography and stereographic cinematography — that creates the illusion of actual depth in the image so that the foreground seems to stand out in relief and the various planes of the image appear spatially distinct and separate. The 3-D effect was perfected with still pictures by the late nineteenth century; at that time the stereoscope was a popular parlor item.

The anaglyph process was the earliest attempt at projecting 3-D moving pictures to a wide audience. It involved simultaneously shooting two views of the same scene and then printing them in different colors (usually red and green) on a single reel of two-layered film. The projected image was viewed through spectacles, with each eyepiece in one of the two colors, guiding the eye to the image of the opposite color and blocking out the other. The first feature film utilizing this process, *The Power of Love*, premiered in Los Angeles on September 27, 1922. Paramount also employed the technique in a series of shorts called "plastigrams" in the early 1920s as did MGM with its "Audioscopiks" in 1935.

The problems with the anaglyphic process (i.e., it couldn't create images in full color, the indistinct quality of the picture itself and the tendency of the glasses to cause headaches) led to the development of the Polaroid 3-D system which utilized two lenses to shoot a scene, one passing light waves vibrating on only a single plane and the other passing waves vibrating in a perpendicular plane. The projection of the two images simultaneously through separate projectors achieved — when assisted by spectacles with polarized eyepieces, each with a filter set to pass light at one or the other plane — an effect of binocular vision, with the picture seen as possessing depth.

First applied in the Italian film, *Beggar's Wedding*, and the German work, *You Can Nearly Touch It*, in 1936, the Polaroid process was later adopted by Hollywood as an attempt at pulling people back to film theaters from television viewing in the early 1950s. The earliest entries — Arch Oboler's *Bwana Devil* followed by *Man in the Dark* and *Fort Ti* — clicked with movie viewers due to the novelty of 3-D, particularly the special effect which had objects flying directly at the audience. *House of Wax* (1953) represented the apex of the fad, combining first-rate production values with strong box office appeal. At that point, the majority of studios rushed to produce 3-D films; e.g., *Kiss Me Kate*, *The Charge at Feather River*, *Dial M for Murder*, *Miss Sadie Thompson* and *Sangaree*. By the time they were ready, however, audiences for the process had diminished and interest had shifted to Fox's CinemaScope (e.g., *Three Coins in the Fountain*); accordingly, most of these films were released with flat images.

3-D has been revived a number of times since the early 1950s. In 1967 Oboler produced *The Bubble* in 3-D, and in 1970-1971 there was a brief revival of interest in the process as a promotional gimmick for cheap sexploitation flicks. Andy Warhol's *Frankenstein* (1974) also focused attention on 3-D, as did a rash of horror-thriller films in the early 1980s (e.g., *Jaws 3-D*). In addition, the process has attracted a cult following among videophiles. A number of 1950s classics shot in 3-D have been released on videotape (e.g., *Creature from the Black Lagoon*), including some never released theatrically in that format.

BIBLIOGRAPHY

Crowther, B. "Picture of Hollywood in the Depths; Three-Dimensional and the Movie Industry," *New York Times Magazine*. (June 14, 1953) 17ff.

Haines, A.B. "Hollywood's Reply to Television," *America*. 89 (September 12, 1953) 576-577.

Halliwell, Leslie. "3-D," in: *Halliwell's Filmgoer's Companion*. 8th ed. New York: Charles Scribner's Sons, 1984, p. 606.

Kampffert, W. "Are Three-D Movies Really News?," *Science Digest*. 33 (May 1953) 26-28.

Knight, A. "Hollywood's Defense in Depth," *Reporter*. 8 (June 9, 1953) 32-34.

Konigsberg, Ira. "3-D," in: *The Complete Film Dictionary*. New York: New American Library, 1987, pp. 350-352.

"Making the Decisions on Three-D Movies," *Business Week*. (August 15, 1953) 78-84ff.

Morrison, C. "Three-D High, Wide and Handsome," *Look*. 17 (June 30, 1953) 27-33.

"Movies with Depth, the Answer to TV?," *US News and World Report*. 34 (April 10, 1953) 77-79.

Sisk, J.P. "Passion in a New Dimension," *Commonweal*. 59 (October 23, 1953) 63-65.

"Strictly For the Marbles," *Time*. 61 (June 8, 1953) 66-68ff. Reprinted in the September 1953 issue of *Readers' Digest* (Volume 63; pages 49-53) as "Third Dementia Takes Over in Hollywood."

"Third Dimension," *Time*. 61 (May 18, 1953) 114.

"Third Dimension: an Industry Changes Its Product," *Business Week*. (July 25, 1953) 60-62ff.

"Three-D Bonanza," *Time*. 61 (March 23, 1953) 101.

"Three-D Comeback," *Business Week*. (December 12, 1953) 45-46.

"Three-D Diagnosis," *Newsweek*. 42 (October 12, 1953) 98.

Tyler, P. "Era of the Three-D's," *New Republic*. 128 (May 18, 1953) 22-23.

The Stratemeyer Syndicate

Edward Stratemeyer's establishment of a publishing empire concerned exclusively with juvenile readers, the Stratemeyer Syndicate, ushered in the modern phase of series-book history. Stratemeyer started his career as a writer of serials for various magazines (e.g., *Good News*, *Young Sports of America*, *Bright Days*) between 1886-1892. He soon began writing full scale juvenile novels, contributing to the Log Cabin Library under the pseudonyms Jim Bowie, Nat Woods and Jim Daley. The first hardcover book published under his own name was *Richard Dare's Venture*, or *Striking Out For Himself* (1894), which initiated the Bound to Succeed series. As his works began finding a ready audience with young readers, Stratemeyer stepped up his output; as early as 1897, he had six series and sixteen hardcover titles in print (using both his own name and pseudonyms).

Many of Stratemeyer's early series dealt either with war and patriotism (in order to capitalize on the expansionist euphoria engendered by the Spanish-American War) or with the Horatio Alger theme of getting ahead in life through hard work. After saturating his audience with these themes, he turned to stories of school life and sports. The Lakeport series (1904-1912) and Dave Porter series (1905-1919) reflected this shift in thematic emphasis and served as prototypes for many of his later series.

In 1899, Stratemeyer established the first of his major series with the publication of *The Rover Boys at School*. The Rover Boys sequence encompassed thirty titles and generated sales of 6,000,000 copies. Other important series followed in short order, including The Bobbsey Twins (1904), The Motor Boys (1906), Tom Swift (1910), The Hardy Boys (1927) and Nancy Drew (1930). In order to satisfy the growing demand for his works, Stratemeyer developed the idea of a literary syndicate in 1906. The concept allowed him to delegate much of the writing load to subordinates while still maintaining careful editorial control of his editorial series. The

Stratemeyer Syndicate was responsible for the publication of eighty-one distinct series up through 1930; estimates of the total number of titles produced over the years varies from 700 to 1200.

The phenomenal success of the Stratemeyer titles gave rise to a full-fledged anti-series book movement which lasted from the turn of the century to World War I. The prime instigators of the move-ment—e.g., the Boy Scouts of America, the American Library As-sociation, the American Bookseller's Association, classroom teach-ers and PTA groups—objected to the series books on the basis of (1) the poor quality of the prose, (2) the tendency toward exaggera-tion and sensationalism, and (3) the assembly-line method of crea-tion. The public, however, rejected the punitive and exhortative tone employed by the critics. Later efforts on behalf of critics were diffused by the Great Depression, World War II and the expansion of other mass media formats (e.g., radio, television, motion pic-tures, comic books, pulp magazines). The Stratemeyer Syndicate itself initiated moves aimed at counteracting critics. Many volumes were revised with the villains losing their ethnic characteristics and the exaggerated (often humorous) dialects of minor characters be-coming increasingly Anglicized. In addition, an effort was made to incorporate educational elements as reflected in the transformation of Tom Swift into the Tom Swift, Jr. series.

The success of the Stratemeyer Syndicate has continued unabated to the present day. With Stratemeyer's death in 1930, his daughter, Harriet Adams, carried on, and the firm continued to produce new series (e.g., the Happy Hollisters, 1953; Linda Craig, 1962) as well as new titles for established older series. The Nancy Drew series, alone, had accounted for fifty-three mysteries (and a cookbook) and sales in the range of 55,000,000-60,000,000 prior to the 1980s; during one recent year (1980), 2,300,000 copies of Nancy Drew books were purchased.

BIBLIOGRAPHY

Donelsen, Ken. "Nancy, Tom and Assorted Friends in the Stratemeyer Syndicate Then and Now," *Children's Literature*. 7 (1978) 17-43.
Fenner, P.R. "Tom Swift and the Rover Boys," *Wilson Bulletin*. 9 (June 1935) 542-543ff.

Hall, Joan Joffe. "The Girl Sleuth," *Children's Literature*. 6 (1977) 256-257.

Jones, James P. "Nancy Drew, Wasp Super Girl," *Journal of Popular Culture*. 6 (Spring 1973).

Mason, Bobbie Ann. *The Girl Sleuth; A Feminist Guide*. Old Westbury, NY: Feminist Press, 1975.

Smith, W. J. "Bobbsey Twins at an Orgy," *Nation*. 198 (June 22, 1964) 633-635.

Soderbergh, Peter A. "The Stratemeyer Strain: Educators and the Juvenile Series Book, 1900-1980," in: *Only Connect: Readings on Children's Literature*. 2nd ed., rev. Toronto: Oxford University Press, 1981.

Zacharies, Lee. "Nancy Drew, Ballbuster," *Journal of Popular Culture*. 9 (Spring 1976) 1027-1038.

Striptease

Lydia Thompson's "British Blondes" broke the ice in America. The year was 1868 and their legshow—a chorus line of girls in tights—brought down the house. Branded wicked from the start burlesque went its merry way for another hundred years passing through a number of changes. Burleycue, as it came to be called, began innocently enough. Patterned somewhat after the minstrel show it delivered entertainment in three parts. First, baggy-pants comics told coarse jokes, sang songs, and otherwise tried to get laughs; second, circus acts and perhaps a legitimate singer charmed the crowd; and third, chorus numbers and a "burlesque" on some topical subject led up to the finale when either an exotic dancer gyrated or a wrestling or boxing match commenced. For a while the comics ruled the stage with their funny patter, tricks, and sight gags. But laughter over legs didn't endure; the finale was about to take over. National circuits of burlesque shows continued to offer variety but at the Winter Garden in New York City Minsky's steered in another direction.

Abraham and Billy Minsky were doing well with their nickelodeons before their father built the National Winter Garden Theater (1916). On the building's roof there was a small auditorium that went unleased. The sons appropriated the space and opened a movie house. It prospered though not quickly enough so the Minskys added a new kind of burlesque show. As in the past their comics told ribald jokes and played with the girls on stage.

Ethel De Veaux: Oh, I think I am in love with you! Yes, I am—take my eyes. Take my arms. Take my lips.

Joey Faye: Sure, the best parts you keep for yourself!

Straight Man: (running his hand over the bald comic's head): Ya know, Charlie, your head feels exactly like my wife's backside!

Comic: (running his hand over his own head) Ya know? You're right!

Voice in the Dark: Peanuts, popcorn, rubber balloons.

Another Voice: Help someone—there's a woman here who's fainted!

First Voice: Peanuts, popcorn . . .

New Voice: Fainted? Rub her wrists, rub her wrists.

First Voice: Rubber balloons!

Then they introduced the striptease artists. Of the many burlesque fads the striptease is the most memorable. At first voluptuous girls sans raiment and framed by light and shadow stood immobile on stage and drew applause. Then theatrical producers could get away with exhibiting a girl nude if she posed without batting an eyelash. Censors believed that movement incited lust, though viewing a naked girl frozen, her eyes averted from the audience, was artistic and permissible. This was practically highbrow entertainment so the Minskys discarded the stock girl silhouette and brought in living, breathing strippers.These girls spent a lot of time looking for the perfect outfit that they didn't wear for long. Something in either feather, beads, veils, or flowers to enhance their natural charms. They were not yet at the point of "takin' it all off" down to a G-string. The rage was to watch a beautiful girl exotically clad remove some of her costume but not all of it. That was the tease along with leaning over to expose the breast. One famous act involved a stripper who plucked bananas from her body until exiting at the last moment with one of the fruit still dangling from her crotch. Striptease artists Ann Corio and Gypsy Rose Lee brought style and beauty to Minsky's. They attracted quite a following without having to bare every inch and were the biggest names in the skin game. Their celebrity alone kept burlesque going strong even in houses where they never appeared.

However, graceful stripping gave way to the bump (the girl snapped her hips forward to a drum beat) and the grind (she traced the letter O with her pelvis), which should have been called the grind and bump since the girl had to grind before she could bump. Stripper fashions became popular with the general public. Wearing gorgeous boas for vamping and tight fitting dresses that zipped from back to hem found favor. Burlesque caused its own demise (civic action groups and public taste also helped) when it became less imaginative and more blatant. The pretty girls in frothy costumes who tantalized the crowd lost the stage to a new breed of jaded girls who had to twirl tassels on their breasts to get a reaction. The days of comic genius, too, had passed. W.C. Fields, Al Jolson, Fannie Brice, Bert Lahr, and Phil Silvers — all burlesque headliners — died hard due to the demand for more skin. Burlesque, the once multiform entertainment, by the 1970s had degenerated into a few girls hustling drinks in between turns stripping on a pocket-sized stage. Let the following serve as an epitaph to a dearly-held illusion:

> Chorus: If you love us, please don't mind
> If now and then we bump and grind!
> We will shimmy and we will shake
> But please don't think we're on the make!

BIBLIOGRAPHY

Alexander, H.M. *Strip Tease: The Vanished Art of Burlesque*. New York: Knight Publishers, 1938.

Corio, Ann, and Joe DiMona. *This Was Burlesque*. New York: Grosset and Dunlap, 1968.

Lee, Gypsy Rose. *Gypsy*. New York: Harper, 1957.

Minsky, Morton, and Milt Machlin. *Minsky's Burlesque*. New York: Arbor House, 1986.

Zeidman, Irving. *The American Burlesque Show*. New York: Hawthorne, 1967.

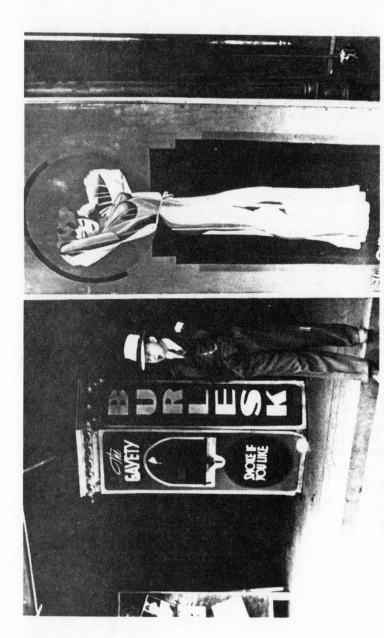

By the 1920s burlesque—a standard art form based on parody—had degenerated into striptease. Gorgeous girls took off elaborate costumes in an attempt to boost attendance. With the passing of a few celebrated strippers, Gypsy Rose Lee being the most prominent, and the hiring of less artistic girls, interest on a large scale waned.

Super Realism

A type of art in vogue from the late 1960s through the 1970s that replicated people and scenes from life with photographic precision. So exact were the painted and sculpted images that the viewer thought they were the real thing. The painted scenes appeared to be windows cut in the gallery wall looking out on a city street; and the sculpted people were even more fascinating—surely they bled if scratched. Super realism mesmerized the public and prompted art critics to write at length about its meaning. One such critic, Edward Lucie-Smith, made this summary statement:

> What one finds in American Super realism is both the uneasy consciousness of the contemporary urban environment, which simultaneously attracts the artist and arouses his disgust, and the equally uneasy recognition of art's minority status, however much it may truckle the mob.

Another critic, Gerrit Henry, suggested a deeper meaning:

> In Photo Realism, reality is made to look so overpoweringly real as to make it pure illusion: through the basically magical means of point-for-point precisionist rendering the actual is portrayed as being so real that it doesn't exist.

Naturally, the contemporary urban environment provided a wealth of subject matter. For example in "Dressing Room with Chandelier" (1978), Jack Mendenhall painted a mirrored room so realistically that it seems to reflect everything near it—including the viewer. Robert Bechtle's "Santa Barbara Motel" (1977), also an oil painting, shows a young woman sitting at a cabana table outdoors; every detail of shrubbery, stone walk, and deepening shadow is a miracle of meticulous replication. Moving on to sculpture, Duane Hanson's "Couple with Shopping Bags" (1976) depicts an overweight man and woman wearing mismatched polyester outfits;

the pair look sullen as if they ate too much or their feet ache. Life-size, composed of cast vinyl and polychromed in oil, the couple are typical mall-walkers who never miss Saturday shopping. Also life-size, John de Andrea's "Seated Woman" (1978) is another star-tling creation, probably all the more so because the woman is nude and desirable. She sits on a chair, her hands crossed loosely at mid-thigh; her dark hair is tied in a bun and she gazes down at the floor. The veins in her body, different skin tones, dirt on her feet, and swimsuit lines from last summer are clearly visible. While viewing her it is hard to believe she is only polyvinyl polychromed in oil. Not to be confused with the Super Realists, the most popular Realist sculptor is George Segal. His work differs from Hanson and de Andrea in that he cast likenesses of human beings in plaster leaving them white and roughly textured. He didn't endow them with real-looking flesh, hair, fingernails, and the like. His stark figures have come to represent modern man's spiritual isolation and feelings of alienation. This is where the Super Realists failed; they achieved precision but forfeited the power of symbolism.

For a decade Super Realism held the mirror up to America and said, "See in the ordinary what you will." Ralph Goings' oil of a pick-up truck, John Salt's ghetto lunch room, or Richard Estes' bus reflected in windows, are some of the all too common sights exalted by this art. In one way the degree to which Super Realism suc-ceeded was remarkable. The camera-like scenes and figures in-spired awe for the artist's ability. Why Super Realism declined can be ascertained from its main characteristics. It was melancholy and often pessimistic; it copied modern life too explicitly; and, after the initial wonder it inspired, its strict objectivity left the viewer feeling cold. In a word, Super Realism was the antithesis of the world's favorite art — Impressionism — and therefore antithetical to what people expect from art.

BIBLIOGRAPHY

Art in America (November-December 1972): entire issue.

Battcock, Gregory, ed. *Super Realism: A Critical Anthology*. New York: E.P. Dutton, 1975.

Lucie-Smith, Edward. *Super Realism*. New York: E.P. Dutton, 1979.

Superman

While Superman is thought by many to have been an overnight success following his debut in *Action Comics #1* (June 1938), he was actually created several years earlier. Author Jerry Siegel and artist Joe Shuster, classmates at Cleveland's Glenville High School, collaborated on a story called "The Reign of the Superman," which appeared in the January 1933 issue of their mimeographed fanzine, *Science Fiction*. Siegel noted that

> ... a couple of months after I published this story, it occurred to me that a superman as a hero rather than a villain might make a great comic strip character in the vein of Tarzan, only more super and sensational than that great character.

Other influences included dual-identity heroes like Zorro, the Shadow and Doc Savage as well as superhuman characters like Samson and Hercules.

The resulting comic book version, in which the hero was depicted as wearing a T-shirt and pants, did not find an interested publisher. The creators remained bullish about their creation, however; the basic concept evolved out of their own fantasies. The inherent appeal of Superman, along with his timid alter ego Clark Kent, is that most people are Walter Mittys and ugly ducklings inside, no matter how secure a front we present to others.

After numerous rejections by comic strip syndicates and comic book editors, the concept was finally accepted by DC. According to Shuster, the first story was taken directly from sample newspaper strips.

> They were in a rush to meet the deadline on the first issue. Everything happened very fast. They made the decision to publish it and said to us, 'Just go out and turn out 13 pages based on your strip . . .' The only solution Jerry and I could

come up with was to cut up the strips into panels and paste the panels on a sheet the size of the page.

DC executives did not foresee Superman's great potential. The editor of *Action Comics*, Vincent Sullivan, claims he simply bought the feature because "it looked good. It was different and there was a lot of action. This is what kids wanted." The public, however, recognized Superman as something special almost from the moment they saw the famous debut cover depicting him holding a car over his head. By the fourth issue, *Action Comics* had spurted well ahead of its competitors. A brief market survey indicated to DC that the portion of the magazine devoted to Superman was vastly preferred to all other features carried by the title. By 1941, *Action Comics* was selling 900,000 copies a month. A new DC title, *Superman*, was started in 1939 and quickly achieved a circulation of 1,250,000.

The Superman phenomenon soon spread to other media. He appeared in a newspaper strip, distributed by the McClure Syndicate, which provided the first detailed account of his origins. Some of the best-known lines associated with Superman originated on the radio show which started on a national basis in early 1940: "Up, up, and away!"; "This is a job for . . . Superman!"; "Faster than a speeding bullet, more powerful than a locomotive, able to leap tall buildings at a single bound . . . "; "Look! Up in the sky! It's a bird! It's a plane! It's . . . Superman!" In the early 1940s, Paramount Pictures released a series of animated shorts devoted to the character under the direction of the Fleisher brothers (also known for their Betty Boop and Popeye cartoons).

The appearance of Superman almost single-handed propelled the comic book industry into its "Golden Age" (1938-1945). By 1942 American consumers were spending appproximately $15,000,000 annually on them, with most of the successful titles a part of the costumed-hero bandwagon. Notable imitators included Batman (DC, 1939), the Blue Beetle (Fox, 1939), the Human Torch (Marvel, 1939), Sub-Mariner (Marvel, 1939), the Green Lantern (DC, 1940), Flash (DC, 1940), Wonder Woman (DC, 1941), Captain Marvel (Fawcett, 1940) and Captain America (Marvel, 1941).

The preoccupation with different concerns during World War II and the growing sophistication of post-war America caused Superman's popularity to diminish considerably by the mid-1940s onward. However, he remained sufficiently popular to be treated in a television series (starring George Reeves) during the early years of that medium. The mid-1970s brought a revival of interest with the appearance of Paramount's first of the Superman film cycle, headlining Christopher Reeve. DC's well orchestrated fiftieth anniversary celebration in 1988, accompanied by a comprehensive merchandizing campaign, resulted in a continued high level of success for the superhero, both in comic books and various other media tie-ins. More than one scholarly source has termed Superman the most significant character in American fiction. Certainly his continued survival is guaranteed for many generations to come.

BIBLIOGRAPHY

Barol, Bill. "The Year of Living Dangerously: Superman, the Golden Gate and Spam Turn 50, Products of the American Heebies-Jeebies," *Newsweek.* 109 (June 8, 1987) 84-85.

Cohn, Lawrence. "Man of Steel Polished for 50th Anni; Comics at Core of Spinoff Coin," *Variety.* 327 (July 8, 1987) 27ff.

"The Talk of the Town: Fifty," *New Yorker.* 63 (June 8, 1987) 25ff.

Collingwood, Harris. "A Midlife Crisis for Superman," *Business Week.* (April 18, 1988) 38.

Edelman, Rob. "Vintage '40s and '50s Film Serials Were Smashes Before TV Did 'Em In," *Variety.* 327 (July 8, 1987) 29ff.

Flatow, Sheryl. "Leaps and Bounds," *Public Relations Journal.* 44 (February 1988) 13ff. Covers DC Comics' publicity campaigns for Superman.

Friedrich, Otto, with Beth Austin and Janice C. Simpson. "Up, Up and Awaaay!! America's Hero Turns 50, Ever Changing But Indestructible," *Time.* 131 (August 14, 1988) 66-74.

Goulart, Ron. "The Kid from Krypton," in: *Ron Goulart's Great History of Comic Books.* Chicago: Contemporary Books, 1986. 83-92.

Hamburger, P. "Television: Superman," *New Yorker.* 29 (December 12, 1953) 165-167.

Kuperszmid, Celia. "Superman Faces Midlife Crisis," *Public Relations Journal.* 42 (September 1986) 15.

McCarthy, Todd. "Salkind's Lucrative 'Superman' Films Also Costly and Litigious," *Variety.* 327 (August 1987) 32.

Nordell, R. "Superman Revisited," *Atlantic.* 217 (January 1966) 104-105.

Sciacca, Tom. "Evolution of Superman Comics Over 50 Years: Imprints Left by Originators and Successors," *Variety.* 327 (July 8, 1987) 28ff.

"Will Superman Fly?," *Chain Store Age-General Merchandise Trends.* 63 (June 1987) 69. Covers the licensing of Superman products.

Surf Music

Surf music was the first variant of the West Coast Sound (which would come to include soft rock and the San Francisco Sound) to hit the big time. The earliest hits of the genre tended to be instrumentals, dominated by a twanging, heavily reverbed guitar in contrast to the sax-oriented sound typifying much of the rock 'n' roll of that era. Surf music responded to the tastes of suntanned young men who lived for the next wave; as a result, it became a key ingredient of the subculture growing up around the Southern California beaches. The first star to employ this style was journeyman Dick Dale who, while occasionally including vocal lines in his material, provided the impetus for a school of pure instrumentals like The Chantays, The Marketts and The Surfaris.

The Beach Boys irreparably changed the course of pop music history by wedding 1950s Tin Pan Alley vocal harmonizing (e.g., The Lettermen, The Four Preps) and surfing lingo to already established instrumental style. With the release of "Surfin'" in late 1961, surf music expanded from its regional base to the entire nation (and eventually the international scene). Brian Wilson, the band's chief composer, brilliantly encapsulized the world of affluent California high school kids where one seemingly could party without end amidst the sand and sun, and all boys and girls were blond and beautiful in their baggies and bikinis. Hollywood surf and beach-party films extended the fantasy by concocting sugar-coated plots portraying what was arguably the first genuine counterculture—a self-contained lifestyle full of teen love, panoramic beaches and freeway cruising while virtually devoid of adults save for an occasional straw authority figure to ultimately overcome.

It was the music, however, with The Beach Boys in the vanguard between 1962-1966, that was most responsible for delineating this hedonistic lifestyle to those baby boomers sharing the affluence and leisure-time interests of their Southern California brethren. Considered the most vital American pop music form of that period (with the possible exception of the Motown Sound), the lengthy list of surf music classics included:

The Beach Boys — "Surfin' Safari" (Capitol, 1962)
The Beach Boys — "Surfin' U.S.A." (Capitol, 1963)
The Beach Boys — "Surfer Girl (Capitol, 1963)
The Chantays — "Pipeline" (Dot, 1963)
Chubby Checker — "Surf Party" (Parkway, 1963)
Dick Dale & His Del-Tones — "Let's Go Trippin'" (Deltone, 1961-1962)
Jan & Dean — "Surf City" (Liberty, 1963)
Jan & Dean — "Honolulu Lulu" (Liberty, 1963)
Jan & Dean — "Ride the Wild Surf" (Liberty, 1964)
The Marketts — "Surfer's Stomp" (Liberty, 1962)
The Marketts — "Out of Limits" (Warner Brothers, 1963-1964)
The Sunrays — "I Live For the Sun" (Tower, 1965)
The Surfaris — "Wipe Out" (Dot, 1963; 1966)
The Surfaris — "Surfer Joe" (Dot, 1963)
The Surfaris — "Point Panic" (Decca, 1963)
The Tradewinds — "New York's A Lonely Town" (Red Bird, 1965)
The Trashmen — "Surfin' Bird" (Garrett, 1963-1964)
The Ventures — Surfing (Dolton, 1963)

The decline of the genre was the result of the following factors:

1. because it was such a calculatedly teen-pitched fantasy, youths felt almost obligated to outgrow it;
2. the rise of social relevancy in the mid-1960s which led to folk rock and progressive rock;
3. Brian Wilson's desire to be taken seriously, resulting in such complex studio productions as Pet Sounds, "Good Vibrations" and "Heroes and Villains."

However, the influence of surf music has continued to manifest itself in the appearance of genres such as beach music (actually a cultural phenomenon largely built around classic oldies of the

1960s) and artists like Blondie, The Go-Go's and The Raybeats. The Beach Boys themselves have become an American institution, content to evoke the aura of bygone years via their tours and frequent reissues of 1960s material on sound recordings.

BIBLIOGRAPHY

Belz, Carl. "The Surfing Scene and Its Music," in: *The Story of Rock*. 2nd ed. New York: Oxford University Press, 1972, pp. 94-101.

Edelstein, Andrew J. "Endless Summer — The Beach Boys and Surf Music," in: *The Pop Sixties*. New York: World Almanac Publications, 1985, pp. 8-10.

Leaf, David. *The Beach Boys and the California Myth*. New York: Grossett & Dunlap, 1978.

Preiss, Byron. *The Beach Boys: The Authorized Biography of America's Greatest Rock and Roll Band*. New York: Ballantine, 1979.

Tobler, John. *The Beach Boys*. London: Phoebus, 1977.

Swing Music

Swing as a jazz style originated around 1930 when New Orleans jazz (i.e., Dixieland) was waning in popularity and creative vitality. Its chief features — relative to its jazz precedents — included a greater emphasis on solo improvisation, larger ensembles (the thirteen-piece dance band, established in 1932, initially set the standard until the appearance of significantly bigger orchestras in the early 1940s), a repertory based largely on Tin Pan Alley songs and more equal weight given to the four beats of the bar. Associated changes in instrumentation involved the tuba being superseded by the double bass, the banjo by the rhythm guitar and the snare drum by the hi-hat cymbal. The increased attention paid to instrumental virtuosity led to the rise of many musical celebrities, most notably cornetist Henry "Red" Allen, saxophonist Coleman Hawkins, drummer Gene Krupa, saxophonist Johnny Hodges, vibraphonist Lionel Hampton, saxophonist Lester Young and trumpeter Harry James as well as bandleaders like Glenn Miller, Count Basie, Duke Ellington, Fletcher Henderson, Jimmie Lunceford and Artie Shaw.

The figurehead of the swing movement was Benny Goodman. Steady touring and a six-month engagement at the Congress Hotel (Chicago) in 1936 rendered the clarinetist the biggest act in the music business, the so-called King of Swing. The style gained wider visibility when he starred in *The Big Broadcast of 1937*, the first Hollywood film to feature a big band, which was followed by a long string of cameo film appearances for Goodman and his ensemble. The Carnegie Hall concert of January 16, 1938 — the first full-scale presentation of jazz in that venerable house — resulted in swing's acceptance by the last holdouts in American society, the cultural elite.

The genre continued to prosper as part of the popular music mainstream until the demise of the big bands, first stricken by the World War II draft of musicians, the 1942-1944 ban on recording

by union czar James Caesar Petrillo, and the twenty percent tax
levied on dance halls, and later superseded in importance by the
crooners initially hired to front them. While a new generation of
jazz musicians turned to other styles—first be bop in the late 1940s,
and then to cool jazz in the 1950s—swing has continued to attract a
small hardcore following up to the present day, fueled in part by the
nostalgia industry. Its legacy has remained visible in the rhythm
sections and brass choirs utilized by much rhythm and blues and
rock 'n' roll.

BIBLIOGRAPHY

Dance, S. *The World of Swing*. New York: Scribner's, 1974.

McCarthy, A.J. *The Dance Band Era: the Dancing Decades from Ragtime to
Swing, 1910-1950*. Philadelphia: Chilton, 1972.

Miller, Paul E. *Down Beat's Yearbook of Swing*. Greenwood, 1978. Reprint of
the 1939 edition.

Robinson, J. Bradford. "Swing," in: *The New Grove Dictionary of Music*, edited
by H. Wiley Hitchcock and Stanley Sadie. Volume Four. London: Macmillan,
1986, p. 339.

"Seems We've Heard That Song Before," *Down Beat*. 16 (January 14, 1949) 10.

Simon, George T. *Simon Says; the Sights and Sounds of the Swing Era, 1935-
1955*. New Rochelle, NY: Arlington House, 1971.

Tamony, P. "Swing, the Big Word," *JEMF Quarterly*. 16 (1980) 59.

Treadwell, Bill. *Jazz: Big Book of Swing*. Cedar Knolls, NJ: Wehman, n.d.

Goodman, Benny

Connor, Donald R. *BG—Off the Record; a Bio-Discography of Benny Goodman*.
Fairless Hills, PA: Gaildonna, 1958.

Swing Time meant hot music, hot dancing, and a cool drink to quench your thirst. To foster the spread of this brassy entertainment urban sophisticates enticed country people to come out and let the music ripple up their spines.

Taxi-Dance Hall

This form of male entertainment originated in San Francisco during the World War I years spreading rapidly to other major American cities. Men frequented the halls to dance with young women for whom they paid a price. Like a taxi-driver in his cab the women were for public hire hence the name, "taxi-dancer." Any man who asked for a dance and had a ticket bought the woman and couldn't be turned away. At the end of the evening each dancer got to keep half of her take, the other half went to the owner of the hall. Not called taxi-dance halls as such, these establishments were advertised as dancing academies. The euphemism was partly true since a few male clients did actually dance with the women to perfect their steps. But the majority of men either went to make conquests, to leer at the women, or simply to take in the spectacle.

Most of the dancers adopted a certain look and manner to please the men. They wore jaunty hats, stylish fur coats, silken dresses, daubed their faces with garish make-up, and smacked chicle. They kept their figures trim and exuded a youthful air of confidence and enthusiasm. When the orchestra struck up, "Baby Face, You've Got the Cutest Little Baby Face" or "I Like Your Size, I Like Your Eyes, Who Wouldn't?," the women started tapping their feet. The dancers certainly earned their money. The more popular ones rarely got a break and had to smile at every would-be Fred Astaire who trampled toes. By design each musical piece lasted only ninety seconds and cost ten cents. Thus a full evening of dancing got expensive — monetarily for the men and physically for the women. Even though wall signs warned "No Improper Dancing Permitted" and officers of the law supervised the hall, desirous males clutched their prey and fights broke out over the dancers. On slow nights to stir interest two dancers might stage a fake fight, rolling around on the floor, the slit in their dresses exposing ample thigh. A surefire gimmick, after the scuffle most every man in the hall wanted to dance with the hot-blooded disputants.

The taxi-dance hall came into being due primarily to the closing of saloons and vice districts by moralistic citizen groups. An outlet for sensual pleasure had to resurface somewhere even during a time of sweeping social change. However, the halls didn't operate unnoticed; some reformers were convinced they were dens of prostitution. Sociologist Paul G. Cressey, in a lengthy study of the taxi-dance hall, squelched that notion with this distinction: "While promiscuous sex behavior and extramarital alliances of varying types are all too frequent, prostitution of the older forms is not common."

BIBLIOGRAPHY

Cressey, Paul G. *The Taxi-Dance Hall: A Sociological Study in Commercialized Recreation and City Life*. Chicago: University of Chicago Press, 1932.
Swift, Arthur L. *The Dance Hall: A Problem of Social Control*. M.A. Thesis, Columbia University, 1925.

Shirley Temple

The most popular child star in the history of the cinema, Shirley Temple provided a badly needed dose of escapism to a country mired in the depths of the Great Depression. The peak of her career was concentrated into a four-year period from 1934 through 1938 in which she starred in more than twenty features, including *Little Miss Marker*, *The Little Colonel*, *Wee Willie Inkie*, *Heidi* and *Rebecca of Sunnybrook Farm*. Temple's impact reached beyond mere top-ranked box office status; she became an institution. The nation's adoration was manifested in a vast array of products—e.g., Shirley Temple dolls, toys and clothes—and her distinctive curly hairdo was adopted by young girls all over America. She even received a special Oscar in 1934 in tribute to her contributions to the medium.

Temple's success appears to have been the result of both her charismatic personality and the redundancy of the roles she played. Her films functioned as well-defined morality plays in which her unflagging optimism, common sense and inherent goodness ultimately overcame all odds. For example, during this period she played an orphan nine times; in the end she always found a family, more often than not a wealthy one. As a diplomat—no matter how grand the scale (e.g., terminating war in India)—she was equal to any situation. She exhibited no racial or class prejudices. In short, Temple embodied all of the ideals that Americans cherished but seldom practiced.

Relegated to stereotypical teenage roles in the 1940s, Temple's movie career stalled. After a brief stint as the host of a TV series, "The Shirley Temple Storybook," she went on to excel in real-life roles within the realm of diplomacy, including U.S. Representative to the U.N. (1968), U.S. Ambassador to Ghana (1974-1976) and U.S. Chief of Protocol (1976-1977).

BIBLIOGRAPHY

Basinger, Jeanine. *Shirley Temple*. New York: 1975.

Burdick, Loraine. *The Shirley Temple Story*. Middle Village, NY: 1975.

David, Lester and Irene. *The Shirley Temple Story*. New York: 1983.

Eby, Lois. *Shirley Temple: The Amazing Story of the Child Actress Who Grew Up to Be America's Fairy Princess*. Derby, CT: 1962.

"Temple, Shirley," in: *The International Dictionary of Films and Filmmakers: Volume III; Actors and Actresses*, edited by James Vinson. Chicago: St. James, 1986, pp. 607-608.

Windelen, Robert. *The Films of Shirley Temple*. Secaucus, NJ: 1978.

Windelen, Robert. *Shirley Temple*. London: 1976.

Tin Pan Alley

In the 1880s and 1890s American popular song writing began to centralize in New York City. By 1900 several of the largest sheet music publishers had offices on 28th Street between 5th Avenue and Broadway near Union Square. Songwriters who pounded away on tinny-sounding upright pianos took their musical wares there to what became known as Tin Pan Alley. Alley historian, Isaac Goldberg, writes this about the derivation of the name:

> Tin . . . it is the one metal to suit the dull reverberations of the passing popular song. Pan . . . the one instrument to sound its flat repetitions, its tinny monotony.

Not a golden endorsement, to be sure, but one that is mostly accurate. Tin Pan Alley did usher in a new era of disposable songs. Many of the songs, though, were not ephemeral — some achieved immortality; it was in the tossed off manner of writing and publishing them that gave rise to faddish entertainment. The Alley flourished until the 1940s turning out one hit song after another. The bottomless cornucopia proved to be a lucrative business. It put a lot of people to work as an anonymous wag attested:

> Sing a song of Tin Pan
> And Cock Robin, too.
> Who really scores the hit
> That magnetizes you?
>
> "I," says the Lyricist,
> "With my words and patter;
> Take my lines away
> And the rest doesn't matter."
>
> "I," cries Composer,
> "With my tune and tinkle.

Without them the song
Would be dead as Van Winkle!''

(Arranger looks on
With a cynical frown.
''He thinks up the tune,
But I set it down.'')

''You?'' sneers the Plugger.
''Go tell that to Grover.
You guys set it down
But I put it over!''

Mr. Publisher smiles.
''And whose shekels stake it?
If it wasn't for me,
How could you fellows make it?''

From the wings speaks a ghost.
''How these kids run amuck!
Shall I tell them the truth, —
That it's me, — Lady Luck!''

Paul Dresser wrote some of the first big Tin Pan Alley songs which because of their sentimentality were not typical of what was to come. ''Just Tell Them That You Saw Me'' (1895), ''On the Banks of the Wabash'' (1899), and ''My Gal Sal'' (1905) were his most endearing compositions reminiscent of Stephen Foster. A few years earlier Charles K. Harris' ''After the Ball'' (1892) had sold five million copies. Also wildly successful were Charles B. Ward's ''The Band Played On'' (1895), Maud Nugent's ''Sweet Rosie O'Grady'' (1896), George Evans' ''In the Good Old Summertime'' (1902), George M. Cohan's ''Give My Regards to Broadway'' (1904), and Gus Edwards' ''By the Light of the Silvery Moon'' (1909). As these song titles suggest Tin Pan Alley was in the business of making people feel good about life and love. Since these commodities are always in demand Americans in that simple prewar time couldn't get enough of them.

The eminent American composer, George Gershwin, was a Tin Pan Alley artist first. He had this to say about the quick write for profit of which he was a past master:

Often one hears that composing a song is an easy affair. All a number needs for success, it seems, is thirty-two bars; a good phrase of eight bars used to start the refrain is repeated twice more with a new eight-bar added which is much less important. It sounds simple, of course, but personally I can think of no more nerve-racking, no more mentally arduous task than making music.

Eventually Tin Pan Alley shifted from the Union Square area to West 28th Street, then to the Brill Building and others near it on Broadway close to 50th Street, before fading away. During its tenure of fifty-plus years it practically invented the popular song market, then responded decisively to America's insatiable appetite for song. Lyrics and melodies just kept bouncing out of the song hopper to keep the public cupping an ear.

BIBLIOGRAPHY

Ewen, David. *The Life and Death of Tin Pan Alley*. New York: Funk and Wagnalls, 1964.

Goldberg, Isaac. *Tin Pan Alley: A Chronicle of the American Popular Music Racket*. New York: John Day, 1930.

Meyer, Hazel. *The Gold in Tin Pan Alley*. Philadelphia: Lippincott, 1958.

Whitcomb, Ian. *Tin Pan Alley: A Pictorial History (1919-1939)*. New York: Paddington Press, 1975.

Tiny Tim

On the strength of his trembling falsetto, strange appearance (big nose, stringy hair and bag-man clothes) and androgynous mannerisms, Tiny Tim became a highly successful camp novelty artist in the late 1960s. The former Herbert Khaury was a fixture at low-rent Greenwich Village nightclubs for years before his trilling of fluffy comedia pop tunes from the 1920s to the accompaniment of his ukelele began to gather a cult audience in the mid-1960s. Bookings on "The Tonight Show" and "Laugh-In" made him an instant national celebrity. In spring 1968, his debut album on Reprise, *God Bless Tiny Tim*, was released; one of its cuts, "Tiptoe Through the Tulips," became a Top Twenty hit.

Tiny Tim's most notorious moment came on December 17, 1969 when he and seventeen-year-old Victoria May Budinger (known to his audience as "Miss Vicky") were married live on Johnny Carson's late night program. The couple is reputed to have spent the first three nights of their honeymoon apart in keeping with Tim's bizarre sexual code.

By early 1972, when they first filed for divorce, Tiny Tim was out of public favor and broke. He toured the backwater lounges of America for a time in the 1970s as part of a traveling vaudeville show whose other acts included Zippy the Chimp and a fireater. During their separation it was revealed that Miss Vicky had had to work as a go-go dancer at Minnie's Lounge in Camden, New Jersey and accept welfare in order to survive. Tim offered to take her back if she'd undergo a VD test; she refused, and the couple was divorced in 1977.

Tiny Tim continued to perform on occasion in the 1980s; however, his shtick has paled in comparison to weirder gender-benders for some time.

BIBLIOGRAPHY

Aronowitz, A.G. "It's High Time Fame Came to Tiny Tim," *Life*. 64 (June 14, 1968) 10.

Dunne, J.G. "Souls and Spirits Within Me," *Saturday Evening Post*. 241 (August 10, 1968) 16.

Edelstein, Andrew J. "A Rogue's Gallery of '60s Celebs: Tiny Tim," in: *The Pop Sixties*. New York: World Almanac Publications, 1985, p. 231.

Goldman, Albert. "And He Keeps His Ukulele in a Sleeping Bag," In: *Freakshow; The Rocksoulbluejazzsickjewblackhumorsexpoppsych Gig and Other Scenes from the Counter-Culture*. New York:Atheneum, 1971, pp. 116-120.

"Last Innocent," *Newsweek*. 71 (May 20, 1968) 113.

"Puff-Up Time," *Time*. 94 (December 26, 1969) 47.

"Purity of Madness," *Time*. 91 (May 17, 1968) 66.

Schneck, S. "Larry Love, Alias Julian Foxglove, Alias Derry Dover, Alias Herbert Khaury, Alias Tiny Tim," *Ramparts Magazine*. 7 (August 24, 1968) 28-37.

"Tiny Tim," in: *The Rolling Stone Encyclopedia of Rock & Roll*, edited by Jon Pareles and Patricia Romanowski. New York: Rolling Stone Press/Summit Books, 1983, p. 556.

Walsh, J. "Meeting with Tiny Tim," *Hobbies*. 74 (September 1969) 37-39ff; 74 (October 1969) 37-40ff.

J.R.R. Tolkien

It has been said that J.R.R. Tolkien's *The Lord of the Rings* burst on the campuses of American colleges in the mid-1960s like a rainstorm over a parched desert. Large numbers of intelligent, educated young Americans found no pleasure in the present, no solace in the past, and little hope for the future. "Be here now" and "do your own thing" reflected the agonizing, hedonistic frenzy of a confused culture. A benign cynicism toward existing institutions inspired a search for new gods: the occult, mysticism, psychedelics, Eastern philosophy, ecology and back-to-the-land movements. In ancient cultures mythology provided reassurance that acts of hope and heroism were possible. In the West, organized religion and, later, the rise of science and industrialization superseded mythology. Tolkien wrote *The Lord of the Rings* as an attempt to modernize the old myths, thereby rendering them credible. The great success of Tolkien's work can be attributed to the care with which his alternative realm was constructed — a world in which moral problems were taken seriously and where it was possible to make the right decisions — as well as the public's thirst for a new mythology.

The Lord of the Rings, written over a fourteen-year period, is a 1200-page trilogy consisting of *The Fellowship of the Ring* (1954), *The Two Towers* (1954) and *The Return of the Ring* (1955). During the 1950s, the Tolkien works were cult items. In 1957 Tolkien received the "Hugo" for the best fantasy of 1956, the first of his major literary awards. By 1961, excitement generated by the trilogy had expanded from academia to science fiction fans. However, the appearance of both Ace and Ballantine paperback editions in 1965 (the work was not copyrighted in the U.S.) led to its becoming one of the most popular works of fiction in American history. By the end of 1968, it was estimated that more than 50 million people had read his work. Even *The Hobbit*, which had always sold well as a children's book, found its way to the adult book section and sold more than one million copies less than eighteen months after Ballantine released the revised version in paperback.

Some of the comments that the trilogy generated included:

- — A mother packing it in her child's luggage said "to go to college without Tolkien is like going without sneakers."
- — At Erasmus High anyone who wants to be sophisticated or snobbish feels he has to read the work.
- — It was a "ritual of passing," according to a student at Bryn Mawr College, where "all the nicest people" read and discussed Tolkien.

The story took place in an imaginary world called Middle Earth and told of a conspiracy by an evil wizard called Sauron to take control of the One Ring, which would enable him to dominate everything. Frodo Baggins, a hobbit (a three-foot tall humanlike creature with hairy feet) had come into possession of the Ring; his mission was to bring it to fiery Mt. Doom where it could be destroyed. The only problem was that the Ring corrupted anyone who possessed it.

Tolkien died in 1973. The posthumously published "prequel" to the trilogy, *The Silmarillion* (1977) sold well, but not nearly so much as *The Lord of the Rings*. Two animated features, *The Hobbit* and Ralph Bakshi's *The Lord of the Rings — Part 1*, were theatrically released in the 1970s and continue to generate interest via video sales/rentals and cable TV showings.

BIBLIOGRAPHY

"Ace Books Reaches Agreement with Tolkien," *Publishers' Weekly*. 189 (March 14, 1966) 37-38.

Carter, Lin. *A Look Behind The Lord of the Rings: Tolkien*. New York: Ballantine, 1969.

Crist, Judith. "Why Frodo Lives," *Ladies Home Journal*. 84 (February 1967) 58.

Edelstein, Endrew J. "The Lord of Fantasy — J.R.R. Tolkien," in: *The Pop Sixties*. New York: World Almanac Publications, 1985, pp. 207-209.

Elliott, C. "Can America Kick the Hobbit?," *Life*. 62 (February 24, 1967) 10.

Grotta-Kurska, Daniel. *J.R.R. Tolkien: Architect of Middle Earth*. Philadelphia: Running Press, 1976.

"Hobbit Habit," *Time*. 88 (July 15, 1966) 48ff.

Mathewson, J. "Hobbit Habit," *Esquire*. 66 (September 1966) 130-131ff.

Norman, P. "Prevalence of Hobbits," *New York Times Magazine*. (January 15, 1967) 30-31ff.

Plotz, R.D. "Face to Face: with R.D. Plotz, Founder of Tolkien Society of America," *Seventeen*. 25 (April 1966) 153.

Ready, William B. *The Tolkien Relation*. Chicago: Regnery, n.d.

Resnick, H. "Hobbit-Forming World of J.R.R. Tolkien," *Saturday Evening Post*. 239 (July 2, 1966) 90-92ff.

Roos, R. "Middle Earth in the Classroom: Studying J.R.R. Tolkien," *English Journal*. 58 (November 1967) 1175-1180.

Schroth, R.A. "Lord of the Rings," *America*. 116 (February 18, 1967) 254.

Sklar, R. "Tolkien & Hesse: Top of the Pops," *Nation*. 204 (May 8, 1967) 598-601.

TV's Bizarre Families

Beginning in the 1950s and continuing into the 1960s television programs about families portrayed everyday life in which a strong father-figure and a home-maker wife worked together to solve domestic problems. Their homes were neat and tidy, their lawns manicured, and their neighbors "swell people." It seemed all of America was one big Norman Rockwell painting of happy people doing happy things. The two best known examples are "The Adventures of Ozzie and Harriet" — the Nelsons — (1952-1966, 435 episodes) and "Father Knows Best" — the Andersons — (1954-1963, 191 episodes). Strong family units and wholesome fun characterized these two extremely popular television programs. Then "The Addams Family" and "The Munsters" moved in to ruin the neighborhood. These two situation comedies shared much in common. "The Addams Family," based on the celebrated cartoons of Charles Addams appearing in *The New Yorker*, aired from 9/18/64 to 9/2/66 on ABC; "The Munsters," from 9/24/64 to 9/1/66 on CBS. So they arose and expired simultaneously. The Addams family displayed humorous idiosyncrasies but looked somewhat normal; their faces were ashen, Morticia's long, black hair hung straight over her black dress, and Lurch/Thing stared absent-mindedly into space. While the Munsters were a family of recognizable movie monsters, both families thought they were normal and the rest of the world abnormal. This inverted perception provided the foundation for most of the plots and laughs.

Gomez Addams (played by John Astin), Morticia Frump Addams (Carolyn Jones), Uncle Fester (Jackie Coogan), Lurch (Ted Cassidy), Grandmama Addams (Blossom Rock), Pugsley (Ken Weatherwax), Wednesday (Lisa Loring), Cousin Itt (Felix Silla), and Thing (Ted Cassidy) comprised the Addams family. In the Munster family portrait there was Herman (played by Fred Gwynne in the guise of the Frankenstein monster), Lily (Yvonne DeCarlo as a female vampire), Grandpa (Al Lewis as Count Dracula), Eddie (Butch Patrick as a werewolf), and Marilyn (Beverly Owen, 1964; Pat Priest 1964-66 as an oddball pretty girl). The plots were ridiculous, but before long faithful viewers found the episodes believable within the context of the family. In "The Addams Family Splurges" they plan a vacation trip to the moon; in "The Addams Family Tree" Gomez and Morticia trace their roots to see if their ancestors were properly bred. The Munsters also faced difficult life decisions. In "Low-Cal Munster" Herman diets so he can fit into his old uniform for his Army reunion; in "Bats of a Feather" Eddie takes Grandpa, who has turned into a bat, to the school pet fair but trades him for a squirrel.

It was fitting that the two most eccentric families on television came and went at the same time, lasting only two seasons apiece. They were an anomaly in the first place spliced in between balanced families that viewers regarded as exemplary. Yet the Addams family and the Munsters cared for one another just as much as the Nelsons and the Andersons did for their families. Albeit they acted strange, most of the time they had hearts of gold.

BIBLIOGRAPHY

Brooks, Tim, and Earle Marsh. *The Complete Directory to Prime Time Network TV Shows 1946–Present*. 3rd ed. New York: Ballantine Books, 1985.

Eisner, Joel, and David Krinsky. *Television Comedy Series: An Episode Guide to 153 TV Sitcoms in Syndication*. Jefferson, NC, & London: McFarland & Company, Inc., 1984.

The Twist

The Twist phenomenon had its genesis in 1958 with the release of a song written by a rhythm and blues journeyman from Detroit named Hank Ballard. Ballard and his back-up group, The Midnighters, hit the pop charts for the first time that year with "Teardrops on Your Letter." The flip side of the single, "The Twist," drew its inspiration from a new dance Ballard had seen teenagers doing in Tampa, Florida.

"The Twist" went largely unnoticed until the dance spread across the country. When it became the most popular dance on "American Bandstand," MC Dick Clark tried to get Danny and The Juniors interested in recording a cover version of the song. When they didn't come up with anything, Clark called the executives at Cameo-Parkway, Philadelphia's most successful record label, and suggested that Chubby Checker, one of its promising young artists, put out the song.

Checker's version was almost a duplicate of the original single; even the vocals, down to the final "eee-yow!," resembled Ballard's. Ballard himself, upon hearing the cover on the radio, is said to have thought he was listening to himself. Spurred by several appearances on "American Bandstand" in which Checker gave "Twist" lessons, the record sped up the charts, reaching number one on September 19, 1960.

After "The Twist" had run its course, Checker continued to release dance records: "The Hucklebuck"; "The Pony," which also rose to the top of the charts; and "The Mess Around." The Twist appeared to have been one of many short-lived teenage dance crazes. Then society columnist "Cholly Knickerbocker" mentioned that Prince Serge Obolensky had been observed dancing the Twist at Manhattan's Peppermint Lounge; as a result, it caught on with adults worldwide, first with the Jet Set, and later, with the rank and file. Checker appeared on "The Ed Sullivan Show" on October

22, 1961 to sing The Twist, prompting its re-release. The single rose to number one again; the only instance during the rock era in which a chart topper returned there after having fell off the charts. A slew of Twist songs charted in 1962, including "Peppermint Twist–Part 1," by Joey Dee and The Starliters; "Dear Lady Twist," by Gary U.S. Bonds; "Twistin' the Night Away," by Sam Cooke; and Checker's own "Slow Twistin'." Checker and Dee went on to star in three Hollywood films: *Hey Let's Twist, Twist Around the Clock* and *Don't Knock the Twist*. Checker was marketed with a line of Twist products. These were Twist shirts, cufflinks, wallets, pajamas, candy, Thom McCan "Twister" shoes and a Twist hairdo that bounced and rotated to the dance's rhythms. Newspapers and magazines provided a steady stream of pertinent news notes to help fuel the craze: for example, New York's Safety Council said that in one week in October 1961, forty-nine out of fifty-four cases of back trouble resulted from too much Twisting; in Syracuse, New York, the widow of an auto salesman who died of a heart attack after Twisting at a company party sued for workmen's compensation under the state law and won.

By 1963, however, a seemingly endless wave of new dances – the Hully-Gully, Mashed Potato, the Frug, the Watusi, the Limbo, the Monkey – all of which attempted to repeat the formula established by the Twist, rendered the original item as dated as the Lindy Hop. The dance left its impact on pop music dance styles in that couples virtually ceased dancing together for almost two decades. The dance continued to live on in cover versions of classic Twist songs such as The Beatles' "Twist and Shout" (1964; 1986) and Rod Stewart's "Twistin' the Night Away" (1972). Checker himself has been reborn artistically and commercially via his featured role in The Fat Boys' 1988 rap remake of "The Twist."

BIBLIOGRAPHY

Belz, Carl. "The Twist and Other Dances," in: *The Story of Rock*. 2nd ed. New York: Oxford University Press, 1972, pp. 90-94.

Bronson, Fred. "The Twist (by) Chubby Checker," in: *The Billboard Book of Number One Hits*. New York: Billboard Publications, 1985, p. 74.

Busner, Gene. "1962–The Twist and Other Dance Crazes," in: *West Coast Story*, by Rob Burt and Patsy North. Secaucus, NJ: 1977, pp. 202-210.

"Checker Climbs Chart with 'The Twist'," *Billboard*. 72 (September 5, 1960) 18.

"Chubby Checker Gets More Cash," *Billboard*. 72 (December 26, 1960) 8.

Clark, Dick. "How the Twist Discovered Bandstand," in: *The Sixties; the Dance Remembered Now, By the People Who Lived It Then*, edited by Lynda R. Obst. New York: Random House, Rolling Stone Press, 1977, pp. 42-43.

Edelstein, Andrew J. "The Twist," in: *The Pop Sixties*. New York: World Almanac Publications, 1985, pp. 156-158.

Fishwick, Marshall. "Twist," *Saturday Review*. 45 (March 3, 1962) 8-10.

Grevatt, Ren. "The Most Vulgar Dance Invented," *Melody Maker*. 36 (December 16, 1961) 13.

Holder, G. "Twist? It's Not a Dance," *New York Times Magazine*. (December 3, 1961) 78ff.

Rolontz, B., and J. Maher. "Is the Bossa Nova the New Twist?," *Billboard*. 74 (October 13, 1962) 4.

Rothberg, Gerald, ed. *Let's All Twist*. New York: Esquire Publications, 1962.

Stambler, Irwin. "Chubby Checker," in: *Encyclopedia of Pop, Rock and Soul*. New York: St. Martin, 1974, p. 106.

"Twist; New Dance Step at Peppermint Lounge," *New Yorker*. 37 (October 21, 1961) 46-47.

"Twist Wiggles Into Big Time," *Business Week*. (December 2, 1961) 44-46.

Uncle Tom's Cabin

Harriet Beecher Stowe's realistic tale of American slavery caused a mild sensation when it was published in 1852. Since much of the novel was in dialogue it adapted easily to the stage. As a play it reached even more people and the mild sensation turned into a brilliant triumph. The images were indelible: the slave Eliza jumping from one swiftly moving ice floe to another while she clutched her son, Harry, to her breast to avoid capture by Haley, the slave dealer; the death of Little Eva, the daughter of Tom's master, from neglect which no black family would have allowed; and finally the long-suffering Uncle Tom succumbing to death after the Yankee planter, Simon Legree, had him beaten senseless for withholding information. Appearing eight years before the outbreak of the Civil War, this "fiction" struck a responsive chord in abolitionists and other people of conscience. After the war some commentators suggested that *Uncle Tom's Cabin* had precipitated the conflict and eventual freeing of slaves.

In play form it was America's first long-running hit and dominated the stage until the beginning of the twentieth century. During those years as many as five hundred Tom companies toured the United States. Some actors and actresses spent their entire careers playing the Tom characters. An actor could gain instant fame if his Tom or Legree were good enough; an actress, her Eliza or Little Eva. The adaptations varied from short one-act plays to six hour spectacles complete with live animals, several hundred jubilee singers, and real cotton ginned on stage. Tom mania built to the point that it produced dozens of songs about the characters, "authentic" Tom recipes and crockery, restaurants, and board games. It is difficult to imagine that what we put up with today—cheap commercialization of anything the public takes a fancy to—could have been present over a hundred years ago. But it was and *Uncle Tom's*

Cabin was a marketing delight. In Europe where the mania spread Berliners dedicated "Oncle Tom Strasse" and the French coined a new word "l'oncletomerie."

Melodrama with a serious purpose was quite a departure from what had gone before, or for that matter, from what would come after. The stage versions of *Uncle Tom's Cabin*, excluding the minstrel show type, were even more stark and penetrating than the novel. George Aiken's dramatization—the one that took the country by storm—retained all the major scenes and abetted the author's intention to expose the horrors of slavery. Aiken left out Stowe's comic relief depicting happier days among the slaves, so that one tragedy followed another in unrelenting gloom. Thus the play was more powerful than the novel and perplexed audiences used to seeing shuffling, grinning blacks on stage. It was a testament to the emerging morality of a nation that Americans could sit through an "entertainment" that disturbed them so deeply. But then there was the crass commercialization of Tom products and the willing rush to watch the play over and again. Long after the Emancipation Proclamation people still anticipated a new production. Did Americans seek catharsis and exculpation for their sins? Or did they just enjoy a good melodrama? What was it about *Uncle Tom's Cabin* that started a wildfire everytime it hit town? And for sixty years? Stowe's theme of man's inhumanity to man lodged in America's psyche like no other work of fiction.

The great entertainer, P.T. Barnum, who rarely missed an opportunity to turn a profit, ran this advertisement for his production of the play in New York City:

It represents Southern Negro
SLAVERY AS IT IS
embracing all its abhorrent deformities, its cruelties, and barbarities. It does 'nothing extenuate nor set down in malice,' while it does not foolishly and unjustly elevate the negro above the white man in intellect or morals. It exhibits a true picture of negro life in the South, instead of absurdly representing the ignorant slave as possessed of all the polish of the drawing room and the refinement of educated whites. . . .

BIBLIOGRAPHY

Gerould, Daniel C. *American Melodrama*. New York: Performing Arts Journal Publications, 1983.
Gossett, Thomas F. *Uncle Tom's Cabin and American Culture*. Dallas: Southern Methodist University Press, 1985.

Underground Newspapers

Underground newspapers were created in response to the counterculture's mistrust of the "establishment" press. The underground publications could be distinguished from other publications in light of the following characteristics:

1. editorial integrity;
2. participative journalism;
3. amateur production methods;
4. leftist politics;
5. concern with alternative lifestyles;
6. local community — i.e., grassroots — involvement;
7. coverage of national and international issues, events, etc., not found in mainstream papers; e.g., student and worker movement in the Third World, the secret activities of the CIA, confrontation politics in Berkeley or Madison.

The term "underground" is generally taken, in contemporary usage, to refer to various movements, mostly active in the 1960s and early 1970s, that focused on the nature and quality of the United States' moral stance in the world. There has always been an underground in America in the sense that certain groups have pointedly refused to subscribe to the dominant values or modes of living of their time (e.g., Tory resistance to the Revolution; Southern abolitionists during the Civil War; communist sympathizers during the Great Depression); however, the phenomenon arising from Vietnam War protests and the civil rights activism of the 1960s differed from its predecessors in several ways:

1. it was a truly national movement existing mainly on university campuses;
2. it covered a wide breadth of issues — political, social, economic and personal concerns were viewed as part of the same fabric;
3. it produced a diverse array of publications dedicated to chroni-

cling the movement, the most notable of which was the underground newspaper.

The "big four" of the movement were the *Los Angeles Free Press*, *The Berkeley Barb*, New York's *East Village Other* and San Francisco's *Oracle*. Every major city and college town had at least one such paper; e.g., Chicago's *Seed*, Detroit's *Fifth Estate* and Philadelphia's *Different Drummer*. In 1966 thirty of them banded together to form the Underground Press Syndicate, for the free interchange of articles and ideas between the various publications.

The decline of the movement has been attributed largely to the breakup of the counterculture as well as rising publishing costs. The former resulted in part from the persecution of the New Left by the Nixon Administration. Although evident much earlier, illegal but official police and political harassment increased and often contributed directly to the folding of many undergrounds. Those surviving generally went aboveground, by the mid-1970s becoming a phenomenon called "alternative weeklies," which specialized in highbrow features and advertising geared to an upwardly-mobile readership. This transition is reflected in the evolution of *Rolling Stone* from a hip subculture fanzine to a tastemaker periodical for today's yuppie.

It could be argued that the underground newspaper reflected the counterculture movement more accurately than any other mass medium. While it was biased, strident, crude, sexist and frequently inaccurate — it represented the collective consciousness of the New Left and its effect on American political and social life.

BIBLIOGRAPHY

"Admen Groove on Underground; in Tabloids, the Record Industry Has Found a New Advertising Channel," *Business Week*. (April 12, 1969) 84-86.

Alternative Press Index. Northfield, MN: Alternative Press Centre, Carlton College, 1969- , quarterly.

Danky, James. *Undergrounds: A Union List of Alternative Periodicals in the Libraries of the U.S. and Canada*. Madison, WI: Wisconsin State Historical Society, 1974.

Didion, J. "Alicia and the Underground Press," *Saturday Evening Post*. 241 (January 13, 1968) 14.

Edelstein, Andrew J. "Underground Newspapers," in: *The Pop Sixties*. New York: World Almanac Publications, 1985, pp. 211-213.

"Making It, Underground," *Newsweek*. 71 (March 4, 1968) 58.

Pepper, T. "Underground Press: Growing Rich on the Hippie," *Nation*. 206 (April 29, 1968) 569-572.

Sanford, D. "Seedier Media: Underground Press," *New Republic*. 157 (December 2, 1967) 7-8.

Shiflet, Lee. "The Underground Press," in: *Popular Culture and Libraries*, by Frank Hoffmann. Hamden, CT: Library Professional Publications, 1984, pp. 249-261.

"Tribe is Restless; Rebellion at Underground Newspaper, the *Berkeley Barb*," *Time*. 94 (July 18, 1969) 46.

"Underground Alliance; Shoestring Paper of the Strident Left," *Time*. 88 (July 29, 1966) 57.

"Underground Press: Symposium," *Wilson Library Journal*. 43 (March 1967) 640-656.

Video Games

By 1982 it was clear that video games were a national obsession. National tournaments sponsored by the manufacturers attracted many participants, and books and magazines devoted to the games were thriving. New arcades were everywhere, and unless they were banned, machines could be found squeezed into delicatessens, pizza parlors, cinema lobbies, bars, diners, laundries and even colleges and churches.

It was estimated that twenty billion quarters were devoured by arcade machines in 1981; in addition, consumers paid an estimated one billion dollars that year for video-game consoles that connected to home TV sets and for cassettes containing the various game programs. For purposes of comparison that figure represented about twice the take in 1981 of all the casinos in Nevada. It was almost twice the $2.9 billion box-office gross of the U.S. film industry for that period.

Space Invaders, designed in Japan and marketed in the U.S. by Bally, launched the video game craze in 1979. However, the genre possesses a lineage reaching back far before the twentieth century. Its prehistory consisted of the many variants of pinball. Pong, introduced by Atari in the early 1970s, ushered in the modern form of electronic games. Primitive in comparison to its descendents popular in the 1980s, Pong featured electronic paddles which slapped a white blip back and forth across a black-and-white display screen. Users soon tired of the limited depth of that — and related — products.

The industry stagnated until *Space Invaders* — with its electronic columns of squiggly, glowing monsters that marched toward earthmen with a measured "thump, thump, thump" — captured the imagination of users due to its ability to increase the fury of the attack as players improved. While the arcade machines provided the original impetus for the rapid growth of the industry in the early

1980s, a second arm appeared in short order: the home video game system. Atari, a major player in the arcade division as well, dominated the home market, Mattel's Intellivision and Magnavox's Odyssey 2 providing the primary competition.

One particular video game, *Pac-Man*, introduced into U.S. arcades in the beginning of 1981, rapidly became a household word. Termed by one industry executive "the Mickey Mouse of the 1980s," *Pac-Man* had sparked an amazing variety of spinoffs by 1982. Coleco Industries produced a battery-run table-top model to complement Atari's home video version, while Milton Bradley offered a puzzle, a card game and a nonelectric board game. In addition to toys, pajamas, lunch boxes and bumper stickers, there were Hallmark cards and gift wrapping, Dan River sheets and pillowcases and J.C. Penney children's clothing. A Columbia Records single, Buckner and Garcia's "Pac-Man Fever," reached the Top Ten on *Billboard*'s Hot 100 in March 1982 and book publishers weighed in with titles such as *How to Win at Pac-Man* (Pocket Books) and *Mastering Pac-Man* (Signet), the latter of which made the *New York Times* bestseller list.

Critics of video games noted that players often exhibited signs of addictive behavior, spending far more time and money than some parents and authority figures might deem appropriate. However, anthropologist Richard Morris noted that "It would be naive to think that most of the time and money spent on these video games would be channeled into anything society would label as productive." In fact, experts in various fields at the time cited a host of positive influences from the games. These included,

1. the enhancement of hand-eye coordination;
2. kids across social classes being given access to and experience with executive organization (i.e., perceptibly and strategically in charge of a sophisticated control system);
3. youth being equipped with computer-related skills for the future;
4. a vehicle for research (e.g., the Epilepsy Center at Johns Hopkins University Medical School employed Atari games to determine the effects of anti-convulsive drugs on learning and ability).

By 1983 the industry had undergone a perceptible drop in popularity, primarily due to the loss of novelty and the onslaught of newer, more attractive media (e.g., home computers, home video, compact discs). However, home video games have found a new lease on life, albeit a less intense magnitude of popularity, via an interface with home computer software. Many of the new programs have integrated text with a more subtle form of video graphics than was possible in the home video games of the early 1980s. By the middle of the decade the arcade games had also undergone a significant change; in 1984 a game called *Dragon's Lair* merged existing video game technology with the state-of-the-art visuals of video discs.

BIBLIOGRAPHY

"Arcade Video Games Start to Flicker," *Business Week*. (December 6, 1982) 39ff.

"Children and Video: Computing the Effects," *Consumer Research Magazine*. 69 (June 1986) 19-22.

"Computer Gaming," *Futurist*. 20 (January/February 1986) 34.

Gutman, D. "Video Games and National Character," *Psychology Today*. 17 (March 1985) 9.

Hacker, R. "Video Games," *Rolling Stone*. (January 21, 1982) 57ff.

Kanner, B. "Can Atari Stay Ahead of the Game," *New York*. 15 (August 16, 1982) 15-17.

Shapiro, N.L. "New Video Games Put You in the Action," *Popular Mechanics*. 159 (April 1983) 98-99ff.

Skow, John. "Games That Play People," *Readers' Digest*. 121 (November 1982) 67-72. Condensed from an article originally appearing in the January 18, 1982 issue of *Time*.

Stuller, J. "It's Going to be a Blip, Zonk, Whap, Bang Christmas," *Saturday Evening Post*. 254 (December 1982) 42-45.

Surrey, David. "It's, Like, Good Training for Life," *Natural History*. 91 (November 1982) 70-83.

"That's Entertainment," *Science Digest*. 94 (January 1986) 77. Re. computer games.

"Video Games are Suddenly a $2 Billion Industry," *Business Week*. (May 24, 1982) 78ff.

Pac-Man

"Pac-Man Fever; Working Up a Playroom Seat," *Time*. 119 (April 5, 1982) 48.

Taylor, A.L. "Pac-Man Finally Meets His Match," *Time*. 120 (December 20, 1982) 62.

Wandering Portraitists

Colonial Americans were easily convinced to have their portraits done in oil or some other medium for posterity. Their grandchildren would want to know what they looked like. If they feared not living long enough to reach old age, then it was advisable to sit for a portrait when the opportunity came along. The better artists conducted a lively trade by moving from one city to the next catering to the wealthy, while their lesser brethren walked the highways and byways of rural America in search of clients. Both provided a much sought after service which can't be called faddish except for a certain standardization of depiction and technique. For instance, sea captains were painted with red faces, standing before a red curtain, holding a telescope in hand. The artist would show his client an example before starting work. The client, thinking the canvas sea captain a master of the ocean, would nod approval and sit for an imitation of the original. Bogus sea captains might as likely have appeared since art made the man. Other occupations probably benefited from this copycat approach. Another method of popular portraiture was for the artist to have already painted a number of set busts and backgrounds for selection. Within a short time the face could be brushed in and the portrait was done. This expedient measure didn't seem to bother the sitter whose prized portrait looked like his neighbor's. If the artist made the client resemble an aristocrat all the more wonderful. Those artists who could transform ordinary folk into elegant people rarely starved in garrets.

In addition to oil, wax portraiture was much in demand. It involved pressing wax, color by color, into a mould of the client's likeness. The wax portrait was then removed from the mould and accessorized with real lace and seed pearls. The final creation was mounted on glass. These were all the rage until word got around that after awhile the wax turned yellow. Clients, not wanting to look sallow before their time, went back to oils. Eventually a clever artist devised a way of keeping the wax from turning yellow and wax portraiture came back into vogue newly mounted on black velvet.

For those who couldn't afford oil or wax portraiture, silhouettes did nicely. Because of the rapidity of execution a silhouette artist could cut a likeness out of a piece of paper in no time at all. People clamored for variety. Some silhouettes were pasted on a wash background. Bored by that a new twist produced a black paper silhouette mounted on a white card. When that became ho-hum silhouettes were outlined on silk, glass, ivory, and metal and then painted in. The art form became so popular that exhibitions were held to display what nimble hands could do.

BIBLIOGRAPHY

Bolton, Ethel S. *Wax Portraits and Silhouettes*. Detroit: Gale Research, 1974.
Eberlein, Harold D. *Practical Book of Early American Arts and Crafts*. Philadelphia: J.B. Lippincott, 1916.
Wright, Richardson. *Hawkers and Walkers in Early America*. New York: Frederick Unger, 1965.

"White Christmas"

Introduced by Bing Crosby and Marjorie Reynolds in the film, *Holiday Inn* (1942), Irving Berlin's "White Christmas" became an instant Yuletide classic, second in America to "Silent Night" in seasonal repetitions. In 1942 it was heard fifteen times (ten versions tied for the first position) on "Your Hit Parade"; it was performed on that program at least once every year up through 1955. In 1954, the song provided the title for the film starring Crosby, Danny Kaye and Rosemary Clooney.

The chart history of "White Christmas" attests to its extraordinary popularity, particularly during the first year of its release (see Figure 3).

It is probably the second most-recorded song of all time** ("Silent Night" again holds the top spot); notable renditions exist by artists such as The Ames Brothers, Paul Anka, Eddy Arnold, Pat Boone, Vic Damone, Eddie Fisher, Ella Fitzgerald, Jascha Heifetz (a violin transcription), Steve Lawrence, Peggy Lee, Elvis Presley, Kenny Rogers and The Supremes. By 1982 an estimated 142 million recordings of "White Christmas" had been sold, with Crosby's total alone exceeding thirty million. In addition, Whitburn rated it eighth in terms of the amount of sheet music copies sold;*** it should be noted that none of the top seven songs were published after World War I, a time when the heyday of sheet music had long

---

**Whitburn, in his *Pop Memories, 1890-1954*, ranks it as the eighth most-recorded song of that period. However, none of the songs ranked above it (with the exception of "Silent Night") — i.e., "St. Louis Blues," "Stardust," "Body and Soul," "Summertime," "The Old Folks At Home," "Tea For Two" — have been recorded nearly as frequently as "White Christmas" since 1954.

***Again, the ranking covers the period up through 1954; only "White Christmas" of Whitburn's top eight is likely to have been selling sheet music at any appreciable rate over the past thirty-five years.

since passed. In short, the song has ascended to the status of an American institution, likely to live on as long as the holiday itself.

BIBLIOGRAPHY

Baratta, P. "Irving Berlin: a Songwriter for All Times," *Songwriter*. 3 (May 1978) 25-32.

Coleman, R. "Christmas Bingo!," *Melody Maker*. 39 (December 19, 1964) 13.

Ewen, David. *The Story of Irving Berlin*. 1950.

Freedland, M. *Irving Berlin*. 1976.

Green, A. "Most Valuable Popular Song; 'White Xmas' Amazing Totals," *Variety*. 233 (December 18, 1963) 1ff.

Morath, M. "Irving Berlin, Greatest of All," *Music Journal*. 33 (May 1975) 8ff.

Whitburn, Joel. *Pop Memories, 1890-1954; The History of American Popular Music*. Menomonee Falls, WI: Record Research, 1986.

"'White Christmas,' 'Rudolph' Prime Another Yule," *Variety*. 229 (December 12, 1962) 1ff. Includes a tabulation of record sales for the two songs.

Wood, T. "'White Christmas': from Pop Tune to Picture," *New York Times*. 103 (October 18, 1953) section 2, page 5.

FIGURE 3. Chart History of "White Christmas"*

Artist	Position Reached	Year
Bing Crosby	1 (11 weeks)	1942
Charlie Spivak	12	1942
Gordon Jenkins	15	1942
Freddy Martin	24	1942
Bing Crosby	6	1943
Bing Crosby	5	1944
Frank Sinatra	7	1944
Bing Crosby	1 (2 weeks)	1945
Freddy Martin	16	1945
Frank Sinatra	5	1945
Frank Sinatra	6	1946
Jo Stafford	9	1946
Bing Crosby	1 (1 week)	1946
Eddy Howard	21	1947
Perry Como	23	1947
Bing Crosby	3	1947
Bing Crosby	6	1948
Bing Crosby	5	1949
Bing Crosby	13	1950
Bing Crosby	1	1952
Mantovani	23	1952
Bing Crosby	21	1953
Bing Crosby	21	1954
Bing Crosby	7	1955
The Drifters	80	1955
Bing Crosby	65	1956
Bing Crosby	34	1957
Bing Crosby	66	1958
Bing Crosby	59	1959
Bing Crosby	26	1960
The Drifters	96	1960
Bing Crosby	12	1961
Bing Crosby	38	1962
The Drifters	88	1962

*The chart listings were based upon a combination of the "Juke Box Charts" (to June 17, 1957), "Best Selling Records" (to October 13, 1958), "Disc Jockey Charts" (to July 28, 1958), the "Top 100" (November 12, 1955-July 28, 1958) and the "Hot 100" (August 4, 1958-present), as compiled by Joel Whitburn in his books, *Pop Memories, 1890-1954* and *Top Pop Singles, 1955-1986.*

Tom Wolfe

Tom Wolfe was arguably the chief exponent of New Journalism, a genre which demanded that reporters abandon their pose as "the gentlemen in the grandstand" and immerse themselves in their subject; in short, they sought to get inside the head of the character being studied, and make it read like fiction. Wolfe himself delineated his aims as follows:

> I believe that it is possible to achieve a nonfiction form that combines the emotional impact usually found only in novels and short stories, the analytical insights of the best essays and scholarly writing, and the deep factual foundation of "hard reporting."

Wolfe made a spectacular entrance onto the American literary scene in the mid-1960s through a succession of outre articles covering various facets of pop culture (e.g., stock car racing, gangster society in Las Vegas, Cassius Clay, disc jockey Murray the K, Cary Grant, lives of the nouveau riche, aerial combat in Vietnam) which appeared in *New York* (then a supplement to the Sunday edition of the New York *Herald Tribune*) and mass circulation magazines such as *Esquire* and *Harper's Bazaar*. The majority of his bestselling books—e.g., *The Kandy-Kolored Tangerine-Flake Streamline Baby* (1965), *The Pump House Gang* (1968), *The Electric Kool-Aid Acid Test* (1968), *Radical Chic & Mau-Mauing the Flak Catchers* (1970), *The New Journalism* (1973), *The Painted Word* (1975), *Mauve Gloves & Madmen, Clutter & Vine* (1976), *The Right Stuff* (1979), *In Our Time* (1980), *From Bauhaus to Our House* (1981), *The Purple Decades* (1982), *The Bonfire of Vanities* (1987)—consisted of compilations of his short pieces. His talent has been perhaps most evident in the multitudes of Wolfeisms entering the common vernacular, including "good old boy," "radical chic," "the Me Decade" and "the right stuff."

According to Wolfe, his breathless, stream of consciousness style — full of ellipses, capital letters, exclamation points, the unorthodox use of italics, repetitions of letters to suggest prolongation of vowels, interior monologues, etc. — had its genesis quite by accident. In 1964 he had an *Esquire* deadline to meet covering custom-car shows; in the eleventh hour he collected his notes and frantically began typing them in the form of a memo to the magazine's editors. The approach clicked and Wolfe quickly supplanted Edward Albee as the chief subject of controversy at literary cocktail parties in the United States. Liz Smith noted that

> Wolfe caused severe jealousy and outrage pangs throughout the U.S. literary establishment when he sprang right out of Pop Culture's forehead to become a star practically overnight . . . His subject matter often trembled like Jell-O about to collapse . . . but there was no one else around who could touch him. The other "soft" journalists just stood tongue-tied atop Roget's *Thesaurus* and watched him, the noiret of the bête noires, absquatulate with most of the fame and fortune.

His success stimulated many other writers to adopt the tenets of New Journalism, most notably, Gay Talese (whose *Esquire* profiles read like short stories), Truman Capote (works like *In Cold Blood* established him as the premier exponent of the nonfiction novel), George Plimpton (*Paper Lion*), Hunter Thompson (*Hell's Angels: A Strange and Terrible Saga*) and Toby Thompson (*Positively Main Street*).

Wolfe has remained a commercially successful writer; however, New Journalism, at least in name, is a dead letter, a casualty of rising publishing expenses, Watergate (which inspired everyone to try their hand at investigative reporting), the legitimizing of gossip via *People Weekly*, and the rise of self-help magazines.

BIBLIOGRAPHY

Bellamy, Joe David. "Introduction," in: *The Purple Decades; A Reader*, by Tom Wolfe. New York: Farrar, Straus, Giroux, 1982, pp. vii-xvi.

"Big Bad Wolfe?," *Newsweek*. 67 (January 31, 1966) 60.

Compton, N. "Hijinks Journalism," *Commentary*. 47 (February 1967) 76-78.

Dandy, E. "Tom Wolfe . . . But Exactly, Yes!," *Vogue*. 147 (April 15, 1966) 124-125ff.

"Department of Amplification," *Newsweek*. 65 (May 3, 1965) 82-83.

Edelstein, Andrew J. "Tom Wolfe and the New Journalism," in: *The Pop Sixties*. New York: World Almanac Publications, 1985, pp. 200-201.

Epstein, J. "Rococo and Roll," *New Republic*. 153 (July 24, 1965) 27-29.

Frankel, H. "Author," *Saturday Review*. 48 (July 31, 1965) 23-24.

"How You Can Be As Well-Informed As Tom Wolfe," *Esquire*. 68 (November 1967) 138ff.

"In Chic's Clothing," *Time*. 86 (July 2, 1965) 59-60.

Simonds, C.H. "Popcult Orgy," *National Review*. 17 (November 2, 1965) 989-990.

Smith, Liz. *Status*. 2 (January/February 1966) 42ff.

"Talk of the Town," *National Review*. 17 (May 4, 1965) 359-360.

"Whisper," *Time*. 85 (April 16, 1965) 60.

"William and the Wolfe," *Newsweek*. 65 (April 19, 1965) 62ff.

"Wolfe, Tom," in: *Current Biography*, *1971*, edited by Charles Moritz. New York: Wilson, 1971, pp. 446-448.

"Yankee Doodle"

Perhaps the most popular American song of the colonial era, "Yankee Doodle" appears to have been rooted in southern Europe in the Middle Ages. Around 1500, it was popular with harvesters in Holland, who began the verses with the meaningless words: "Yankee dudel doodle down." In England the song was sung to small children during the Elizabethan era; later, the Cavaliers changed the words to ridicule Oliver Cromwell as he rode down from Canterbury to assume command of the Puritan forces.

The words that gained widespread renown in the U.S. have been attributed to an English army surgeon in Albany, Dr. Richard Schuckburgh. Whether or not this is the case, the verses appear to have been composed during the 1750s and were used by the British to make fun of the provincial colonial troops. However, it became very popular with the Americans as well; by 1967 — the date of the earliest written reference to it (i.e., the libretto of *The Disappointment*, a comic opera published in New York) — many versions were current in the colonies. The first complete rotation of the verses in America appeared in the *New York Journal* on October 12, 1768, which included the now famous refrain:

> Yankee Doodle keep it up,
> Yankee Doodle dandy,
> Mind the music and the step,
> And with the girls be handy.

The British continued to use the song in derision of the American troops during the Revolutionary War. After their victory at Concord in 1775, however, the Yankees sang it while pursuing the retreating enemy. The British General Gage is said to have exclaimed at this time, "I hope I shall never hear that tune again!" From that point on "Yankee Doodle" became an American patriotic air. While the

U.S. has discovered new anthems over the years, American school children continue to learn the song as part of their national heritage.

BIBLIOGRAPHY

Kendall, Raymond. "Yankee Doodle," in: *World Book Encyclopedia*. Volume 21: W-Z. Chicago: World Book, 1988, p. 554.

Lane, S.G. "Bicentennial Bowdlerizing; or, the Rape of Yankee Doodle," *School Library Journal*. 23 (September 1976) 34-35.

March, T.H. "Real Yankee Doodle," *Hobbies*. 69 (June 1964) 80ff.

"Yankee Doodle," in: *The Encyclopedia Americana*, edited by Alan H. Smith. Danbury, CT: Grolier, 1985, Volume 29, page 648.

Yankee Doodle: the Great American Classic with All the Verses. Introduction by N. Goldberg. New York: Hart, 1977. Reviewed in *Tennessee Folklore Society Bulletin*. 43:4 (1977) 224-225.

The Ziegfeld Follies

Utilizing the motto, "Glorifying the American Girl," Florenz Ziegfeld (1869-1932) established an onstage model of feminine beauty, with an emphasis upon slenderness and grace, which dominated American fashion during the early decades of the twentieth century. His prime vehicle was *The Ziegfeld Follies*, a musical revue instituted in 1907 and followed by more than twenty consecutive annual editions. The *Follies* were spectacular displays, combining lavish and imaginative sets and costumes with a steady procession of entertainers. He hired leading composers and lyricists of the day as well as the cream of the vaudeville comic talent, including Fanny Brice, Eddie Cantor, W.C. Fields and Will Rogers.

The girlie numbers, however, comprised the heart of his revues. At the critical moment, the Ziegfeld Girls would appear onstage accompanied by a lilting tune like Irving Berlin's "A Pretty Girl Is Like A Melody." Accenting the pelvis and lifting the shoulder, each girl—projecting an aloof and expressionless bearing and swathed in feathers and chiffon—would undulate slowly into the spotlight, pause, flash a quick smile, and then slink slowly offstage. Audience interest was hyped by gossip column coverage of the girls' madcap, scandal-ridden lives.

In addition to the *Follies*, Ziegfeld enjoyed outstanding stage successes with *Sally* (1920), *Kid Boots* (1923), *Rio Rita* (1927), *Show Boat* (1927) and *Bitter Sweet* (1929). While the Great Depression hastened the demise of his revues, the format he popularized continued to attract a large audience via the Hollywood musicals of the 1930s (most notably the films of Busby Berkeley such as *42nd Street*).

BIBLIOGRAPHY

"Beauty, the Fashions and the Follies," *Ladies Home Journal*. 40 (March 1923) 16-17.

Cantor, E., and D. Freedman. "Ziegfeld and His Follies," *Collier's*. 93 (January 20, 1934) 22ff; (January 27, 1934) 24-25ff.

"Glorifier of the American Girl," in: *This Fabulous Century; Volume II, 1910-1920*, edited by Ezra Bowen. New York: Time-Life, 1969, pp. 262-271.

"Great Ziegfeld as He Might Have Done It Himself," *Newsweek*. (April 18, 1936) 29.

"Portrait," *Delineator*. 104 (June 1924) 13.

"Portrait," *Literary Digest*. 121 (April 4, 1936) 22.

"Showman's Shifting Sands," *Ladies Home Journal*. 40 (June 1923) 23.

Tittle, W. "Ziegfeld of the Follies," *World's Work*. 53 (March 1927) 562-568.

"What Becomes of the Ziegfeld Follies Girls?," *Pictorial Review*. 26 (May 1925) 12-13.

Cross-References

The Beach Boys *See*: Car Songs; Surf Music
Beadle and Adams *See*: Dime Novels
The "Beat Generation" *See*: "On the Road"
Beatlemania *See also*: British Invasion; Paul McCartney Is Dead;
  Sgt. Pepper's Lonely Hearts Club Band
British Invasion *See also*: Beatlemania
Buffalo Bob *See*: "Howdy Doody"
Cartoons *See*: Betty Boop; *Gertie the Dinosaur*; Mickey Mouse
"Charlie's Angels" *See*: Farrah Fawcett-Majors
Cody, Buffalo Bill *See*: Buffalo Bill
Comic Books *See*: *Batman*; *Superman*
Comic Strips *See*: *Peanuts*
Disney, Walt *See*: Mickey Mouse
Elvis Is Alive *See also*: Elvis Presley
Goodman, Benny *See*: Swing Music
"Gunsmoke" *See*: Adult Westerns
Haley, Bill *See*: "Rock Around the Clock"
Hootenannies *See*: Commercial Folk Music
"J.R. Ewing?, Who Shot" *See*: "Dallas"
Jazz *See*: Original Dixieland Jazz Band; Ragtime; Swing Music
Kerouac, Jack *See*: "On the Road"
MaCay, Winsor *See*: *Gertie the Dinosaur*
Moore, Clement *See*: The Night Before Christmas
Nancy Drew See: The Stratemeyer Syndicate
New Journalism *See*: Tom Wolfe
A Nightmare on Elm Street See: Freddy Krueger
Pac-Man *See*: Video Games
Paul McCartney Is Dead *See also*: Beatlemania; *Sgt. Pepper's
  Lonely Hearts Club Band*
Posters *See*: Peter Max; Psychedelic Posters
Presley, Elvis *See also*: Elvis Is Alive

Psychedelic Posters *See also*: San Francisco Sound

Rock 'N' Roll *See*: Answer Songs; Ayatollah Songs; Beatlemania; British Invasion; Car Songs; Death Songs; Elvis Is Alive; Glitter Rock; The Monkees; Paul McCartney Is Dead; Elvis Presley; "Rock Around the Clock"; San Francisco Sound; *Sgt. Pepper's Lonely Hearts Club Band*; Surf Music

Sgt. Pepper . . . See also: Beatlemania; Paul McCartney Is Dead

Soap Operas *See*: "Dallas"; "General Hospital"; "Mary Hartman, Mary Hartman"

Stallone, Sylvester *See*: Rambo

Television *See*: Adult Westerns; Batman; Milton Berle; "General Hospital"; "Hopalong Cassidy"; "Howdy Doody"; "Mary Hartman, Mary Hartman"; "The Monkees"

"Texaco Star Theater" *See*: Milton Berle

Walt Disney *See*: Mickey Mouse

Westerns *See*: Adult Westerns

The Wild West (Show) *See*: Buffalo Bill

Index

Vaughan, Sarah, 59
Vawter, Keith, 77,78
Video games, 349-351
Vietnam War, 261-262,271-272,345
Vincent, John Heyl, 77
Vince Vance and the Valiants, 21
"Virginian, The", 1

"Wagon Train", 1
Walker, George, 57
Wallace, George, 8
Wallach, Eli, 31
Ward, Charles B, 326
Warhol, Andy, 242-243,296
Waronker, Si, 81
Washington, George, 27,137
Waters, Muddy, 11
Watusi (dance), 338
Weatherwax, Ken, 335
Weavers, The, 89
Weil, Cynthia, 184
Weintraub, Fred, 210
Weiss, Charles, 19
Wesselmann, Tom, 242
West, Adam, 31-32
West, Benjamin, 228
West, Mae, 41
Westerns
  adult, 1-2
  as movie serials, 198
Wheeler, Edward L., 108

White, Barry, 110
White, Jules, 87,88
White, Pearl, 197
"White Christmas", 355-357
Whitman, Robert, 131
Who, The, 250
Wild West, Buffalo Bill Cody's, 83-85
Williams, Bert, 57
Williams, Paul, 183
Willis, Nathaniel Parker, 278
Willson, Meredith, 7
Wilson, Brian, 61,62,65,313,314
Wilson, J. Frank, 103
Wilson, Wes, 249
Wilson, Woodrow, 138-139
Wolfe, Tom, 359-361
Women, as writers, 277-279. *See also*
  names of specific writers
Wood, Grant, 7-9
Wooley, Sheb, 16
Worley, Joanne, 271

"Yankee Doodle", 363-364
Yarbrough, Glenn, 168
Yellow Submarine, 163,282
Young, Lester, 317

Zanuck, Darryl, 53
Ziegfeld Follies, 75,365-366
Zukor, Adolphe, 235
Zurbel, Victor, 163